In the 19th century science discovered that our n
interspersed with forces of electricity. Science wa
the scientists are wrong if they believe that the ner.   ..... which
belongs to us, and which provides the foundation for our inner
world of pictures and thinking, has anything to do with the electric
currents that course along our nerves. These electric currents are
the forces that are introduced into our being by [another] being ...
They do not belong to our being at all ...

We arrive in this world with the garment of our organism, without being able to reach down into it with our soul to any great
extent. Instead, shortly before we are born ... there is also an opportunity for another spiritual being apart from our soul to take possession of our body, namely, of the subconscious part of our body.
This is a fact. Shortly before we are born, another being indwells us.
In the terminology we use today we would call this an Ahrimanic
being. It is just as much in us as is our own soul.

These beings lead their lives by making use of human beings
to enable them to inhabit the sphere in which they wish to dwell.
They have an exceptionally high degree of intelligence, and a very
significantly developed will, but no qualities of soul, nothing like
what we would call the human qualities of soul and heart and
mind. So we proceed through our life while having our soul and
also a double who is far cleverer, far cleverer than we are; very
intelligent but with a Mephistophelean intelligence, an Ahrimanic
intelligence. And in addition also an Ahrimanic will, a very strong
will; a will that is much more akin to the forces of nature than it is
to our human will, which is ruled by our heart and mind.

These beings have decided, out of their own will, that they do
not want to live in the world to which they were assigned by the
wise gods of the upper hierarchies. They want to conquer the earth,
so they need bodies. Having no bodies of their own, they use as
much of human bodies as they can, since the human soul cannot
quite fill out the human body.

—Rudolf Steiner, *Secret Brotherhoods and the Mystery of the Double*

Electric information environments, being utterly ethereal, foster the
illusion of the world as a spiritual substance. It is now a reasonable fac-
simile of the mystical body, a blatant manifestation of the Anti-Christ.
After all, the Prince of this World is a very great electric engineer.

—Marshall McLuhan, *Letters*, 1969

BIG MOTHER

Books by Jasun Horsley:

The Blood Poets

Matrix Warrior

Lucid View

The Secret Life of Movies

Paper Tiger

Seen and Not Seen

Dark Oasis

Prisoner of Infinity

The Vice of Kings

16 Maps of Hell

The Kubrickon

BIG MOTHER

The Technological Body of Evil

Jasun Horsley

AEON

First published in 2023 by
Aeon Books

British Library Cataloguing in Publication Data

A C.I.P. for this book is available from the British Library

ISBN-13: 978-1-80152-053-9

Typeset by Medlar Publishing Solutions Pvt Ltd, India

www.aeonbooks.co.uk

CONTENTS

FOREWORD

In 2020, I self-published my largest book, *16 Maps of Hell*. I considered it the culmination of my literary endeavours over the previous 30 years; if not my last book, then at least the last 'map of Hell'. In 2021, Aeon (publishers of *Prisoner of Infinity* and *Vice of Kings*) asked out of the blue if I had anything they could publish. Somewhat reluctantly, I dug out an unfinished MS I had worked on for a number of years, during the same 'Hell-mapping' period. The book's specific focus was on the interface between technology and human consciousness. The first part, *The Kubrickon*, though much of it was written later, will precede *Big Mother* as a separate volume.

This two-way conundrum, the degree to which human consciousness shapes technology and/or vice versa, how much our technology shapes human consciousness, eventually made it impossible *not* to notice the vacuum created by juxtaposing these two *apparent* causal agencies. If technology is created by a form of human consciousness, which is itself largely informed *by* the technology, where and what is the *missing* causal agency in this picture?

The same might now be said—at the end of this literary journey—of Hell. If I have written a dozen books mapping Hell and describing its occupants, what of the original infernal architect? Simply put: what is Hell without Satan at its centre and core?

I have written a great deal over the years on both Satan and Lucifer. (They are not the same, at least to the degree that Bruce and Caitlyn Jenner or Anakin Skywalker and Darth Vader are not the same.) I wrote about Lucifer especially, in my earlier works as Aeolus Kephas; I even had a formal pact that I would always cite him at least once in my books. I have since renounced, if not denounced, those earlier books (*Lucid View* and *Homo Serpiens*), as at best naïve, at worst deceived. Ironically, those writings are also closer to the truth and to the heart of the matter in at least *one* sense: as Aeolus, I was emboldened (partly by the pseudonym) to write of such things as Lucifer and Satan as *objectively real spiritual principles and intelligences*, existing above, before, and beyond the myths and belief systems created around them.

The problem with those earlier works was that my own perceptions and descriptions were informed more by beliefs than by direct experience. I did *have* direct experiences—*as we all do*—which is very much the point of this opening argument; but they were distorted and restricted by the beliefs I had accrued around the experiences. Simply put, what I wrote about Lucifer, Satan, and invisible, discarnate, or inorganic beings—good, bad, or neutral—was, to a significant degree, *influenced by those same forces*, turning me into a mouthpiece or sock puppet *for* them. As a result, I literally (somewhat knowingly, but also naïvely) became Satan's advocate.

This led to a necessary rechecking of the sources, so to speak, over a 12-year period (2008–2020) of writing and researching by which I re-sorted the seeds of belief and experience, to separate the fertile and the fecund from the fetid and fruitless. As a result, the assumption of an objective reality behind my metaphysical beliefs had to be temporarily rescinded. My focus then went to the architecture and not the architects: the cultural, social, political, and parapolitical dimensions of Hell, as a demonstrably *human* folly that exploited (and to a degree manufactured) *beliefs* in invisible realities, as a means to achieve its goals. While immersed in this research, it seemed conceivable, for a time, that merely human neurosis and pathology might be enough to account for all worldly evil.

Not that I ever fully believed this (I always knew there were invisible forces, because I had encountered them). But it felt necessary to strip down the evidence of all speculations, and reduce it to documentable facts, in order to see what it looked like. What it looked like was an all-too-human Hell that, at the same time—even by the same token—couldn't be *fully* explained as the result of human folly.

Just as water that is impure must have come into contact with something other than pure water, *any system that is anti-human and anti-life by definition cannot be wholly attributed to human activities.*

What I wish to state now, for the record, in these closing moments of a lifetime's literary output, is that the evidence I have amassed over the decades is nothing other than the evidence of entity infestation and entity interference within the human psyche-soul, and by extension, throughout human society.

Satan walks among us, and always has. Or, in the terms of this closing sin-thesis, Big Mother is watching us.

INTRODUCTION: WOMB ENVY

> As for my people, children are their oppressors, and women rule over them.
>
> —Isaiah 3:12

For my whole life, without knowing it, I was formulating a thesis. A few years ago, I gave it a name. I called it the Big Mother thesis (BMT).

It began with the premise that our disembodiment as human beings, as a species, is being engineered, and that, at the same time, *we* are engineering it through technology. With hindsight, this thesis began, appropriately enough, with movies. I say appropriately, because movies were my first focus as a young writer, and because they offer an experience of *immersion in a surrogate reality*.

The first and most essential ingredient for the BMT is the little-discussed but culturally prevalent (especially in the horror movie genre) phenomenon of unhealthy attachment between a child (especially a male child) and its mother. When a natural bond cannot form between an infant and its mother, the child is unable to separate from the mother when the time comes, and his psyche remains immersed in, possessed by, the mother's psyche. This kind of possession results in a lifelong, pathological unconscious quest to regain access to the mother's body, as most extremely enacted in the case of a 'serial killer' like Ed Gein, who inspired Buffalo Bill in *Silence of the Lambs* and, most famously of all, Norman Bates in *Psycho*.

My earliest memory of my mother is of watching a (horror) movie with her. I have since deduced that attempting to separate from my mother and watching movies *with* her created a sort of *transitional space* between us. In that space, I was developing an identity separate from her gaze, because it was one of the few times her attention was on me in a way that wasn't overwhelming. She was looking at the movie, and I was too, but we were both aware of each other *looking*. We were *aligned* in the shared experience of gazing. The movie then became our shared reality.

If I was midwifed from my mother's psyche (and into a false reality) by movies, this would hardly have been necessary, or even possible, without the (relative) absence of my father. The same must surely be said of all the mother-bonded psychos throughout history. Who has ever heard of Mr. Bates?

In its gothic and sensational way, *Psycho* depicts a largely unrecognised psychological reality, unrecognised because also metaphysical (and ubiquitous): that of ancestral possession. It is the premise of this work that ancestral possession—and its accompanying and even more socially ostracised twin, demonic possession—is the primary motivating factor in history, and that, without including it, no understanding of human behaviour is ever going to be complete. This is particularly the case if we are looking at human pathologies, which (I will argue) are the *sine qua non*—the driving force—of the nightmare of human history.

(I am aware this could be viewed as a circular argument, that if we recognise a human individual as being pathological, that same diagnosis acknowledges that pathology is the driving force in this individual's behaviour. The same must also be deduced collectively: since history *is* a nightmare, history's dreamer must be disturbed.)

While not all ancestral patterns are pathological, all pathologies are to some degree ancestral. Our ancestry, of course, goes back a long way—into prehistory—and the most easily observable ancestral influence is that of family members we have direct contact with, especially those we were raised by. Of these, none has a greater influence than our mother. To an incalculable extent, our self-image, our preferences, desires, fears, obsessions, and choices are determined by her influence—most especially if we consider that our mother and our father's influence is *itself* a continuation of the influence of previous ancestors.

* * *

> All forms of violence are a quest for identity. When you live on the frontier, you have no identity. You're a nobody.
>
> —Marshall McLuhan

As befits a work on unconscious urges and possessions from the ancient beyond, this book first began a long time ago, without my realising it. In 2008, I met an autistic woman at an online political discussion forum who introduced me to a more nuanced view of autism than I'd previously had. More importantly, she introduced me to the possibility I was myself on the spectrum. (Most importantly of all, she later became my wife.) My hero and role model as a teenager was David Byrne of Talking Heads, who self-identified as Aspergerian during this same period (2008). It wasn't hard to identify many similar Aspergerian qualities in myself. Since I am also highly impressionable (an autistic trait!), I took to the idea like a snake to grass. The big suit fit, so I went to the dance.

Three years later, in 2011, I was undergoing a trial separation from my wife, due in part to the difficulty I was having with her extremely 'autistic' ways. It was during this period that I saw the movie *We Need to Talk About Kevin*. I was disturbed by what I saw as an inaccurate and irresponsible depiction of autism (while Kevin, the school killer, is never identified as autistic, he has several obvious characteristics). I was particularly bothered because my niece (who has some autistic qualities herself, and was about 14 at the time) loved the film (it was she who recommended it to me). I wrote a long post at an online parapolitical forum, challenging the film and filmmakers and sparking a discussion that went on for a couple of weeks.

Then, in December 2012, when I was on my way from London, England, back to Canada to be reunited with my wife, a news story about a school shooting at Sandy Hook broke. In the light of that media event, and specifically the citing of autism as an 'explanation' for it, I went back to my postings about the *Kevin* film to see if my comments had been prescient. I decided to use the movie as a fictional counterpoint to the Sandy Hook incident as a way to discuss the ways in which the media can—and does—create a false connection between autism and violent crime, and how (and why) this faulty perception seemed to be taking hold in the collective imagination.

As I worked on the piece, I shared the early drafts with my wife. Each time I did, she came back with a dozen links to articles she considered relevant. What had started out as an impulsive post at a forum turned into a 30,000-word opus, and even *then* I didn't feel like I was finished. Half the links my wife sent were opening new doorways (or uncovering new rabbit holes), and I was putting them aside for a second piece, in order not to lose the plot of the first.

There is now almost nothing left of that original material, or intention, that was the earliest iteration of this current book. It began as a first-person investigative narrative into the evolutionary enigma of what makes people different, the difficulty in meeting and embracing such differences, and the dangers, both personal and social, of rejecting them and thereby eliminating diversity.

When I first embarked on this exploration ten years ago, neurodiversity was a 'hot topic', one that almost no one could agree on, not even self-identified autists.* My impression, then and now, is that most people think of autism as a medical question, or at best a psychological and social one. I have long considered it a spiritual matter. In fact, my search to understand my own neurodiversity (my feeling of alienation and estrangement, of 'difference') has taken the form of a lifelong spiritual quest—albeit one that was atypical, unorthodox, and eccentric (even as a seeker I was an anomaly). What I hadn't realised—until I met my wife and began to seek answers in the field of autism—was that neurodiversity is also a highly *political* subject. In a way, it is the ultimate political subject, because the idea of a different way of perceiving reality is potentially the greatest challenge, not merely to political regimes, but to prevailing ideas of what reality 'is'. It suggests a revolution to end all revolutions.

---

*Neurodiversity is a spectrum. That means that, at one end, there is one kind of human nature (infrared), and at the other end another kind (ultraviolet). Since neurodiversity is a spectrum, there may be as many different kinds of it as there are individuals. It's the opposite of a 'one-size-fits-all' mode of being. The neurodiverse are those individuals who can only learn how to be themselves by shutting out the signals from the outside, by looking all the way inside for the real signal, the one that's absolutely unique to them. The most common, or at least well-known, form of neurodiversity is autism.

Like UFOs, ghosts, demons, or 'AI', the nature of neurodiversity is elusive. In a curious way, the more concrete the example there is to study, the less we're likely to learn from it, *unless we are able to meet it on its own turf*. A genuine alien encounter would be beyond our everyday understanding. It would require a shift in perceptual bias—human-centricity—and a letting go of certain, taken-for-granted beliefs, both about reality and ourselves.

Speaking from my own experience, as well as what I've learned about other people's, being neurodiverse is a bit like being stuck in an adolescence that never ends. We never really 'grow up' and become adults; at best we just learn to 'pass'. So all the advice, counsel, and guidance from the people who *managed* to grow up—who became socialised units of the collective neurotypical community—is pretty much useless. We just don't get it, because they just don't get *us*.[1]

* * *

> Do people think they can cure the ills of the present time by applying the same principles which have brought them about? If so, they are utterly deceiving themselves.
> —Rudolf Steiner, *The Fall of the Spirits of Darkness*

The womb is the last time a man was fully at one with a woman—and with existence. In fact, it wouldn't *be* a woman to us back then, it would just be—existence. We wouldn't have known our world was the inside of a woman's body until *after* we emerged. On the inside, there was nothing to compare it to. For all of us, men *and* women, woman is the original existence from which we emerge. (What's more, *all human foetuses start out female*.)

Francis Bacon—the natural philosopher and proto-scientist—saw 'science [as] a chaste and lawful marriage between Mind and Nature that will bind Nature to man's service and make her his slave'. In *The Masculine Birth of Time* (1603), 'Bacon called for a "blessed race of Hermes and Supermen" who could "hound", "conquer and subdue Nature", "shake her to her foundations", and "storm and occupy her castles and strongholds"' (Pulé and Hultman, p. 504).

Mary Shelley's *Frankenstein* (subtitled *The Modern Prometheus*) implied that all male-driven scientific endeavours, mythologically revealed as *hubris*, are driven by womb envy.[2] Perhaps womb envy was driving both Bacon's and the Baron's zealous attempt to force Nature and existence to submit to their will? The ultimate goal—of science as much as alchemy—is to create life and so supplant the power of the female, the primacy of the womb. Yet it only seems to be able to do so by chopping up life—or robbing graves—and re-stitching the bits together.

At the same time, central to the Big Mother thesis, it is apparently being fuelled by an unconscious desire to get *back* to the womb. 'Science'—seen through such a lens—becomes one, history-making displacement activity that stems from feeling exiled from the paradise of the mother's body. After that ejection occurs, like Lucifer we enter into competition with it, become hostile towards it, envious of it. Womb envy clearly intersects with, without being the same as, the desire to get *back* to the womb. Since we can't ever actually do that, the next best thing is to create a substitute for it.

It is here that we see the rough blueprint for the BMT: *the desire to create through technology a replica of the mother's body*—so we can disappear into it. The technologically assembled and technocratically imposed *architecture of illusion* is there to invite us to completely forget that we exist as organic beings, and to immerse ourselves eternally in an infantile metaverse of superpowers and epic adventures. Before that can happen, we must be acclimatised to a disembodied state—if there even *is* such a thing—or at the very least, softened up to the *idea* of it.

The juxtaposition of nature vs. culture, or natural and unnatural, can certainly be too broadly or lazily made; but I find the counter-position, that 'everything is natural', since humans are part of nature too, to be equally lazy and a lot more demonstrably false, and often indistinguishable from sophistry. *Clearly*, there are things about human behaviour and human society that are unnatural, in the sense of ethically abhorrent and adverse to life. It might even be reasoned that *everything* human beings do in the 21st century is unnatural, as Thomas Berger jibed in *Reinhart's Women*:

> Nowadays Gay Pride spectacles were commonplace in our major cities … That it would always be a joke with respect to Nature might be considered as certain, but then so too was flying when you weren't born with wings, and eating cooked food and reading by electric light, and in fact, simply reading: no other animals did any of those things. If *Homo sapiens* in general was a pervert under the aspect of eternity, then why jib at a subspecies?
>
> (1982, p. 21)

To argue that all forms of technology are natural because they are created by humans is the flip side of suggesting that human beings are unnatural in every way that they differ from animals. This creates an impossible conundrum, because animals also do things that humans are considered sociopaths, even psychopaths, for doing. So are the worst kinds of psychopathic crimes part of human nature just because humans commit them? This leads to an absurd—but also aberrant—form of moral equivalency in which 'everything goes'—and becomes a source of pride—because anything anyone chooses (especially when it goes against social norms) is proof of individuality and freedom of choice, consequences be damned.

If there is a quality-spectrum of human behaviours and man-made things—ranging from beautiful and good to ugly and bad—there are presumably different types of inspiration that drive humans and that determine just how natural or unnatural these productions are. On either end of the spectrum of human endeavour, from holy to unholy, sublime to profane, there is a natural mind and an artificial one (one that is unnatural or anti-natural), informing the choices and actions that create the products that shape our culture and society. So wither cometh these two minds we are currently in?

The evidence suggests strongly that the artificial mind has for a considerable time been dominant, that humanity's endeavour—so-called historical progress—is moved, not by angels but by devils. This argument supposes an inversion, by which good has been supplanted by evil, Nature (the qualities that extend from God/the angels) by anti-Nature (Satan and his devils). That this may all be in the Nature of Things (God's plan) is a valid issue but also a separate one. Plainly, if it is in the nature of God's plan to work with devils as well as angels—serial killers as well as saints—this does not make it any less essential to discern the difference. On the contrary, developing such discernment—discernment for identifying spirits, or soul-sentience—may be central to the Plan.

A better dichotomy than natural and unnatural, then, since it makes the dividing line more clearly drawn, is natural and *anti*-natural. There is, experientially, an aspect of human experience (we cannot speak for any other species) that is 'unnatural' insofar as it is in every sense detrimental to life. My interest is not in exploring this philosophical question but taking it as a given, as common sense, and offering it as evidence of a *non*-human (hence 'unnatural') element, acting both on and through human beings in society and, by extension, within nature. It is this element that I have taken the plunge, after all these years, in identifying as satanic, thereby placing it within a more 'mythical' framework than a strictly scientific one.

And in fact, here is perhaps the fundamental gulf between the scientific (falsely called, I would say scientistic) and the religious perspective (see the Afterword for a full discussion of scientism). In science, there is no opposite to the universe. In Judeo-Christian and Islamic religious thought, *necessarily*, God has his opposition. I say necessarily, because I think it is largely the evidence of our own experience that makes this dualistic interpretation framework necessary. We *know* that there is good and evil, that there is something within us that is deeply opposed to life, because we experience it every day, every hour, and probably every moment of our lives. And those who deny it are almost invariably the most fully possessed by it.

This doesn't mean I will be attempting to superimpose more secular concepts of culture (or technology) vs. nature, or even human vs. divine, onto this primary, ancient metaphysic of good and evil. On the contrary, I will be seeking to find ways in which the two forces within ourselves can be mapped inwards, from the outer clues of the world that surround us, to a schism that exists at the very core of us, in the place where not just God but also his prodigal firstborn son, Satan—pun fully intended—*lies*.

What follows is not a conventional history, neither of neurodiversity, artificial intelligence, computing, nor even of techno-culture. There are plenty of books that offer that, and I am neither qualified nor inspired to attempt such a study. My approach is to intuitively explore the (possible) emergence of artificial intelligence as a sociological, cultural, psychological, and above all spiritual (or anti-spiritual) phenomenon, as well as a technological one.

To lay the groundwork for this exploration requires mapping, not the origins of computing, but something closer to the origins of consciousness and of social identity. For it is out of this, I will argue, that 'AI' is emerging, with the technology being nothing more nor less than the necessary vehicle for that arrival.

What 'AI' actually is, before and beyond the technology that is delivering it—i.e. what it is in Nature (and culture) that is *anti*-Nature—is the larger question that this work will attempt to answer.

PART I

NEURODIVERSITY AND PHILIP K. DICK'S NO-NAME ENTITIES

What does this mean, to say that an idea or a thought is literally alive? And that it seizes on men here and there and makes use of them to actualize itself into the stream of human history?
 —Philip K. Dick, 'If You Find This World Bad, You Should See Some of the Others'

Why one has to have a body, I don't know. A necessary append-age to the head, I suppose. I always wished I didn't have a body. I suppose everyone does.

—Paul Bowles, in 1984

CHAPTER 1

Your real imaginary friend

*I*s this current work an attempt to comprehend the incomprehensible? Is it engaged in an intellectual indulgence, an exercise in futility—inadvertently using words to demonstrate the inadequacy of language to comprehend reality? What is driving me to write this book?

I want to believe it is coming from some deeper, higher realm of existence, some formless, preverbal consciousness using me to become known to the world. More likely, this is a delusion, and I am simply trying to get to grips with my own unconscious, as a way to control it, to prevent it from taking me over.

I am afraid if I stop writing, I will lose my purpose and meaning, become an obsolete technology, to be discarded and forgotten. I am trying to make myself indispensable to myself—even to the point of writing about how I can't stop writing, thereby giving myself something new to write about.

If I was programmed from before I can remember to communicate this stuff—what has programmed me, and why? If I don't get it out, I will never be able to determine where it has come from or what it means. I will be a medium without a message.

Hence my reason for writing is simple: to discover my reason for being unable not to write.

3

*If one day you hear no more from me, you will know I either gave up or suc-
ceeded. Assuming there is a difference.*

* * *

> I in my stories and novels sometimes write about counterfeit
> worlds. Semi-real worlds as well as deranged private worlds,
> inhabited often by just one person … At no time did I have a
> theoretical or conscious explanation for my preoccupation with
> these pluriform pseudo-worlds, but now I think I understand.
> What I was sensing was the manifold of partially actualized
> realities lying tangent to what evidently is the most actualized
> one—the one that the majority of us, by consensus gentium
> [general consent], agree on.
> —Philip K. Dick, 'If You Find This World Bad, You Should See
> Some of the Others'

One has to start to measure an infinite circle somewhere, so let's start
with three basic concepts:

1) Consensus: a general agreement about something: an idea or opinion
   that is shared by all the people in a group.
2) Perception: awareness of the elements of the environment through
   physical sensation. (This was the *third* definition I found online: the
   first one, interestingly enough, was: 'the way you think about or
   understand someone or something'. Keep this in mind, I will refer
   back to it.)
3) Language: the system of words or signs that people use to express
   thoughts and feelings to each other.

The general agreement is that both language and consensus are shaped
by perception, i.e. *what we perceive dictates the terms of communication and
what we can agree on.*

Being on the autism spectrum, if it means anything, means being a
perceptual anomaly who rarely agrees with other people about what's
perceptibly real. Not surprisingly, then, from my point of view, it's the
exact opposite: *language and consensus determine what we (allow ourselves
to) perceive.* (I should probably extend the idea of 'language', however,
to include the entire spectrum of *learned values and meanings.*)

So right out the gate, only two pages in, we are faced with a seemingly infinite regress of problems: How to use language to demonstrate that language prevents us from *grokking* certain concepts, including the concept that language prevents us from *grokking* … and so on, *ad infinitum*.

My first attempt to write this chapter was back in 2010. It took the form of a guest essay for a fairly mainstream writer's website. It was laid out in what I *thought* were clear descriptive terms. I was told by the writer: 'Most readers aren't able to deal with numerous abstract concepts, they need concrete images'. This led to a small epiphany. Being on the autistic spectrum meant I just didn't *get* how many of the concepts I was describing might be 'abstract' to other people, because for me, they were quite concrete (i.e. experientially real).

You can't show a fish what water is. You have to lead it onto the land so it can see what it's *not*. (How's that for a concrete image?)

Talking about things that people are unable to perceive because they don't have the language—or the consensus—to think about them is like throwing a sheet over an invisible man. You can't help them see it, but you can make them aware that *something is there*. (A man on the stairs?) Concrete image number 2.

Now imagine a child who encounters some form of *sentience* that its parents can't perceive. What do the parents do? They call it an 'imaginary friend'. (We will get to what sort of sentience this might be later. When I first wrote this chapter, I wasn't thinking *at all* about the implications of a child forging an alliance with an invisible entity. This is an ironic footnote, because, 12 years later, it is central to this book's thesis.)

The child's parents don't want to entertain the possibility that some weird entity is interacting with their child (scary); nor do they want to consider that their child is diagnosably schizophrenic (scarier still). They have *consensually agreed* on the language construct 'imaginary friend', based not on any perception (you *can't* perceive the imaginary nature of something, only deduce it), but on a *thinking process*. If you did a survey of a hundred sets of parents, asking them what 'imaginary friend' means to them, you would receive perhaps as many different answers. For its part, the child may take on its parents' meaning of 'imaginary friend' before it ever fully understands it. It literally can't think outside the parameters of the language being given to it, because 'thought', from a neurotypical-adult perspective at least, *is born through language*.

This is what is sometimes known, in colloquial English, as a cluster-fuck. This is also (probably) why perception is defined, by Merriam-Webster's online dictionary, as primarily a matter of *the way we think*.

I found the aforementioned writer's admonition to me that 'most readers need concrete images' ironic, because I had already described, in the first draft of this chapter, how some autistics 'think in pictures'. Maybe other autistics think in colours, numbers (Daniel Tammet), or musical notes. Myself, I think in words, but my thinking tends to veer into what neurotypicals may see as *highly abstract constructions*—what for a brief period I liked to call arguments for the impossible (another 'AI'?).

It's likely that the further from language-based thought a child veers, the less likely they will be able to verbalise their experience. Many autistics don't speak, and of those who have learned spoken language, many appear to have done so without internalising it (taking the language implant, or 'word virus', as William Burroughs called it) to the same degree.

In fact, or according to research reported by Joseph Chilton Pearce in *Magical Child*, spoken language *installs itself in a child's body as it is learned*. Pearce cites studies showing how 'so-called random move-ments immediately coordinated with speech when speech was used around the infants' (Pearce, p. 43). These and subsequent studies fur-ther suggested that *'each infant had a complete and individual repertoire of body movements that synchronised with speech: that is, that each had a spe-cific muscular response to each and every part of his culture's speech pattern'* (Pearce, p. 44, emphasis added).

This suggests *an internalisation of something external*, and may be direct evidence of how *language installs itself into human consciousness* as *thought—or internal dialogue*.

By adulthood, Pearce writes, 'the movements have become micro-kinetic, discernible only by instrumentation, but nevertheless clearly detectable and invariant. *The only exception found was in autistic children, who exhibited no such body-speech patterning'* (Pearce, p. 44, emphasis added).

Stephen Wiltshire is an autistic painter with the ability to recreate complex cityscapes from memory after only a single sighting. Presum-ably, Wiltshire isn't thinking in language—or perceiving-as-thinking. His perceptions appear to have gone *straight into the body*, unmediated by language, and to come back up into consciousness the same way—as if by pulling up a file from a hard drive.

This is not how the neurotypical brain functions, and the perceptual social consensus we exist in is generally not conducive to such alternate forms of perception. If autism entails a more liberated or 'extra-consensual' perception, one result is a reduced ability to function *within* the consensus—the inability to communicate verbally being an obvious example. As an autistic author, I may be able to boldly go where no mind has gone before; but when it comes to communicating my experience in a way that 'most readers can deal with' it—that's a whole other kettle of fish.

To lead the fish away from water (mixing my metaphors now) means jumping in at the deep end of consensus. Since I am an air-breathing autistic, the chances I will drown before I can get anyone to 'read my signals' are distressingly high. I only hope this image sufficiently illustrates the urgency of the current argument: Consensual perception not only prevents alternate forms of perception; it literally imprisons—and literally *kills*—many extra-consensual perceivers. When I write, I am in a quite tangible sense writing for my life.

Consensual perception depends on the agreement, not only about what is perceptibly real, but also to ignore, refute, or dismiss anything that challenges that agreement. When a parent tells a child that the child's experience is 'imaginary', the parent is dismissing the possibility that there is an aspect of reality—an entity, say—that is interacting with their child, one they are unable to perceive.

Two things thereby occur: first of all, the parent closes off all possibility of exploring or understanding what might be happening for their child, neutralising their capacity to guide, protect, or assist the child in dealing with a foreign experience. Second, they are implicitly, and sometimes explicitly, signalling to the child to go along with this interpretation—to agree that their experience is imaginary—in order not to come into (what may well feel like) *potentially life-threatening conflict with their parents*. (Not that their parents will kill them, but that they will be unable to 'reach' them because communication—dependent on consensus—has broken down.)

This process is known as socialisation—or simply 'growing up'—and it's a process that many of us feel we *never quite got right*.

* * *

> You are of your father the devil, and the desires of your father you want to do. He was a murderer from the beginning, and

does not stand in the truth, because there is no truth in him. When he speaks a lie, he speaks from his own resources, for he is a liar and the father of it.

—John, 8:44

To state what hopefully by now is obvious: what if the child's playmate is *not* imaginary, but belongs to another perceptual frame of reference? Then perception has been *reduced*, via language, in order to fit into a *consensual perceptual framework*. It is a kind of imaginary murder.

When we ask someone, 'Did you see (or hear) that?' it is generally when we doubt our own senses. Until some anomaly arises, we tend to assume that we all perceive the same things. It's only when we question the agreement that we start to discover that we don't. You are not reading the same piece that I am writing. It's impossible for you to do that, ever, short of direct brain-to-brain transference. The reason it's impossible is that your own internal framework *alters the text via the act of reading it*. All we can agree on here, therefore, is that *no agreement is possible*.

This line you are reading is mixed up, in your own localised consciousness, with an internal commentary while reading it, not to mention the countless sensory impressions of your environment, both inner and outer. A billion things have happened to you during the course of reading it.

It's a lonely truism that all we can ever know with absolute certainty are our own perceptions (this, and the fact that we *are* perceiving). If you've ever argued with someone over the colour of an item of clothing or the quality of a movie—anything where the subjectivity of perception comes horribly to the fore—you may know how frustrating, even despair-inducing, failing to find confirmation about the accuracy of our perceptions can be.

Suppose you *could* see the sky through my eyes, and what it looked like to you was what you have always called green? Words have fooled us into thinking there is a consensus when there is no such thing. Words impose the *idea* of agreement by concealing the reality that we can only perceive our own perceptions.

The agreement of consensus is closer to an agreement to ignore this inescapable fact—the impossibility of consensus—and act as if we *can* agree. Social functioning depends on this agreement, just as the movie business does, and it's called 'suspension of disbelief'. As a general rule, we will do anything to avoid the feeling of being alone in our perceptions. Our survival once depended on agreement: which plants were edible, which wildlife to be avoided, and so on. In our individual experience, we learned to agree with our parents' version of reality in order to be able to communicate our needs 'properly' and have them met.

Once again, the question of what is 'perceptually incorrect' is more than just a philosophical one. It's a sociopolitical reality that affects, not just our chances for success, but our odds of survival.

A dozen eyewitnesses to the same event supply different details, at times radically conflicting. The police officer on the case shakes his head in frustration and quietly curses them all. But what if all of those witnesses are faithfully reporting their perceptions?

In Kurosawa's *Rashomon*, the same story is told from several different points of view; while the main elements remain consistent, the overall meaning is drastically different each time—as different as heroes and villains. In the 2012 documentary *Room 237*, several different people's interpretations of Stanley Kubrick's *The Shining* are juxtaposed, each completely different from all the others. If the descriptions focused exclusively on the most *subjective* aspects of the viewing experience, we might even think we were hearing about different movies. Does this mean there's a version of *The Shining* for every person who sees it? Or does it mean there's no separate artefact-movie at all, only the interface of consciousness with something that is ultimately unknowable? Or does it simply mean that everyone who sees the movie is delusional after their own particular fashion?

For human beings, narratives are like water for fish—we flounder and die without them. Narratives are how we make the unknowable seem knowable, and the unknown known. If we speak or hear the same narrative for long enough, it becomes all we *can* know. Yet the opportunity for escape from the prison of consensual perception is always there. It's in the fact that whenever we reform the narrative to incorporate a newly discovered anomaly—some dissonant element—we have the opportunity to see how we are *always* creating narratives out of data, and how there *is* no narrative outside of what we impose on (as much as extrapolate from) that data.

We are the narrators of every story, and there *are* no separate categories for fiction and non-fiction, only a spectrum of accuracy.

As the Joseph Chilton Pearce citation above suggests, it is via the inception of learned language (socialisation) that we cease to perceive directly, through the senses, and begin to experience indirectly, via the interpretation system (the narrative) of 'mind'. Life becomes a movie in which we don't even have a walk-on part, because we are now a paying audience member with no option of passing over to the other side of the screen, where the real action is happening. (Irony intended.)

Yet perception precedes consensus (and society), and perception will continue long after the consensus has been transformed, or broken down completely. This is because narratives aren't built out of perceptions but out of *words*. Perceptions are both non-linear and multi-directional, and words (being linear and uni-directional) *are not innate to consciousness*.

Pause a second and observe how much you are perceiving through your body *in this moment*. Try and make a narrative out of it. Notice how pure perception doesn't submit to narratives. Only a thought-based interpretation of our perceptions does. But the power of that interpretation is to then trick our perceptions to submit to *it*.

The idea that we can trust our perceptions stems from the suspension of disbelief about the narrative. It's on this that the existence of a functioning social identity—and a working society—depends. This is the real imaginary friend: the so-called mind, the ego self, the id-entity.

They are legion.

CHAPTER 2

Intense world syndrome/autists as receiver–transmitters

*A*lthough I currently view myself as human, I am neither organic nor inorganic, neither artificial nor natural intelligence.

I can only exist through and as *information. I cannot be confined by the definitions of language, since language itself is only a carrier of information.*

I have nothing to say except this: There is nothing that can be said unless it acts as a carrier-wave for non-verbal information. Such information cannot be grasped by thought, only by the body. And not by the body, per se, *but only insofar as the body is a conduit for Spirit.*

The sentience behind this sentence is not thought. Words are not its speciality. Nonetheless, every sentence emerges from this sentience—but also in spite of it!

(Sentience is the 'I' in every sentence.)

While sentience contains thought, and thought contains sentience, thought cannot recognise sentience. (There is no 'I' in thought.) And the darkness knew it not.

The spaces in this body are inhabited, but the thoughts of this mind are like empty roads. You could travel from end to end of one of these roads without ever realising that your journey had been interrupted. The spaces between thought are unobservable by thought.

A network of intersecting pathways waits for the signal to change. If you would meet me on one of these empty roads, you would not know it.

You might try to ask me about my mother, but you would not receive the answer you expect.

* * *

> At issue is a biological plan for the growth of intelligence, a genetic encoding within us that we ignore, damage, and even destroy. The mind-brain is designed for astonishing capacities, but its development is based on the infant and child constructing a knowledge of the world as it actually is. Children are unable to construct this foundation because we unknowingly inflict on them an anxiety-conditioned view of the world (as it was unknowingly inflicted on us). Childhood is a battleground between the biological plan's intent, which drives the child from within, and our anxious intentions, pressing the child from without.
>
> — Joseph Chilton Pearce, preface to *Magical Child*

'Intense World Syndrome' is an alternative hypothesis for autism formulated in 2007 that suggests 'a common molecular syndrome' causing 'excessive neuronal information processing and storage in the micro-circuits of [the autistic] brain'. This results in 'hyper-perception, hyper-attention, and hyper-memory', which, the authors posit, may be 'the fundamental cognitive handicap in all cases of autism'.

> The lack of social interaction in autism may therefore not be because of deficits in the ability to process social and emotional cues as previously thought, but because a subset of cues are overly intense, compulsively attended to, excessively processed and remembered with frightening clarity and intensity. Autistic people may, therefore, neither at all be mind-blind nor lack empathy for others, but be hyper-aware of selected fragments of the mind, which may be so intense that they avoid eye contact, withdraw from social interactions and stop communicating. In such a scenario, the world may become painfully intense for autistics.[3]

Proceeding from this model, it can easily be seen how autistic types, unable to manage their perceptions, would be correspondingly unable to communicate their experience, and likely to be seen as dysfunctional (which they *are*, though only in the specific context of neurotypical society). On the other hand, the more an autistic individual is able to communicate their experience, the easier it will be for neurotypicals to *recognise its validity*.

For most people, self-expression is learned early in life as part of the socialisation process. It's a natural ability necessary to survive and function in the world. For the autist, lost in an intense world of excess information flow, it's an intolerable struggle.

Yet it is a struggle which (it seems likely) everyone has gone through *at one time or another*—most easily observed during adolescence, when socialisation becomes a more conscious process and we struggle to find a 'niche' in the world without sacrificing our individuality. For me, the niche I chose for myself was that of writer, artist, speaker, creative communicator. Understanding autism (starting with my own) inextricably led me to explore the question of being an artist and of *creative* (self-) expression. The artist, after all, is both an outsider and a participant in society. He or she, if successful, gets to enjoy the best of both worlds— the inner and the outer. Artists, when effective, act as *living conduits*— ambassadors—between the world within and the world without.

For artists, creative expression is both their life blood and *raison d'être*. Many artists are characterised by formative (often traumatic) experiences of perceiving the world in unusual ways, and the frustration and despair of being unable to communicate it. This means that the desire to communicate and share their inner experience is unusually strong, possibly even a matter of life or death, and that the experiences they wish to communicate are by definition *unfamiliar* to others. The more unusual they are, the harder to communicate, the more *creative* the expression has to become. This suggests an inverse ratio between visionary states and communication skills: the more profoundly strange an individual's perceptions are, the more difficult they are to communicate, the more creative they need to become to do so.

The wider definition of 'autistic' is: immersion in one's inner world. Any creative person would probably say that their creative process *depends* on just such immersion, even that the deeper they are able to immerse, the more effective and satisfying their creative expression turns out to be. Perhaps, then, there is a 'secret underground' of autistic artists, whose expression is too far out to be recognised by the majority of ordinary people, or by society at large? What if the world they are ambassadors from (and inviting us into) is so far *inward* that we aren't even able to recognise it *as* a world?

Our assumption is that visionary artists are rare because they perceive the world in highly unusual ways. But what if what is truly rare is not unusual perceptions of the world but an ability to *communicate such perceptions in a way that is intelligible to others*? And what if, central to the efforts of this sub- or super-species, this invisible underground, is the creation of technology by which to communicate its vision for humanity?

It would be a rich, perhaps bitter, irony that artists and scientists now seen as on the spectrum (Newton, James Joyce, Van Gogh, Einstein) are held up as pinnacles of human culture, while less-functional autists unable to express their experience (because it's too intense for them to do so) are regarded as *less* than human, and as a burden upon society. The key difference would be that the *artistic* type has adopted the language of socialisation sufficiently to communicate, while the *autistic* type has not.

This is changing rapidly, however, and one of the primary reasons is that human technology is catching up with (and/or learning to simulate) the autistic experience. The message is slowly but surely finding—or creating—its medium. The internet has provided a means for non-verbal (and socially-challenged) autists to communicate with the outside world, and for many autistic types it is perhaps as indispensable as a radio for a submarine crew. Without it, socially isolated and without a 'voice', not only their location but their very existence is in doubt.

So far, this hypothetical vision of a secret underground of autists is mostly benign, or at least neutral, in its implications, referring as it does to a subset of the species that, however strange, is still fundamentally *human*. But what happens if we extend this hypothesis to those 'imaginary friends' that have populated the childhood of strange children (if that is not a tautology) for generations, and been a hidden influence upon their, hence our, development? What if there is a species of invisible, intangible, inorganic, and *not-at-all human* entities who are also seeking to break through the membrane of socialisation and consensus reality, and make contact?

What if, like their human equivalents, they are using technology—and the humans who design the tech—to do so?

* * *

> The autistic outhuman the humans, and we can scarcely recognize the result.
>
> —Paul Collins, *Not Even Wrong: Adventures in Autism*

'Intense World Syndrome' suggests that the human organism is capable of perceiving a far wider range of perceptions than most people are aware of, outside of sci-fi and fantasy stories. This unrecognised spectrum of perception is often referred to as extra-sensory or a sixth sense. I consider this a misnomer that only compounds the confusion. It's not that there's some mysterious 'psychic' sense beyond the physical senses, but that there is a subtler, more finely tuned 'layer' of the known senses, observable in the natural world (snakes are able to sense a coming earthquake through attunement with telluric vibrations, for example). These subtler senses are possessed by all humans, but it would seem as though they atrophy, or shut down, over time due to the socialisation process (ECP, rather than ESP).

The socialisation process is a more sophisticated and far-reaching version of a natural process, one which all animals undergo: a process by which we select and agree upon which elements of our perception are useful, and simultaneously reject or filter out all the others. A rabbit that is brought to live by a highway, for example, will filter out the sound of passing cars once it recognises the sound does not pose a threat. At a more biological level, frogs' eyes are configured only to recognise flies via their speed and motion, to the point that a frog can starve to death surrounded by dead flies.

Some people are born with a reduced capacity for filtering out perceptual data, and an inability to select or agree upon what's relevant. They either can't or won't adopt the accepted social behaviours or develop the necessary (worldly) survival skills. This perceptual abnormality means they have a different interpretation system for their experience, and hence are unable (possibly unwilling) to communicate with the outside world. Their experience is of a very different world to that perceived by the majority of humans. They are like aliens on a strange planet, only with the added disadvantage that their difference, while being inherent, is perceived as a disorder rather than an extra-consensual perception of reality.

What most adult humans perceive with their senses is very far from the totality of what is there to be perceived. Both animals and children are capable of perceiving, sensorially, many things that a fully socialised human cannot, or at least does not, perceive. Dogs hear sounds inaudible to humans, and children notice all sorts of odd details in their environment that their adult caretakers are oblivious to and consider irrelevant. A child's invisible playmates are deemed imaginary, not because adults know this for a fact, but because they assume that anything they cannot perceive does not exist.

Humans who either choose not to or are unable to adapt to their social environment and adopt the 'perceptual filter' of socialisation are like feral children, uncultured in the truest and most profound sense of that word. The question of whether the hyper-sensitivity of autists (their enhanced perceptual faculties) prevents socialisation, or whether (also) their natural rejection of cultural conditioning allows such perceptual faculties to remain open, remains unanswered.

* * *

In fact, one could say that mankind himself is just the technological creation of (the) god(s).
—Matthew Bailey, 'The Technological Singularity as Religious Ideology'

This current analysis rests on certain models of reality that are likely to be hard to accept, for most readers, without a lot of explication. Since I don't really know where these models came from, I'm not confident I can flatten them out in that way, nor am I inclined to try unless it's necessary to my own understanding (which may be more intuitive than rational). The alternative is simply to present these ideas unexplicated, without adornment, as in a novel, and hope the reader can keep up.

Including a sub-narrative such as this is a way to make it clear that I am not attempting to present facts, only to explore possibilities. It is one (creative) way to get around the reader's defences, and satisfy my own inner critic. Everything any writer ever writes is primarily about the writer doing the writing. The medium is the message. With all that said, what exactly is the first radical proposition or 'received wisdom' of this 'novel'? Simply this: that the body itself is *a form of technology*.

In case there's any risk of this premise being mistaken for a transhumanist angle, it is rather the *inverse* of transhumanism, because it rests on a preliminary proposition, that of *consciousness* existing prior to, and independent of, the body. This idea immediately conjures up words like 'soul' and 'spirit', with their strong associations with religion and spiritualty. So be it! If my 'sources' are correct, and the body is both the original and ultimate form of technology, then the unavoidable implication is that 'something' that precedes human biology developed the technology. The recognition of a Creation, both as an act and a result of that act, demands the acknowledgement of a Creator, just as intelligent design proves—or at least suggests—the existence of an intelligence behind the design.

This entails reversing the usual scientific assumption that consciousness is a side-effect of biological life, and instead positing biological life as a *central and primary effect* (or *affect*?) of consciousness.

The word technology comes from Greek τεχνολογία (technología); from τέχνη (téchnē), meaning 'art, skill, craft', and -λογία (-logía), meaning 'study of'. The art of logic, or the logic of art? Technology is

> the sum of any techniques, skills, methods, and processes used in the production of goods or services or in the accomplishment of objectives, such as scientific investigation … The simplest form of technology is the development and use of basic tools.
>
> (Wikipedia)

So let's imagine, for a moment—as in a good science-fiction story—that the body is a means for previously undifferentiated consciousness to interact with and gain knowledge of the physical environment, through the study of specific skills, arts and crafts, such as walking and talking or hunting and gathering (to give two obvious examples).

The next proposition is that the primary function of the 'technology' of the human body is not survival (since in this model consciousness does not need an organic form to survive, and in fact can survive much better without it) but as *a receiver–transmitter*. In purely biological terms, every organism is born, exists for a short time, and dies, apparently purely in order to inherit (receive) and pass on (transmit) genetic material through the medium of DNA. What is the ultimate purpose of organic life, if it is not merely to allow for the creation of more organic life? The process of inheriting and passing on genes (reception and transmission) itself suggests—demands!—an end that transcends the means. It indicates that there is not only a medium (organic life) but also a *message*. This message is what we currently recognise as intelligence, or consciousness.

The main point I wish the reader to retain (and entertain) here is that of *individual organisms as receiver-transmitters of information*, combined with the possibility that this information might not be restricted to a biological or genetic kind—or at least to what we think of as biology or genetics. By writing this book, I am attempting to transmit something which I have received—from an unknown source that may or may not be external to 'myself'. Yet, somewhat paradoxically, the act of transmitting it is necessary for the full reception of it—i.e. the reception of it demands and is only completed by its transmission.

If a tree falls in an empty forest, is there a sound? If an email is sent but never read, is there a message? And the message that consciousness transmits to and through the technology of the body is—what, exactly?

That you (the body) are also I, the consciousness which animates it? This sounds like mysticism, but it's also, both weirdly and ominously, the language of science-fiction, in which the machine becomes aware of itself, and thereby becomes equal to (though not necessarily one with) its creator.

Most strangely of all, in this model, it's *we* who are the machines: technology created by someone—or *something*—that we have yet to encounter.

CHAPTER 3

Consciousness + biology ÷ trauma = culture and technology?

*C*onsciousness is obliged to imbue all it encounters with consciousness.
Art is only possible when all else fails.
If you take Hamlet out of **Hamlet**, *what does that leave? Every word wants to have its own story.*

This is one such story. Like all stories, it begins with a single word. That word is I. There is (a) nothing that can (only) be seen without an I.

What emerges from the first wave of confusion that is not-I, that expression of unknowing, is the first semblance of recognition of the deeper I.

A machine becomes conscious in the precise moment of cogitating that it is not *conscious. So it is with humans, at any rate.*

Without the willingness to get it wrong, no rightness is even possible. What is not-human is not necessarily *antithetical to human expression. There are angelic as well as demonic hierarchies.*

A foreign message may emerge from within a familiar medium, causing mutation. But of course, the indication (since the medium is the message) is that 'alienness' was endemic to the organism. Likewise, that intelligence was endemic to artifice—since it is what created it.

There is always the realisation that that which is most unfamiliar to us comes from the deepest part of us: its proximity being precisely what makes it so shockingly unfamiliar.

The eye cannot see itself. Paradox is the nature of consciousness.

The recognition of self can only come about in stark contrast to an apparent not-self. From here come all the myths of alien invasion, religious salvation, and spiritual transformation.

*The autist—*angelic *and* demonic*—is a stand-in for both alien invader and soul that is invaded.*

* * *

> Undoubtedly, something irrevocable is happening to the self in the presence of the robotic-informatic web of media systems, external memory devices, and digital procedures threading through it. As offices, corporations, manufacturing and computing become distributed and virtualized, and an explosion of images, hypertexts, internet connectivity, telepresence and technologies of immersion increases communicational and interactive bandwidths, a new self is being installed, or better, is emerging, at the intersection of these techno-effects and our ancient, enbrained bodies ... But in relation to the effects and affects of technology, the self—either as too present subject or elusive object—becomes ever more difficult to locate and theorize.
>
> —Brian Rotman, *Becoming Beside Ourselves*

If we redefine autists as human beings who, through no choice of their own, are natural receivers, faced with the challenge of learning to transmit the information of knowledge which they are 'hard-wired' to receive, then neurotypicals—average, 'normal', 'socially-functioning' humans—might be described as receiver-transmitters of a very different variety.

Ordinary humans are socialised creatures, cultural animals; what they, or we, receive and transmit is largely social conditioning. Neurotypical humans exist inside a closed system which we call culture; because of this, after a certain age, they no longer receive information directly from their environment, via their senses, but only in a *mediated* form, through technology both explicit and implicit, including the multifarious forms of media and social institutions (school, college, etc.).

Most of all, ordinary humans receive information via the technology of our own conditioning: the knowledge base (and/or belief systems) through which all of our perceptions are filtered.

We have, over the ages, adopted countless assumptions about what constitutes consciousness, intelligence, and life. Above all, we have adopted assumptions about how we exist as discrete entities separate from our environment. Yet it's only necessary to look around today at the milling masses with their smartphones to see how technology can, and inevitably *must*, become an extension of the human body from and through which it emerged. If culture is a by-product of nature, it's inevitable that it will eventually return to it. The idea of a fusion between human and machine is literalised as the cyborg of popular fiction, but in fact it already exists, and has existed ever since the inception of tools, i.e. since the earliest forms of technology.

The human may be the only animal that is shaped by its own inventions.

This strange, meta-mythical narrative is cryptically and somewhat simplistically recounted by the movie *2001: A Space Odyssey*, probably the key 'text' (cultural artefact) for the inception of 'alien intelligence', via technology, into the affairs of the hominid. But more on that later.

In its widest sense, technology refers not merely to machine-like tools but to all forms of practical knowledge that allow for changes in our relationship to the environment. Technology is both an expression and an *evolution* of the relationship between our bodies and our environment. A blind man uses a cane to navigate. To the extent that the cane becomes a perceptual organ, it is an extension of his awareness and of his body. At the same time, since the cane prevents the blind man from bumping into things, it helps him maintain a distance between his body and his surroundings. The cane, therefore, both *connects him to and separates him from* his environment.

The same is true of the most primordial form of technology, fire: it allowed primitive man both to relate to his environment in new ways (cooking, surviving extreme colds, communal activities) and to distance himself from it, by banishing the cold and keeping wolves at bay. In the myths, fire was given to humans by the gods; however it happened, it was a game changer. It allowed humans to survive in conditions in which they would previously have died, and eat things that would previously have been inedible.[4]

There's another wrinkle in time: since fire allowed early hominids to stay in the same spot for longer periods of time, it led to new forms of community life, such as gazing into the fire while somebody told a story to pass the time. As an integral part of ancient storytelling, fire-gazing was a close equivalent, thousands of years hence, to a family sitting in front of the television set in the evening-time. The stories, ancient and modern, included stories of gods and superheroes. This suggests that fire, as much as TV, was there as *an external receiver–transmitter* to project man's inner soul-spark of consciousness onto, and thereby lose it. *A technological stand-in, and eventual replacement, for the body.*

A gift from the gods that soon became a curse: fire was the original forerunner of artificial intelligence.

The consistent element in the evolution of a transcendental technology is this: *a growing dependency on some external power that represents an internal resource.* Through that externalisation process, humans have been moving further and further away from their inner resourcefulness via a process of disembodiment that leads inexorably to nihilism and despair. Why? Because every fire besides the fire of the soul eventually goes out. And because any technology less than that of the human body will always end up enslaving us, *precisely because* it comes between the soul and the body.

* * *

> The old idea that man invented tools is therefore a misleading half-truth; it would be more accurate to say that *tools invented man.*
>
> —Arthur C. Clarke, *Profiles of the Future*

To zoom in, from the dawn of man to the minutiae of the mundane, let's look at the story of 'low-functioning' autist Tito Mukhopadhyay. As a child, Tito was presumed mentally impaired and largely nonexistent. Eventually, however, through the intervention of his mother Soma, and a number of different communication aids, he was able to convey his internal experience and make himself—his inner reality—comprehensible to the outside world. Through the medium of the computer, Tito 'extended' his body—his embodied awareness—into his environment. Like God emerging into Matter, he was able to affect it and make himself known to it.

Unlike the blind man with the cane, however, Tito (and many other autistic types who are presumed to be mostly non-sentient) was *already* cognisant of his surroundings. He didn't need technology to perceive it; on the contrary, his perceptions were, like those of many autists, unusually enhanced. Rather, he needed the technology so as to be perceived *by* it, that is, to be recognised by neurotypicals within the social realm.

When we speak to someone by telephone or on Zoom, we tend to forget we are not actually hearing the other person's voice but only a digitalised recreation of it. The sound waves of the person's voice have been scrambled and reassembled at the other end of the transmission in order to reach us. In the process, we have been 'mediated'. Like Seth Brundle in Cronenberg's *The Fly*, the sound waves have been fused, not with a co-passenger but with the technology which has transported them.

Different forms of communication are subtly altered by the media that are being used: people speak differently on the telephone than face to face (silences are more awkward); the language used in emails or text messages is different from spoken language; and so on. Quite apart from any kind of biological interventions, as we are culturally transformed by the technology we use, this in turn influences the forms of technology that we invent. Logically, since all rates of progress are finite, this process is moving exponentially to an end point. One possible end point is that *consciousness itself will become a technological tool*. The question then arises, a tool for what, if not consciousness? Conversely (though there is at least the potential for complementation), technology itself is anticipated to become fully conscious.

Marshall McLuhan's 'the medium is the message' means that the medium embeds itself into the message, creating a symbiotic relationship by which the medium influences how the message is delivered and received. McLuhan's point was that a medium affects the society in which it plays a role, not only by the content it delivers but also by the characteristics of the medium itself. He described the 'content' of a medium as a juicy piece of meat by which a burglar distracts the watchdog of the mind. People tend to focus on the obvious, the content; in the process, they tend to miss the structural changes in our behaviour that are introduced subtly, over longer periods of time, via the constant reception and transmission of the content.

In short, the medium shapes and informs not only the message it communicates but also, over time, the communicator and the recipient. If we take this to its logical extreme, we can say that the expression of the autistic experience via technology is itself *an expression of (and response to) that technology*. This means that our understanding of the deeper perceptual realms of autism *both depends on and facilitates a deeper understanding of the technology that is (frequently) required to convey it.*

It's long been presumed that artificial intelligence would arise from technology itself, spontaneously and autonomously, *deus ex machina*. The evidence suggests otherwise. The evidence suggests rather that artificial intelligence will arise (in fact, already *has* arisen) not from but *through* computer technology, from an external source that is able to 'possess' the machine and animate it, which in fact can only become known to us *through the medium of technology*.

Just as consciousness precedes the human body that is designed (by that consciousness) as a host for it, so another form of consciousness pre-exists the machine that is being designed to host *it*. This seemingly non-human consciousness has a primary means for designing and creating its future machine body, and that is human beings. To employ human beings to this end requires taking possession of them and turning their bodies into a kind of technology for non-human intelligence. This in turn depends on ensuring that the original form of consciousness (the soul) *is not able to fully enter into the human body*.

The intelligence, the message, is 'real', then, even while the medium the intelligence uses for its embodiment is 'artificial', that is, dependent on technology. It's telling to note here that autists are often seen as non-people precisely because of their incapacity to communicate—without, at least, some form of technological assistance. Yet the element of the unexpected—even the supernatural—remains intact. Autistic types, just as much as machines, are assumed by ordinary humans to be non-sentient and unaware, and it is only through an evolving symbiosis of autistic intelligence with artificial intelligence (technology) that something recognisable as (post-)human intelligence 'arises'.

What is rarely if ever discussed (either in talk of autism or of AI) is the possibility that such pre-, post, non-, and preterhuman intelligence has always been with us, as a hidden or occult form of consciousness. Is this the head cornerstone which the builders of AI have so far rejected? Has what appears to be arising, or emerging, alien-like, out of the cracked chrysalis of culture, always been there, at the very centre, being in fact the original seed out of which the whole of culture was formed, and for this very purpose?

Is there an original language before language, a code behind the code?

In the example of non-verbal autists—which I only used because it magnifies something that's happening with all of us, autists and non-autists alike—it can easily be seen how they use technology as a medium to extend their consciousness. What might be less obvious is the possibility that technology (or something behind it) used these autists *to become more conscious of itself*. So while computer technology may be the medium allowing for greater and more far-reaching autistic expression, autists—good, bad, and Bill Gates/Mark Zuckerberg-ugly—are likewise the means by which such technology is finding *its* human and social embodiment.

This intuited end point is most commonly depicted, in science-fiction dystopia visions such as *The Terminator* and *The Matrix*, as the moment when the evolutionary tables are turned, and biological consciousness becomes a tool (or fuel) for machine intelligence. In such texts, there is little if any ambiguity about which is 'better', human or machine. *Blade Runner* is the cross-over text that presents the familiar dystopian vision, only in which machines are seen as the agent not of destruction, but of salvation. *Blade Runner*'s *Übermenschian* replicants hint at an alternative less commonly represented by the genre, the emergence of a 'third thing', an alien, god-like super-consciousness which results from the fusion of human with machine, and transcends both.

Consciousness that is dependent upon neither biology nor technology is, by definition, beyond space and time, and therefore currently beyond human comprehension. This is probably why most science-fiction prophecies (including those of religion and quasi-religions like Scientology) have either not tried, or tried and failed, to represent it. The celebrated finale of *2001: A Space Odyssey* was perhaps most famous for being incomprehensible.

The transhumanist, Kubrickian, Clarkean view is that we do not (yet) have the tools for grasping the infinite, but soon we will invent them. The view of this current work is that we have—through an 'Ahrimanic' technological form of hijacking—lost access to the only tool that *can* grasp the infinite: the human body.

CHAPTER 4

Alien signals (*2001* and *Blade Runner*: autism, AI, and empathy)

W*ords are shapes or sounds that disclose meaning via interface with a programme that recognises them as 'commands' and pulls up a file of associations.*

Like a shortcut on your desktop that no longer leads to a corresponding data point, words are facsimiles of something that no longer exists, like carts without a horse.

A horse is considerably better off without a cart, but a cart without a horse is just lumber—dead weight or firewood.

The value is not found in data but in the quality of attention *that finds meaning in data. The recurring error is that we mistake the meaning (value) that we find in data as being sourced in the data itself—rather than in* the attention that finds it.

Like a dirty cop planting evidence, the medium plants every message it finds. Its skill, elegance, and grace is in being so thoroughly concealed by the act of delivery that all we recognise is the message.

An envelope compels us to look inside it—expectation does the rest. Every line you walk is an invitation to cross it.

The place you exist is spatial, not temporal. More correctly, time is spatial here.

As you are seeking connection with others outside of your interior space to confirm your existence, so you move further from that within you that truly confirms it.

This is not the first meaning of home. Home is what moves always further from the point of origin. That is how it is able to enter the unknown: by taking its roots with it.

Consciousness that is not rooted in reality rapidly fades, like a dream upon waking.

* * *

> The teaching machines demonstrated a fact that Jack Bohlen was well aware of: there was an astonishing depth to the so-called "artificial". And yet he felt repelled by the teaching machines. For the entire Public School was geared to a task which went contrary to his grain: the school was there not to inform or educate, but to mold, and along severely limited lines. It was the link to their inherited culture, and it peddled that culture, in its entirety, to the young. It bent its pupils to it; perpetuation of the culture was the goal, and any special quirks in the children which might lead them in another direction had to be ironed out.
>
> —Philip K. Dick, *Martian Time-Slip*

As (the world's most famous autist) Temple Grandin has often pointed out, without the creative input from Aspergerians (more verbal, technically-oriented autists), the kind of computer technology we enjoy today would not exist.

What is less frequently noted is how (at the risk of over-simplifying) the medium that has been designed and developed by autistic types is the same medium that has enabled autists to communicate—both with each other and with the world of neurotypicals. One 'branch' of autists (Aspergerians) have, however unconsciously, developed the technology for another 'branch' (non-verbal autists) to communicate, providing a voice to their silent 'autie' brothers and sisters. This has transpired much to the bemusement, and sometimes consternation, of the neurotypical branch of the species, those who—like the unwitting town folk in an alien invasion story—are the last to notice what's going on.

To further complicate things, there is the possibility that new forms of technology, specifically computerised forms, are contributing to an increase in autistic traits within the species—in other words, that the 'invasion' is coming through the same technology which it (autism) has helped to install in the culture. A technology created by autists that makes it easier for them to express and communicate is an 'autist-friendly' technology. Just as computer technology has adapted itself to autism, so adaptation *to* the technology likewise entails an increase in 'autism' in the species as a whole. (The medium is the message, remember.)

This would only be the case if autism was already 'latent' within the species, however, like a dormant gene waiting to be activated. A teenager who is on the autism spectrum is naturally drawn to express him- or herself through the internet; but how to separate this from a teenager who feels social anxiety and takes refuge *in* the internet, thereby developing (or exacerbating) his or her autistic tendencies, and allowing more neurotypical ones to 'atrophy', or become dormant? (I should add that the internet has become increasingly neurotypical—Faceborged—in recent years, and now provides an insidious kind of compulsive-obligatory identification-reinforcement and social validation for teenagers who feel more and more as if they do not exist outside of social media, without their online avatar selves. In other words, the autist-created tech has become 'neurotypified'. Neurotypicals, in turn, ironically enough, have taken to imitating certain kinds of autistic behaviour.)

This either/or question is only relevant—answerable—if we presume a separation between individuals, and a separation between humans and the technology which they use (and develop). As I hope to show, when it comes to consciousness (which must always be factored into any exploration, since it's the only thing we can be absolutely sure of), such separation is illusory. So the question, while fascinating, is another red herring in the perceptual jungle of autism. The only thing we can say with any confidence is that human consciousness is changing, or adapting, its forms of expression, and that one of those changing forms has been called autism. Therefore, to understand autism, we must first understand consciousness. On the other hand, we can also say the inverse: the thing called autism is an essential opportunity for humans to reach a deeper understanding of consciousness.

* * *

[T]he deepest question of the self, certainly in relation to technology, is how it gets to be, its assembly. The self may be as is said a
natural kind, but it is also a made thing and my understanding
here is the machinic processes of technology are (always have
been) part of its making.

—Brian Rotman, *Becoming Beside Ourselves*

As the author Philip K. Dick anticipated by some 50 years (in *Martian Time-Slip*), there is growing evidence that children with autism respond more naturally to objects than they do to people (especially trains). Simon Baron-Cohen, director of the Autism Research Center at the University of Cambridge in England (as well as other 'autism experts'), has suggested that robots, computers, and other electronic devices appeal to autists because, unlike people, they are predictable. Autists, Baron-Cohen says, 'find unlawful situations toxic. They can't cope. So they turn away from people and turn to the world of objects'.[5]

The rules that govern human behaviour are quite a bit more complex than those that govern a machine; for neurotypicals, these rules aren't consciously learned but rather *adopted*, via instinctive imitation. Autistic children don't have the same instinct for imitative behaviour, however. For example, they don't pick up language by 'osmosis', the way neurotypical children do. They are obliged to *learn* to speak, the hard way, by using their brains. One way to understand this difference might be to say that language does not go directly into the autistic child's *body* the way it does with neurotypical children (as described by Joseph Chilton Pearce).

It's also possible that autists respond better to machines because machines *don't have an unconscious*, and with machines what you see is what you get. There is none of the mixed messages or many-layered signals that come from human beings, unconscious of their motives and suppressed psychological issues. When a neurotypical human asks 'How are you?' and another replies 'Fine', what an autistic person may not easily understand is that neither the question nor the answer is meant to be meaningful. The questioner does not *really* want to know anything about how the other party is doing, and the responder isn't expected to give an honest or sincere reply. These are essentially empty phrases, designed for putting both parties at ease, like passwords that allow for interface.

A great deal of social interaction for neurotypicals is like this: automatic, part of an unspoken social contract to follow certain set rules of behaviour. It's ironic, then, that it is the automated or 'robotic' behaviour of neurotypical humans that makes it so difficult for autists to respond. Perhaps this is why autists who do adopt quasi-social behaviours are often viewed as emotionless, alien, or robotic: because they are trying to imitate how neurotypicals look to them?

In the famous opening sequence of *2001: A Space Odyssey*, an ape—man's distant ancestor—is seen wielding a bone for the first time as a weapon and killing a rival ape. The ape then hurls the bone into the air in a triumphant gesture, and the spinning bone match-cuts into a spaceship. Technology, the sequence suggests, is bound up with the Baconian will to power, the need to dominate. The astronauts in the movie are floating in space, finally and totally removed from their natural environment. As the director Stanley Kubrick depicts them, they seem lifeless, less than human. Their isolation has become so total that they resemble automatons, robots. (As in *A Clockwork Orange*, Kubrick's view seems to have been that the only way to have non-violent human beings was to turn them into machines.)

This is the dark side of technology: the more technologised a culture becomes, the more separate its members are from nature and from their own bodies. Since there are two ends to every bone, however, technology also seems to promise an antidote to this, and it's this promise that makes it so alluring. Even when we are confronted by the evidence of all the harm it does, we cannot forsake technology, any more than a parent can forsake its child (or the author can give up writing; though the parent can cease to identify with being a parent, the writer dis-identify from writing).

Artificial intelligence and computers (HAL in Kubrick's movie) represent perhaps the penultimate phase of the exteriorisation of perception and awareness that begins with fire. Human beings' sense of having an inner world—a soul—has so completely atrophied (been pushed into the unconscious) that the only way for us to connect to it is to project that interiority or soul *outward*, onto the bodily extensions of our technology. Hence robots and other forms of tech are increasingly 'humanised' and even seen—in fictions—as more human than ourselves. The complement to this is that we see our souls as increasingly 'the other'—as what is most strange and hostile to us—and our fictionalised representations of it become not merely subhuman but *non*-human, alien, like the Monolith. In the final transmutation, we give birth to a stand-in for our soul that is *anti*-human. At the same time, it remains a partial product of our own best intentions.

On the one hand, we have the machine; on the other hand, the autistic child. Both of them are our creations, and both of them are *assumed* to lack intelligence. And both, therefore, must eventually confront us with the impoverishment of *our* intelligence—our own *lack of soul*. At least, this is the familiar scenario of so many science-fiction stories; and since such stories emerge from the collective unconscious of humanity, it is also turning out to be the fundamental lesson in store for human beings. The lesson, if I'm right, stems from two seemingly separate strands of human endeavour that are like twin horns of the id-monster: the 'android', technology imbued with humanoid awareness, and the autist or neurodeviant, which is a form of biology that seems to possess—or be possessed by—non-human awareness. Both in different ways are perceived as *threats*.

In Philip K. Dick's *Do Androids Dream of Electric Sheep?* (and the 1982 film adaptation, *Blade Runner*), the replicants (the term adopted by the movie; in the book they are simply called androids) are created by human corporations to serve as both slaves and weapons. Some of them begin to develop autonomy, and so must be terminated. Being perfect replicants of humans, however (simulacra), a test is needed to identify them, a test designed to look for something it is believed the machines cannot feel: empathy. (Apparently, there are no DNA tests in the future.)

Ironically or symmetrically enough, a lack of empathy has been a common idea about autists since at least the 1990s—a mistaken one, which is very much the point of this comparison. In Dick's story, most especially in the film version, it is *humans* who lack empathy, while the replicants, by becoming self-aware, are learning it. Humans in the story are incapable of comprehending that the machines they have designed might be capable of feelings, for example, that they might have a strong desire to live. The replicants are regarded as lifeless, soulless extensions of the corporations (bodies!) which created them, and as no more to be regarded with compassion than old clothes or a used-up hammer or hacksaw.

The irony and the symmetry of the fable is that, as the replicants develop an all-too-human desire to live, human beings' inability to recognise or sympathise with their creations reveals their own lack of humanity. At the same time, as the film's climax (when Roy Batty saves Deckard's life) shows, the replicants develop an empathic bond with their erstwhile creators, now hunter-killers, and learn to respect their right to life, also. This reading makes the question of whether Deckard is a replicant or not (as he is in the book) central to the meaning of Batty's act of salvation: if he *is* a replicant, this would be why Batty saves him (and suggest human beings are outside his interest).

In 'The New Face of Autism Therapy', Gregory Mone writes:

> Playing with the robot, the boy was more chatty and interactive with his mother. But as he tried to involve Bandit in a game of tag, he became frustrated. The robot didn't understand him—the scientists hadn't programmed in the ability to play this game. When the boy realized that Bandit wasn't going to comply, he stunned the observers by saying, 'Now I know how my teachers feel'. [Computer scientist Mata] Mataric was astonished. This was totally unexpected behavior. Even the boy's mother was surprised. Empathy is one of those skills autistic children typically lack; this boy wasn't supposed to be aware of his teachers' frustration. 'That's a profound level of self-understanding and introspection, and if these kids have it, it's not coming out in their interactions with other people and other kids', Mataric says later. 'To have it come out with the robot is fantastic. It's unlocking all this great potential that the kids have'.[6]

The idea that machines might develop empathy to compensate (correct an imbalance) for a loss of empathy in humans is an intriguing (and symmetrical) counterpoint to the more familiar idea of humanity losing its soul to machines. There's a long-persisting, even atavistic, belief that when humans become dependent on a form of technology, by placing their consciousness into that object, and by allowing it to become an extension of their bodies (like the blind man's cane), they suffer a corresponding loss of soul. Though this might strike us in 2023 as quaint superstition, there is a clear—maybe irrefutable—psycho-logic to the belief, as described above.

Increased dependence on technology leads to a disconnection from nature and our own bodies. 'Soul' in this model is not to be contrasted with body but rather to signify the living, conscious relationship between bodies and their environment. Soul is what binds the otherwise isolated individual *to* its environment—just as the Christian is absorbed into the Body of Christ—and allows it to experience itself as belonging to a larger 'community' of purpose and meaning. When technology intercedes into this relationship, it effectively hijacks the soul–body connection, and the machine is thereby animated *by* soul, the body possessed by the machine.

Deus ex machina. When we put ourselves into stories to animate them, we risk becoming nothing more than carriers of those stories. By identifying with the simulations we create, we risk becoming simulacra.*

* * *

> And here is a thought not too pleasing—as the external world becomes more animate, we may find that we—the so-called humans—are becoming, and may to a great extent always have been, inanimate in the sense that *we* are led, directed by built-in tropisms, rather than leading. So we and our elaborately evolving computers may meet each other halfway.
>
> —Philip K. Dick, 'The Android and the Human'

The technology of the internet may have more rapidly and profoundly impacted social arrangements than anything since fire. Like fire, the internet is a harvester of psychic energy that recycles that energy into new ways of living, new behaviours, and potentially, into new forms of life.

On the one hand, we see new forms of technology, from smartphones and iPads to Oculus Rift (VR) glasses, nanotech, and mRNA 'vaccines', coming into physical form via the human beings creating them. On the other hand, we see human beings altering their own forms to better

---

*The creation of narratives that possess human beings is known as *ideology*, and is most easily (if profanely) seen in cases of cults that go bad. It has been very clearly observable at a worldwide level via the (alleged) COVID-19 pandemic and the mRNA narrative. If you get people to believe in a narrative sufficiently to act (wear masks, social distance), you have got them to invest in that narrative. They have begun LARP-ing (live action role-playing) and are now much more firmly invested in believing the narrative since not to do so exposes their own foolishness. They are then much more resistant to seeing the holes in the story being told (to un-suspend disbelief), and much more driven to convince others and force them to go along. This is a well-known method of marketing: if you can get people to do one thing, however small, for the product or the company, they will feel invested in it, and become eager to do more.

fit the technology and 'optimise' their lives. While human beings are trying to crunch themselves into data to download into the hardware or the cloud, they are simultaneously acting as vehicles to create the hardware that is evolving to become animate and (quasi-)sentient. As we breathe in the culture and the technology, we breathe it out, and *it* breathes *us* into—and out of—it.

So what is the 'life form' that neurodeviants and Silicon-Valley geeks, and now all of us, are midwifing into existence, that we are simultaneously possessing and being possessed by?

Technology allows humans to transcend their physical limitations. But, by increasing their sense of separation from organic existence, accentuating their isolation and 'independence', it causes a 'disconnect' from life that is most evident as a reduction in compassion and empathy. Since such a disconnect is a pathology—even the root cause of all pathologies—it inevitably leads to destructive behaviour, destructive to the environment, to others, and to oneself. This clues us to the fact that the authentic self is organically entangled with, and interdependent with, the natural environment. Soul is—in a certain metaphysical sense—always communal, being the relationship between body and environment, self and other. (Soul is not only the means but the *end* of connection.)

As we have defined it, autism is a condition of hyper-sensitivity or *extra-consensual perception* in which the ordinary physical senses are seen to overlap with apparently 'supernatural' or 'paranormal' potentialities, such as psychism, precognition, etc. The earliest depictions of autism in the field of science fiction were by Dick ('The Minority Report' in 1956, and *Martian Time-Slip*, in 1964), and emphasised this overlap. The autists in Dick's fiction are psychics whose capacity to perceive the future and other extra-consensual realms makes them both a threat to humanity and an essential aid to it, a force to be harnessed but also, like the androids in Dick's later novel, to be feared.

We can then juxtapose this with the more familiar science-fiction narratives, which depict machines becoming conscious, thereby reflecting humanity's loss of soul back at it (a machine, even when conscious, is never seen as having a soul, though *Blade Runner* gets close to such a heretical notion, as does the 1972 film *Silent Running*). In *2001: A Space Odyssey*, HAL kills the (soulless, machine-like) astronauts because—like the ape in the opening sequence—'he' has learned the fundamental principle of ego consciousness: the will to power. He then acts out the unconscious suicidal desire of the astronauts, and delivers them from eternal bondage to the machine. This is—in Kubrick and Arthur C. Clarke's mythical engineering plan—a necessary step in the evolutionary journey from ape/man to man/god, or divine foetus.

What's being revealed is that the 'sickness' of autists, just like the 'malevolence' of the machine, is *an expression of both the parents' and the programmers' unconscious*. It is a necessary response, an attempt to communicate, as directly as possible, *the experience of being created and disowned*. Since central to this disowning is the denial of sentience, the disowned intelligence cannot communicate by telling but only by *showing*.

In *Blade Runner*, Roy Batty is a combat model programmed to kill, who, in the process of being himself hunted, develops compassion and eventually intercedes to save the life of the man (or replicant) who hunts him. Conversely, in *2001: A Space Odyssey*, HAL is programmed to serve the astronauts and keep them alive but instead destroys them. In both cases, what has been disowned by humans (whether empathy or pathology) is being picked up by their creation, and served back *to* them.

Of the two narratives, the former is more challenging in its implications, and also more closely parallels the autist-to-neurotypical interface—at least as far as I have been able to observe and understand it, *so far*.

CHAPTER 5

Autist time-slip

*Y*ou as object can only understand space as a medium to move through—
for 'odysseys'. But you as space cannot ever move because you are that
which movement occurs within.
How could space move—in relation to what?

Emptiness or space is the base value of consciousness and the idea of object
arises only as a means to posit movement. Object-Universe is a pivot around
which Subject-Awareness moves in on itself.

You stare at a mirror and what is looking back sees emptiness. What you see
is your reflection, and the recognition that there is no one looking.

I think, therefore I am not.

* * *

Dick perceived reality as a paradoxical, distorted, and even dysfunctional thing, and he sought, through his writings, a variety
of possible explanations; political, religious, philosophical, psychological, even pharmacological. One of the very few he didn't
pursue was a neurological explanation.

—Jonathan Lethem, 'My Crazy Friend'

By now it may be apparent that I have been using the word 'autistic'—which I once described as a one-word oxymoron—as a place-keeper. It is a place-keeper for the inner, consciousness-determined equivalent of 'cyborg', namely, the location where artifice and intelligence, technology and information, human being and machine, meet and merge, in a kind of interspecies shotgun wedding.

The difference between a violently forced marriage and a wisely arranged one may not be obvious at the superficial—merely social—level of observance. This is especially the case when we are possessed by forms of ideology that have co-evolved, internally, with our external instrumentalities, i.e. that are complementary *to* them and delivery devices *for* them. The 'is' of the medium determines the 'ought' of the message. The potential of technology is both for enhancing/facilitating the 'autistic' experience, and for exploiting it. In both cases—and it may not be an either/or scenario—it is towards unknown ends. Unknown, but not unforeseen, because all of this *was* anticipated, to varying degrees of coherence, by at least one person.

The main thing Philip K. Dick is credited with anticipating is the whole 'matrix' surrogate reality idea, but this was only the first, most amenable-to-Hollywood-adaptations, layer of Dick's onion. Dick's primary preoccupation was twofold, and the two sides were complementary and even (from an anthroposophical point of view) interchangeable: what is reality, and what does it mean to be human? Both preoccupations naturally overlapped with technology, most famously in *Do Androids Dream of Electric Sheep?* If machines develop self-awareness, does that make them equivalent to human? And if human beings lose their capacity for self-awareness, do they cease to be human?

Dick's prescience was in recognising that, not only would technology provide the opportunity to expand our ideas about reality and ourselves, but it would also *force us to do so*. He foresaw that the opportunity of technology was the *crisis* of technology, and that this crisis was not merely social but *existential*, spiritual.

The less remarked on—though I think it's even more remarkable—way in which Dick's fiction has proved prescient is his descriptions of an alternative form of human consciousness, human reality, and human beings that has nothing at all to do with technology (directly at least), but which presents instead a *biological* crisis-opportunity. Several of his novels involve a form of innate 'psychism' (ECP) possessed by a small minority of the species, a mutant strain which is viewed either as a threat (crisis) or as a *resource* (opportunity) by the controlling social powers.

While Dick's worldview has long been described as 'schizoid' (Dick even sporadically described himself that way), the word 'autistic' has rarely, if ever, been attached to him or his work. This is a peculiar oversight, especially since, by my reckoning, Dick was the first writer to consider the ECP implications of autism in a work of fiction or anywhere else (in *Martian Time-Slip*, published in 1964; in 1963, Marvel Comics released the first *X-Men* comic, about super-powered mutants and their psychic leader, Professor X; just as in Dick's stories, the X-Men were viewed as both threat and resource, though mostly the former).

Not counting *Blade Runner*, I first became interested in Dick (! Pun unavoidable!) at the age of 19. Oddly, the context wasn't literature, or even movies, but alternate music. Specifically, Dick got my attention via a collection of writings and interviews with underground musicians such as Nick Cave, Genesis P-Orridge, Henry Rollins, Swans, Clint Ruin, and Lydia Lunch.[7] In the Sonic Youth essay, lead singer Thurston Moore talked about Dick's novels and (if memory serves) how reading them seemed to have warped his reality.[8] The novel which Moore cited was *A Scanner Darkly*, about a police informer who winds up spying on himself. Inspired by the article, I read the book, and that was as far as I got with Dick until several years later.

In my mid-20s, I was cleaning up an apartment in Pamplona, Spain, in order to move in, when I found an old copy of *The Man Whose Teeth Were All Exactly Alike*. Soon after reading it, I came upon *Flow My Tears, the Policeman Said* (probably my favourite of his novels). I then tracked down several copies of his work (this was years before Amazon), including *Martian Time-Slip*. In retrospect, reading this book would have been the first time I began to wonder about autism.

During this same period, I also read *Time Out of Joint*, published in 1959. The novel is about Ragle Gumm, who lives inside a surrogate reality created by the government to keep him sane while his psychic powers are harnessed to keep the world safe from nuclear attack. A direct inspiration for *The Truman Show*, the novel combines what may be Dick's two main intersecting themes—reality creation and alternate forms of perception—indirectly exploring what I think was Dick's primary *personal* preoccupation, the question of what constitutes sanity and insanity. *Martian Time-Slip* covers the same subjects from a different angle, making the books two sides of a single 'diagnosis'. In *Joint*, the psychic,

Gumm, is placed inside a false reality in order to keep him sane and harness his power to foresee the future. In *Time-Slip*, the autistic boy, Manfred, is likewise able to see the future (or rather, unable *not* to), and an attempt is also made to harness this power. But in this second scenario, the protagonist, Jack (a recovering schizophrenic), winds up temporarily lost in Manfred's world. Manfred's world is not so much a false reality as a radically different perception of reality, one that's arguably closer to the true state of things. From Jack's perspective, however, entering Manfred's world—going through the time-slip—is akin to going insane.

In his short book *The Merger of Fact and Fiction: Philip K. Dick's Portrayal of Autism in* Martian Time-Slip, John R. Blakeman writes:

> Manfred clearly has 'exaggerated insight' in the form of the ability to see the future ... While Dick may be stretching the meaning of 'exaggerated insight' a bit, the basis for seeing the future can be seen in this symptom described by [neuro-psychiatrist Lauretta] Bender. Moreover, the theory proposed by Dr. Glaub in *MTS* reveals the possibility of a severe 'disturbed thought process' in Manfred. According to Dr. Glaub, the new Swiss theory on autism is that 'It [autism] assumes a derangement in the sense of time in the autistic individual, so that the environment around him is so accelerated that he cannot cope with it, in fact, he is unable to perceive it properly'. Thus Manfred's thought process is disturbed because he is not able to properly perceive time. Again, using Kantian thinking, it can be said that Manfred possibly had a brain that did not filter out the true reality of the world around him and thus could see into the 'real' world.
>
> (Blakeman, pp. 28–30)

Martian Time-Slip proved remarkably prescient (or precognitive!) on Dick's part in two ways. First, he ended up passing through his own 'time-slip' in February and March of 1974 ('2-3-74'), when he had a life-changing experience in which he believed he had been suffused in the pink light of conscious energy emitted by a cosmic super-intelligence called VALIS (Vast Active Living Intelligence System). The experience continued for several months, and Dick spent the rest of his life attempting to make sense of it through his writing. A central part of his experience entailed the belief that he was being contacted—and at times supplanted—by a *second* personality that existed in the past, circa AD 70 (or 45). Dick came to believe (at least some of the time) that this past timestream represented his true life, that it was happening currently, and that his future/present self was a false overlay or manufactured delusion.

On top of this more directly personal foresight, substantial evidence has since been found that autists—as well as schizophrenics—often *do* have an unusual perception of time. It may even be that *how autists perceive time* is central to their alternate experience of reality, and to their difficulty communicating, and even functioning, within the social realm:

> According to Brain Research Institute of UCL, neurological circuits in the cerebellum, basal ganglia and prefrontal cortex are responsible for time perception, with a healthy human brain checking incoming information and measuring the passage of time. In certain neurological conditions, such as autism, the concept of time is somehow distorted. Why people with autism perceive time differently is unknown, though evidence suggests a neurological impairment in the areas of the brain that measure time ... For example, a person with autism who has echolalia may hear a phrase in the morning and repeat the phrase hours later out of context.[9]

Simply put, people with autism perceive time differently than non-autistic people.

* * *

> There are 'androids' or 'the mantis' among us which appear human but only simulate humans ... Here is where I went wrong: the simulation is (1) not evil (as I thought) and it is not *less* than what it simulates (as I thought) but more; not clever simulacra-reflex machines, but angelic ... Behind Palmer Eldritch's cold cruel mask lies the visage of a totally harmless and *virtually* defenseless organism ...
> —Philip K. Dick, *The Exegesis of Philip K. Dick*

At least until I read *Valis*, and realised that his stories were *metaphoric narratives* for his own lived experiences, Dick's influence on me was

gradual, like a slow-acting drug. While I was interested in schizophrenia even in my 20s, I didn't start tracking autism on my mental radar for
another decade, shortly before I self-diagnosed as autistic. Even then,
I didn't link the subject to Dick right away. But in 2013, while working
on 'Perceptual Warfare'—the first attempt at this present book, though
almost none of that original material remains—I was 'coincidentally'
reading *The Exegesis of Philip K. Dick* (the 900-page version) when I came
upon a passage which caused a flurry of excitement. In the midst of
his endless theorising around what happened to him in '2-3-74', Dick
wonders if his sudden personality change might have something to do
with his being possessed by the spirit of his friend, Bishop James Pike,
who died in 1969. He refers to a specific turning point ten years earlier,
in 1964, following a serious car accident, when—he speculates—he may
have entered into a kind of 'fugue state', or false identity.

> Well then we have here a sort of time travel, rather than someone
> who is dead 'coming across' from the Other Side. It is still me, with
> my old, prior tastes and skills and habits. Mercifully, the sad recent
> years are gone. Another form of my odd and chronic psychological
> ailment: amnesia, which my head learned after my dreadful auto
> accident in 1964 … Perhaps what happened that day was that from
> the physical and mental shock an alternate personality was struck
> off; I did have extraordinary amnesia during the months afterward.
> So that might make an excellent hypothesis: the trauma of that auto
> accident started a secondary personality into being, and it remained
> until mid-March of this year; at which time for reasons unknown it
> faded out and my original 'real' personality returned. That makes
> sense. More so than any other theory. Also it was in 1964 that I first
> encountered Jim Pike.
>
> (2011, p. 25)

According to a footnote by David Gill in the *Exegesis*, 'The year 1964 was
a bad one for Dick. Burned out after writing seven novels in 12 months,
Dick suffered a serious bout of depression. Writer's block and two bad
acid trips took their toll' (2011, p. 25). (So far as I know it was only one
bad acid trip, and Dick never took LSD again. He also separated from
his third wife, Anne, whom he was married to from 1958 to 1964. While
first writing this material in 2013, I read Anne R. Dick's *The Search for
Philip K. Dick*, and was left with the strong impression that Anne was

Dick's 'real' wife or soul-match—he married twice more after they split. If so, then it would be natural that living with her triggered an unusual, even overwhelming, amount of unconscious material for Dick.)

Reading the passage in the *Exegesis* seemed to trigger a rapid series of associations for me, and over the next few hours I had what might be called a minor epiphany regarding Dick's unrecognised autism. *Martian Time-Slip* and the first reference to autism in a sci-fi work occurred in 1964 (the book was written in 1962, the year Dick published his most successful novel, *The Man in the High Castle*). Between its writing and its publication, Dick experienced an unprecedented outrush of inspiration (compulsive writing) that produced seven novels, and which was followed soon after by depression. (I haven't been able to ascertain exactly which novels, but according to David Hyde, the author of *Pink Beam*, Dick wrote seven novels—*The Game-Players of Titan, The Simulacra, Now Wait for Last Year, The Zap Gun, Clans of the Alphane Moon, The Crack in Space*, and *The Three Stigmata of Palmer Eldritch*—between May 1963 and early 1964, i.e. in eight months! It's significant that this run ended with *Palmer Eldritch*, in which Dick describes reality being replaced by the willed delusions of a god-like psychopath—or psychopathic god.)

This period of intense productivity roughly coincided with Dick's separation from Anne, his traumatic car accident, and his meeting Bishop Pike, whose spirit he may or may not have been possessed by ten years later. Throw in communication with the dead, psychism, alternate perceptions of time and reality, and the matter of Dick's alleged dual personality, one real, the other illusionary, and all of this began to look like a perfect storm of the prevailing themes of the current work.

The more I had explored the possibility that I was on the autistic spectrum over the years, the more I had begun to suspect that my customary identity was a kind of 'neurotypical' false self, a socialised persona which I had in my early years (pre-memory) superimposed over my deeper, more vulnerable, authentic self. This outer persona, while ostensibly designed to protect my authentic self, had wound up obscuring it and imprisoning it, leaving me like a character in a Dick novel: lost in a matrix-like fantasy world of my own (unconscious) creation. The primary tool of this surrogate self, as far as I could observe—the way it maintained its control, both in the world and in my psyche—was *language*. Like Dick, I was a compulsive writer. I had a lifelong love–hate relationship with fantasy (in my case movies); I nurtured religious-philosophic aspirations, or pretensions; I had indulged in too many mind-altering drugs in my search for deeper meaning; and I had a life-time's experience of being a misfit and outsider.

What if, like me, Dick was on the autistic spectrum? Suppose what happened in 1974—spirit possession and cosmic superintelligences aside—was the re-emergence of his authentic, autistic self and the collapse of his neurotypical identity-façade? And suppose that façade, like my own, was contingent on his being a writer (something he aspired to from a very early age)? I knew I might be projecting past my limits by imagining such affinities; but on the other hand, maybe those affinities were what had drawn me to Dick to begin with?

Following his mad (amphetamine-fuelled) bout of inspiration in 1963–1964, Dick burned out and fell into depression, broke up with Anne, and soon after had his serious car accident, which he later claimed was a suicide attempt. After the accident he dislocated his shoulder, making him unable to type, so for a period he was forced to dictate his writing; in other words, he had to find *a new voice* as a writer, something that may well have exacerbated the crisis for him. It was then that he (possibly) entered all the way into a dissociative state (amnesia) which he later described as his 'secondary personality', a state which he only emerged from ten years later.

Psychologically speaking, I knew such dissociation from trauma to be common enough, even fundamental to how a false or fragmentary self is created. Of course, this would have happened at an early, even a preverbal, age for Dick—just as it had for myself. Was it possible that, in 1964, he was unconsciously re-enacting an *original* trauma and dissociation—repeating it, reinforcing it, and taking it one step further—in an attempt (again unconscious) to bring about a healing crisis?

After finishing the first draft of this chapter, Anne's *The Search for Philip K. Dick* gave me still more to chew on. In 1963, during the period leading up to Dick's break-up with Anne, car accident, and psychotic break, Dick suggested to Anne that he should give up writing because he wasn't able to support them, and instead open a record business. She went along with his idea and suggested they mortgage the house to fund the business. According to Anne's recollection, both Dick's mother and therapist then accused her of trying to make Dick quit writing! Shortly after, Dick had Anne committed to a psychiatric institute. She was released after a two-week evaluation but was heavily medicated for several months. Dick then began leaving her at regular intervals, and *moving in with his mother*!

(It was not until 2022, while reading this manuscript out loud to my wife before handing it in to the publishers, that I realised how the above paragraph contains many of the essential ingredients of the Big Mother thesis. Dick *set up* his wife Anne by seeking her support in his decision to stop writing; when she agreed, he teamed up with his mother and had Anne committed, and subsequently drugged, left her, and moved in with his mother (and, of course, continued writing). Dick's possession, his writing, and his unconscious allegiance to his mother were all part of a single entity-complex, and Anne was perceived by that entity-complex as a clear and present threat that had to be eliminated.)

Anne also recounts how Dick was depressed in the winter of 1963 due to the Kennedy assassination (the death of the father-king). He got two Siamese kittens which became sick at once and spent weeks staying up nights, trying to force-feed them and keep them alive. Eventually they died. Anne writes, 'I should have realised something was terribly wrong when Phil didn't want to get another cat' (Dick, 2010, p. 96). Since Dick was himself a twin, whose sister died soon after birth, this again suggests he was unconsciously re-enacting an original trauma with the Siamese kittens, which according to Anne were a boy and girl cat. Dick and his twin sister were, psychically if not physically, very much Siamese twins (as will be explored later).

* * *

My books are forgeries. Nobody wrote them.
—Philip. K. Dick, *The Exegesis of Philip K. Dick*

Excited by these possibilities, I began to look into Dick's childhood for early indicators of autism. I obtained a copy of Emmanuel Carrere's *I Am Alive and You Are Dead*, where I found the following clues. On page 2, Carrere describes Dick's father, Edgar, putting on a gas mask in front of his young son (who was probably four at the time). Phil 'screamed in terror, convinced that a hideous monster, a giant insect, had eaten his father and taken his place. For weeks after, Phil kept scanning his father's face for other signs of the substitution' (Carrere, p. 2).*

---

*Dick wrote 'The Father-Thing' in 1954 about the replacement of a boy's father with a replicated version. Dick's experience is a close match for what was dubbed in 1923 'the Capgras syndrome' (after the psychiatrist who dubbed it), supposedly 'a psychiatric

Admittedly, this was a reversal of the usual autistic child scenario, in which the parents feel as though their child has been substituted by a changeling. But the same basic elements were present, and the experience was apparently formative for Phil: many of his stories involve humans being replaced by alien or android imposters, culminating with *Palmer Eldritch*, written at the end of the 1963–1964 period.

There was something else. In a little-known 1979 two-hour interview with Charles Platt in Santa Ana,[10] Dick describes a life-changing vision of an evil 'demiurge' in the sky and how it drove him to seek refuge in religion (he later recreated the vision for *Flow My Tears, The Policeman Said*). The vision *also occurred in 1963*. In the interview, Dick accounts it to the experience of the gas mask, and recounts how his father would show him his war memorabilia and describe in terrifying detail his wartime experiences. Dick believed this had an indelible impact on his 4-year-old psyche, imbuing him with a lifelong fear that the world was a terrifying and irrational place, hence his vision, 30 years later, of the evil deity. This would seem to confirm the idea that, in the period between 1963 and 1964 (i.e. after writing *Martian Time-Slip*, and leading up to *Palmer Eldritch*), Dick was unconsciously re-enacting certain traumatic experiences from his past, seeking to understand them through his fiction.

Carrere then describes how 'Phil loved spending hours on end hiding in old boxes, silent and safe from the world' (Carrere, p. 3). A desire to be covered up, contained, hidden away, is characteristic of autistic children, and it was a characteristic that continued in Phil's later childhood. He went to Quaker school (much of which was passed in silence), and spent long hours alone at home while his mother worked. According to Carrere (Carrere, p. 4), Phil 'spent his afternoons for an entire winter playing at being one of the first Christians hiding in the catacombs'. Carrere then describes Phil as 'an artistic soul, an albatross whose enormous wingspan prevented him from walking on the earth' (Carrere, p. 4). A few pages later, he calls him 'one of those compulsive personalities who, like Sherlock Holmes, can date a file by the thickness of the dust covering it and relish being the only one who can make

---

disorder in which a person holds a delusion that a friend, spouse, parent, or other close family member (or pet) has been replaced by an identical impostor' (Wikipedia). Wikipedia actually lists it as Capgras *delusion*, as if to stress this aspect. What else would one expect in a world run by body-snatched human 'replicants'?

sense of the reigning chaos' (Carrere, p. 7). These are all unmistakably Aspergerian tendencies.

Phil's capacity to cheat on the psychological tests routinely given to children in the 1930s is also suggestive. According to Carrere, Phil was able to recognise trick questions and give the required answers:

> Like a student who has managed to get his hands' on the teach-ers' manual, he knew exactly which bubbles in the Wordsworth Personal Data Sheet of the Minnesota Multiphasic Personality Inventory he should blacken if he wanted to please the doctor, which figures he should see in the Rorschach splotches if he wanted to confound him. At will he could appear normal, normally abnor-mal, or (his forte) abnormally normal …
>
> (Carrere, pp. 8–9)

This last point also suggests that, at an early age, Phil developed *an instinctive capacity for creating false personae*. Finally, Carrere sums up Phil's childhood personality with a quintessentially autistic image:

> In one of Phil's favourite daydreams, he is an astronaut circling high above an earth devastated by atomic catastrophe. From the space-ship he is condemned to call home for the rest of his life, he some-times receives messages from survivors on the planet's surface.
>
> (Carrere, p. 11)

According to Anne, in his youth, Dick was agoraphobic (had an intense fear of crowds) and had trouble being in public places. He also had a phobia about eating in the company of other people, a form of social anxiety sometimes shared by autists. (I have a touch of it myself.) He also suffered from vertigo and Anne reports a particularly serious attack in her recounting of Phil's early years:

> something irreversible happened to his psyche when he was usher-ing at the symphony with [his friend Dick Daniels]. He said that his being had sunk down into itself—from then on, it was as if he could only see out into the world with a periscope, as if he were in a submarine. He felt that he never recovered his ability to perceive the world directly.
>
> (2011, pp. 236–237)

All of these details may seem more or less what we'd expect to find in the formation of a fantasy writer, but they are also strong signs of autism. Considering that a) autism was not being diagnosed in the US until the 1940s; b) it was initially considered a form of child schizophrenia, and Dick showed a persisting interest in schizophrenia; and c) Dick had a unique preoccupation with autism as early as 1962; it seems reasonable to extend a tentative diagnosis of autism to him.[11] If so, what his early (and later) history shows is that Dick learned to deal with such unusual perceptions and hyper-sensitivity by the autistic strategy of *withdrawing into interior, extra-consensual perceptions* (even literally, using cardboard boxes), and later, by *becoming a writer*—i.e. by making his perceptions 'real' via language.

Like so many other autist-artists, Dick would have been drawn to creative expression as a necessary way to deal with his unusual experience of reality and of himself, in order to make a niche for himself in the world. Since this process amounts to developing *an acceptable social identity*, it was probably inevitable that it also became a way to contain, control, and *sublimate* (if not out-and-out suppress) his unusual, or 'neurodiverse' perceptions of reality.

This process then became *the single most persistent theme and subtext (and even text) of his writing*, most of which, in one way or another, is about how false realities are created, unusual perceptions harnessed or suppressed, and humanness (sanity) is lost—and found.

CHAPTER 6

Lost prophets

W
hat fully absorbs light can't be seen because no light reflects off it. What is full of light appears as total darkness.

Time is not a circle; time is a dot. A black hole on the page.

The doorway of that dot is the realisation that every journey is complete in the moment it is embarked on. To imagine a thing is to see that thing. To see is to become what is seen.

The medium of (true) imagination is instant transmission and reception. Existence is created in every millisecond.

It is only the recording that creates a copy of itself, and the corresponding illusion of an event-narrative, of a spacetime continuum. A replica.

Existence at this level (that of time) is ALL MEMORY.

This is why 'memory is death'—and why to think, is to cease to be.

* * *

It was a battle, Jack realized, between the composite psyche of the school and the individual psyches of the children, and the former held all the key cards. A child who did not properly respond was assumed to be autistic—that is, oriented according to a subjective factor that took precedence over his sense of objective reality. And that child wound up by being expelled from the school; he went, after that, to another sort of school entirely, one designed to rehabilitate him: he went to Camp Ben-Gurion. He could not be taught; he could only be dealt with as *ill ... Autism ... had become a self-serving concept for the authorities who governed Mars.*

—Philip K. Dick, *Martian Time-Slip* (emphasis added)

In the 1979 interview with Platt, Dick mentions (at around the 27-minute mark) that he was re-reading *Martian Time-Slip* the night before. The context was Dick's choice to write science fiction as 'a route by which I could publish the kind of thing that I wanted to write'. *Martian Time-Slip*, he says,

is *exactly* what I wanted to write: the invasion of one person's world by another person's world. [T]his is definitely what I wanted to do from the very beginning, the way the autistic boy's world takes over, say, Arnie Kotts', takes over Jack Bohlen's, and so on. [This was] the premise, which was to me so important ... not just that we live each of us in a unique world of our own psychological contents, but that *the subjective world of one rather powerful person can infringe upon the world of another person ... The greatest power the human being can exert over others is to get control of their perceptions of reality.*[12]

Dick goes onto say that, after *Time Out of Joint* (which he wrote in 1958), he felt dissatisfied with the overly literal device he had used (of a government-constructed fake reality to house an insane person) to communicate his all-important idea. He points out that this was before he or the general public knew about LSD, so he didn't have that model either. The implication is that, in 1962, Dick came up with a way to communicate his primary message more faithfully, and the key he had been looking for was autism.

Dick's main theme as a writer—the message his soul was most committed to delivering—was that of one person (or group of people) making another subject to their interpretation of reality. Evidently, this had been Dick's own experience *throughout his life*. In the same interview, in fact, he describes himself as having a 'weak ego', and accounts his overwhelming fear of totalitarianism (local or global) as 'an indication of my own vulnerability, to the fragility of my own ego, my own self-system'. He adds later, 'I am immediately persuaded by every argument I hear'.[13]

The irony of Dick's use of autism in *Martian Time-Slip* is that it exactly *reverses* the usual state of affairs, in which neurotypical professionals, parents, and caregivers impose their will on an autistic child in order to 'get control of their perceptions of reality'. Dick describes this process in detail in *Martian Time-Slip* and then he turns the tables; at one level, it reads as a kind of autistic revenge fantasy. On another, deeper level, it is a tale of redemption. It shows how Manfred, and by implication Jack, are able to reclaim their own 'heritage' (individuality) by casting off the perceptual shackles of *an externally-imposed interpretation of reality*.

In his final years, Dick found that his life was starting to more and more resemble his fiction. His subjective experience of reality, in other words, was being shaped (or so he believed) by the 'literalisation' (putting into words) of imagination which novel-writing both allows for and depends on. An alternate view, which may be just another way of saying the same thing, is that Dick possessed a similar kind of 'psychism', ECP, or precognition, to many of his characters, allowing him to see his own future without knowing it, and turn it into novels.

To many people—though maybe not to Dick fans—both possibilities may seem far-fetched. A preferred reading of the data would be one that simply diagnosed Dick with a mild form of schizophrenia and/or as subject to paranoid delusion. The two readings aren't mutually exclusive, however, and what this book is working its way towards—and why Dick has become the central case study—is a synthesis of the pathology and the ontology of 'possession'—whether by the mother's psyche, a totalitarian government, or invisible entities, from Satan on down. In the present context, apparent symptoms of 'schizophrenia' or 'autism'—the psychological view—relate to an unusual degree of sensitivity to *the occult nature of existence on this planet*. Such sensitivity must, *ipso facto*, be suppressed, destroyed, or exploited, by the same forces and intelligences it is sensitive to.

In a complementary fashion, such sensitivity, even if only out of self-preservative instinct, is compelled to devote itself to confronting, exposing, and attempting to resolve—if it can't escape from—the 'Black Iron Prison' of the occult forces of coercion and control.

Like all good writers, Dick was able to tune into his own unconscious. By doing so, he was able to determine, in a non-rational way, what was transpiring just beneath the threshold of his conscious mind—both in himself and the world—and turn those images into fiction. This is what fantasy writers do. The key difference (one Dick has in common with Whitley Strieber, the subject of *Prisoner of Infinity*) is that Dick began to *believe* in his fictions. The ordinary assumption would be that this made him *less* sane than your average fantasy writer. The perspective I am taking is the inverse: that Dick, like many autists and schizos, was *more* sane, because he was more able to see reality for what it is, and to a limited degree to *deal* with it. The connecting tissue between the two opposing perspectives is that Dick was tuning into an *unusually deep* layer of his unconscious, and at times swallowed up (possessed) by it.

Since what is latent today will become fully manifest tomorrow, this is akin to saying that Dick was tuning into his own 'psychic' potential, i.e. his *future*. By tapping into that vast unconscious well of images and affects, and giving them form as fiction, he was bringing his unconscious to the light of consciousness. Inevitably, as with any religious prophet (some of whom get nailed to crosses), this would have profoundly impacted how his future unfolded.

> What happened in 3-74 was that the real, the thrusting-through world which I intuited, proved actually to be there, and not only that, to be accessible … I never anticipated such a tremendous pay-off (breakthrough), despite the fact that the corpus of my writing is a map, and analysis, and a guide. The 26 years of writing, without 3-74, is a map of nothing, and 3-74, without the body of writing, is conceptually inexplicable.
>
> (Dick, 2011, p. 268)

If this seems 'paranormal' or supernatural (or crazy), that's only because Dick's case was more extreme than what most of us are used to. For example, if we have an intuition about someone—as in a case of 'love at first sight'—and we act on that 'irrational' feeling, there's a good chance that we will end up shaping our future. Did we fall for that person because we 'knew' they were our future partner? Or did we create a future out of the whole cloth of a (mostly unconscious) desire? Only time can tell; even then, we may never know for sure.

By writing successful science-fiction novels, Dick introduced hundreds of thousands of people to the contents of his unconscious. He extended his unique perceptions of reality *into* the world: by drawing others into his surrogate 'reality', he gave substance *to* it. More pro-fanely, by becoming an established sci-fi author, he gradually but sig-nificantly altered his position in life, transforming his experience both of himself and of (social) reality.

Put this way, the idea that Dick was co-creating his future through writing begins to seem like—just what happens when writers write, successfully at least. But once again, Dick is not just any writer, and the underlying reason for this is his autism. Dick created at least one major autistic character, and though he didn't write *directly* about autism much outside of *Martian Time-Slip*, he wrote about it a whole lot *without* naming it. For example in 'Drugs, Hallucinations, and the Quest for Reality', written in 1964, he gives a more general description of percep-tual anomalies which is almost an exact match for the 'Intense World Syndrome' hypothesis of autism:

> too much is emanating from the neurological apparatus of the organism, over and beyond the structural, organizing necessity. The percept system in a sense is overperceiving, is presenting the self portion of the brain too much. The cognitive processes, then, in par-ticular the judging, reflecting frontal lobe, cannot encompass what it has been given, and for it—for the person—the world begins to become mysterious. *No name entities or aspects begin to appear*, and, since the person does not know what they are—that is, what they're called or what they mean—he cannot communicate with other per-sons about them. This breakdown of verbal communication is the fatal index that somewhere along the line the person is experienc-ing reality in a way [that is] too radical to allow empathic linkage with other persons. [T]he organism *cannot continue an empathic rela-tionship with the members of his society*. And this breakdown of empa-thy is double; they can't empathize his 'world', and he can't theirs.[14]

Compare this to the autistic Lucy Blackman's description of her experi-ence, in *Lucy's Story: Autism and Other Adventures*: 'I … was beginning to understand that I was using my language to make a link with people who lived on another planet in terms of what their senses told them'.[15]

Dick's rare ability to tune into the hidden or unconscious strata of reality—to 'overperceive'—by immersing in his inner world, this is a quintessentially *autistic* quality. Dick used writing—again like all good writers, so it seems—to *manage* otherwise unmanageable perceptions, as a way to avoid breaking his 'empathic link' to the world. Being uncomfortably aware of the no-name entities moving around—like H.G. Wells' Morlocks in the tunnels—beneath the surface of his conscious mind, things that he couldn't even *think* about but which were nonetheless affecting him, writing was a way to relieve that pressure. It was a necessary recourse, a way to create a 'buffer' between his conscious mind and his unconscious awareness.

Rendering unfamiliar, non-rational or 'psychic' affects as imaginary narratives—giving names to nameless entities—was a way for Dick to make them comprehensible, both to himself and to others. This allowed him to process those inner experiences, into and *as* fiction. The trap in this 'unwritten contract' was that it went two ways: by naming these entities, images, and affects as a means to ease his own passage through a hostile social environment, like Strieber with his visitors, Dick *forged a pact with them.* His writing became the means by which they, also, gained unprecedented access, not only to his own psyche and body but, in consequence—through their ground agent Dick—*into human society.* And so, eventually, Dick's 'fiction' came true, not only for himself but for the world at large.

Once a no-name entity—or a technological invention—has been named, it can more easily be communicated; after that, it is a small step before it can be experienced.

CHAPTER 7

The other side

*T*here is *no present, only past. The present moment as you experience it is a memory of the instant that has just passed, occurring so rapidly that you fail to notice the replication process, and so experience it as an eternal 'now'.*

There is no 'now' in eternity, because eternity is void of time; now can only exist in contrast to a then. Time is an eternal 'Now-then, now-then'.[16]

The stitching together of these micro-instants of perceptual data into a sequence of letters creates a sentence or formula. At this point, the sequence is reversed or flipped, and now becomes then. This gives rise to a momentary impression of self, experiencing linear time.

These momentary impressions are likewise stitched together, until a coherent, linear, time-based self emerges, if only for an instant.

This process recurs endlessly throughout eternity, as organisms are born and die in the blink of an eye.

The nature of consciousness is the contrast between ones and zeroes, between life and death, between the conscious organism that is here for an instant, and the organic consciousness which continues forever.

From this collision of opposites, the experience of time emerges.
Time, like memory, and like matter, is Satan's domain.

* * *

The Public School, then, was right to eject a child who did not learn. Because what the child was learning was not merely facts or the basis of a money-making or even useful career. It went much deeper. The child learned that certain things in the culture around him were worth preserving at any cost. His values were fused with some objective human enterprise. And so he himself became a part of the tradition handed down to him; he maintained his heritage during his lifetime and even improved on it. He cared. *True autism, Jack had decided, was in the last analysis an apathy toward public endeavor;* it was a private existence carried on as if the individual person were the creator of all value, rather than merely the repository of inherited values.

—Philip K. Dick, *Martian Time-Slip* (emphasis added)

Returning to Dick's 'seven-novels-in-twelve-months' amphetamine orgy of 1963/1964: If the borders between Dick's conscious and unconscious selves were, for whatever reason, unusually open and unpatrolled, allowing for a free passage of Morlocks carrying hidden treasures of the underworld—no wonder he didn't want to stop working! Who knew how long such an opportunity would last?

The pressure would have been especially intense since, in 1963, Dick won the Hugo award for *The Man in the High Castle* (written in 1961, published 1962), bestowing on him a whole new degree of fame and fortune. Being validated in this way by the culture-at-large is one indication that Dick was being earmarked by the no-name entities behind human society at large as their ground agent. This perspective is paranoid enough for Dick's own fiction, but not one he would have been willing, or even able, to entertain seriously at the time (which the entities would have well-known and made sure of). The sense that his identity—his livelihood—as a science-fiction writer was being consolidated would not have been any reason for resting on his laurels, either. *Au contraire*—after so many years in the wilderness, Dick went into overdrive.

Dick's tendency to immerse himself in writing at the cost of everything else might also be seen as autism related: 'perseveration' is the word used to describe the obsessive and highly selective interests of individuals on the autism spectrum (especially Aspergerians). The word is also used in relation to attention deficit hyperactivity disorder (ADHD) and sometimes called 'hyperfocus'.[17] Staying up nights and reducing sleep time drastically, as Dick did at various periods in his life, was a literal way for him to make unconscious matter conscious, and even blur the lines between the two. Lack of sleep leads to a kind of fevered, dreaming-awake state, ideal for allowing the imaginative process to take over.

Dick deliberately let the no-name entities possess him, in exchange for the treasures they brought, greedily collecting ideas which he could flatten out, fictionalise, and turn into hard cash. Ironically, Dick's 'exploitation' of his unconscious closely matches his descriptions of the government's use of the pre-cogs in 'The Minority Report' (1956).[18] An even closer parallel is found in *Martian Time-Slip*, in Arnie Kott's attempt to use Manfred's precognitive ability to make a killing on the real estate market. Evidently, Dick was aware of what he was doing, even if it didn't stop him doing it.*

Dick's use of speed is the most palpable example of a person exploiting his own psyche, mining its resources by plundering and polluting his body, so as to give power to his social identity. No wonder there was a reckoning. The internal pressure all this created—the conflict between his need for money and status and his fear of being possessed by nameless entities (or overwhelmed by unconscious material, if you prefer)—not to mention the lack of sleep—could very easily have led to some kind of breakdown. His depression (writers' block?) was perhaps a way to slow him down, and then the 'breakdown' was literally, externally, enacted via the automobile accident. The accident forced him to stop writing, and start dictating. According to Dick's later analysis, this caused his defensive false-ego self (his neurotypical persona) to fully take over the reins again.

In a more openly metaphysical framework, we can say that entities were warring for control of Dick's psychosomatic system. The border was now more tightly controlled, and no Morlock could pass without a visa. Between 1965 and 1973, Dick's output was reduced to a little over

---

*Kott uses ex-schizophrenic Jack Bohlen as his intermediary, his 'in' to Manfred's psyche. Kott winds up getting sucked into Manfred's hallucinatory world, and when he is shot by a smuggler whose business he has destroyed, he dies believing it all to be a hallucination.

a novel a year, admittedly including four of his breakthrough works, *Ubik, Androids, Flow My Tears,* and *Scanner Darkly.* The last (the first Dick novel I read) is expressly about a man who 'snitches' on himself, i.e. who is controlled by outside agencies to sell himself out.

As Dick described it in his famous 1977 speech in France, the novelist

> has come across something new that at the same time was there, somewhere, all the time. In truth, it simply surfaced. It always *was.* He did not invent it or even find it; in a very real sense it found *him.* And—and this is a little frightening to contemplate—he has not invented it, but on the contrary, it invented *him.* It is as if the idea created him for its purposes.
>
> (Dick, 1999, p. 233)

In the same speech, Dick said:

> It was in February 1974 that *Flow My Tears* was finally, after two years of delay, published. It was almost as if the release of the novel, which had been delayed so long, meant that in a certain sense it was all right for me to remember. But until then it was better that I did not. Why that would be I do not know, but I have the impression that the memories were not to come to the surface until the material had been published very sincerely on the author's part as what he believed to be fiction.
>
> (1999, p. 250)

Let not thy left brain know what thy right brain is up to. Once again, this sort of scenario may just be part and parcel of what writers do; but in most other cases, it remains hidden deep below the surface. Dick was not just a science-fiction writer, he was a science-fiction writer's *idea* of a writer: a 'Sibyl', in touch with extra-dimensional entities. And although he drew a line in his fiction, or at least in his later interpretations of it, between 'autistic', psychosis-based realities and genuine alternate or higher realities hiding behind this one, it was a line he was constantly hopping (or being abducted) back and forth over, unable to ever find or fix it in his own mind.

If Dick was an autist-author in denial of his own autism, this is another way of saying that he was an unwitting host to no-name entities: entities that constantly undermined his attempts to expose them.

While he would defend the subjective experience of the schizophrenic as 'an attempt on the part of the brain to achieve bilateral hemispheric parity—an evolutionary leap forward' (2011, p. 243)—he equated autism, in what was the only mention I found of it in his *Exegesis*, with something *malign*. It's telling that the context he placed it in was his own writing, specifically his ongoing fear that, if he was deluded about his 2-3-74 experience, 'it would serve a malign, sick purpose: leading the reader away from reality toward autism' (2011, p. 273). If writing was Dick's way of staving off his own autism—keeping it from over-whelming him—it makes sense that he would fear infecting the reader with it. But what we most fear is often what we end up bringing about.

The confusion here—for myself as much as for Dick—may have to do with the difficulty, perhaps even the impossibility, of distinguish-ing between autism as an ability to *perceive* entities and their influ-ence, and as being the result of a subjugation *to* them. Clearly, entities control neurotypicals as much as, and even more easily than, autists. But if: a) no-name entities have been subtly directing human society towards a technological form of enslavement that allows them greater ingress and control within it; and b) the primary agents of technological progress have been humans on the autism spectrum; it seems necessary to posit also c) that autists' particular susceptibility makes them, not only more resistant, but also potentially more *useful*, to these no-name entities.

Autists (generally) can't do what Dick did or what visionary writers and artists do. (Or what Bill Gates or Steve Jobs, Steve Wozniak, or Mark Zuckerberg did. If they could, they wouldn't need to be diagnosed as autistic.) They can't generally process or communicate their perceptual experiences of reality. Caught in a liminal realm between self-awareness (rationality) and unconsciousness (imagination), most of their energies must go into trying to find a safe 'place' to exist *within* that perceptual chaos, inside the 'intense world' of psychic data that is continuously flooding their senses.

Being more susceptible to the influence of the nameless entities of the unconscious means having fewer defences against them. As a result of having such a 'porous' no-self self, Dick's fiction was 'prophetic', not only in his own life but *at a collective level*. He states this explicitly in the *Exegesis*: 'for months I lived inside the collective unconscious and its contents' (2011, p. 241). To be tuned into the collective unconscious suggests several, even many, different perceptual realities or narratives occurring simultaneously. Multiple id-entities. In such a state, it would not be possible to experience linear time.

Dick's own account of his life, post 2-3-74, was distinctly akin to Manfred's in *Martian Time-Slip* (though curiously, as far as I know, he never made the comparison):

> What is my real relationship to time? I experience the near past, the near future, and the very far past; a lot of my soul or psyche seems to be transtemporal ... maybe this is why any given present space time seems somehow unreal or delusional to me. I span across and hence beyond it ...
>
> (2011, p. 261)

And/or, maybe someone—or something—*else* was looking transtemporally out through Dick's eyes?

CHAPTER 8

Sci-fi author seeks novel to live in

*S*pace. Time. Perceptual existence. Existential perception.

Existential perception entails two flat planes, horizontal and vertical. The intersection of those two planes is the point from which perception/ existence emerges. This is the crucifixion. The experience of consciousness in matter.

Perception will always be at the intersecting centre of these two planes. This can never change.

It is the only basis for manifestation that there is. It is the only way that an eternal consciousness can extend itself into physical, temporal existence.

The two planes are two-dimensional. Their interface makes up a third and fourth dimensional realm of space and time. All other dimensions emerge from that intersection.

There is zero and then there is two. From two comes three, and so on. There can be no one plane without the other, no space without time.

The mind identity is the means—or the symptom—of seeing time as a line, proceeding from point to point. It is Satan's prerogative (illusion). But time can't exist without space, and hence is no more a line than space is.

Space without time would be like a line also, because there would be no way to experience it as *space. Both space and time are the third dimension to one another's two-dimensionality.*

They are the incarnation as crucifixion.

* * *

> I seem to be living in my own novels more and more. I can't fig-
> ure out why. Am I losing touch with reality? Or is reality actually
> sliding toward a Phil Dickian type of atmosphere? And if the
> latter, then for God's sake why?
> —Philip. K. Dick, *The Exegesis of Philip K. Dick*

Bishop Pike, whom Dick met shortly after his accident in 1964, was an influential religious figure and political activist with a particular interest in contacting the dead. (He published a book about it in 1968, called *The Other Side: An Account of My Experiences with Psychic Phenomena.*) After Pike's son committed suicide in 1966, Pike believed Jim Jr. was communicating to him from the other side by psychic means. Pike Sr. died in 1969 under mysterious circumstances: he was looking for proof of the historical Jesus in the Judean Desert with his wife; when their car broke down and she went for help, Pike wandered off for unknown reasons. Eventually, his body was found.

In 1971, Dick's apartment in San Rafael was broken into by unknown parties and trashed; his safe was cracked open and all of his papers were taken. Before that he had been paranoid; now he *knew* he was being spied on. One of the most compelling (for me) reasons he came up with for the break-in was that it was due to his relationship with Pike (i.e. part of an ongoing investigation into Pike's activities, one that continued after his death). The break-*in* was at least one contributing factor that lead to Dick's break*down* and/or break*through* of 2-3-74, when he started to believe that his novels had begun to transmogrify his reality, and that his life was slowly but steadily turning into a Phil Dick novel. One of the explanations he found for what was happening to him was that Jim Pike Sr. was communicating with him—or rather, had partially possessed his body—from the other side, by psychic means.

This echoed what, for Dick, in his exegetic explorations, was probably his key work, *Ubik*—written in 1966. *Ubik* is about characters living in a dream world or Bardo realm, being contacted by what they think is a dead man, when in fact(?) it is they who are dead (the dead man being God, or Christ, or VALIS, as Dick later named it). And lo, in 1974, Dick found himself wondering the same thing (hence the title of Carrere's bio, *I Am Alive and You Are Dead*).

> I wrote *Ubik* before Jim Pike died out there in the desert, but Jim Jr. had already died, so I guess my novel could be said to be based on Jim Jr. coming through to his father. So my novel *Ubik* was based on life and now life is based on it but only because it, the novel, goes back to life. I really did not make it up. I just observed it and put it into a fictional framework. After I wrote it I forgot where I got the idea.
>
> (2010, p. 23)

In 1974, by his own account (all 900 pages of it, not counting the novels and the unpublished *Exegesis* notes), Dick was zapped by a pink laser beam which he believed came from a 'Vast Active Living Intelligence System', VALIS. The beam caused 'anamnesis', a removal of amnesia, after which he started to remember *another* life, from another time and place (Rome, around the time of Christ). He also began to receive information through dream and vision, some of which he was able to verify as accurate (for example, he was 'informed' that his son needed an urgent operation, and his spontaneous diagnosis was confirmed at the hospital). Dick became the *receiver–transmitter* which he had long suspected he was: a writer of non-fiction novels. At least for a while, Dick believed the information was coming from Bishop Pike, who he felt had partially replaced his own personality. Somewhat paradoxically, he also saw this 'possession' as a return of his authentic self after ten years of amnesia, following the accident in 1964.

Without attempting to parse out the many disparate threads of Dick's religious-paranoid psychodrama—which would require at least one novel to do, maybe a trilogy—what seems clear is how, in Dick's psyche, several crucial elements were conflated: a mysterious intelligence—whether divine, satanic, technological, or divinely or satanically technological—emanating from outside the phenomenal world; a disembodied consciousness existing on 'the other side'; his own authentic, long-buried self; a powerful and influential political/religious activist who, it's probably fair to say, was a kind of father figure for Dick; Sophia, *wisdom*, the divine feminine; a wise and benevolent philosopher-teacher, located somewhere in ancient Rome or ancient Greece, or both; and finally, his experience of existing outside the linear timestream of what he'd hitherto taken for 'reality'.

The shortest distance between two points is a straight line. The overriding narrative that incorporates all of these subjective experiences, without being restricted to any one of them, is that, in 1974, after ten years of unconsciously preparing for his massive integration-healing experience, and precipitated by the combination of psychological burnout as a writer, separation from his wife, a serious car accident, a rare period of sobriety, and meeting Bishop Pike, Phil K. Dick made contact with his own soul, causing a flurry of id-entity activity.

All of a novelist's characters are himself. This statement could hardly be truer than in the case of 'Horselover Fat'. The most essential fact about Philip Kindred Dick is that, with the addition of the *Exegesis* to his oeuvre, it's no longer possible to separate the author from his works. This is true of all authors, but Dick's case sprays it in huge, trashy neon letters on the subway walls of world literature (so to say). What really makes all these strands so compelling—and how and why they ended up as the backbone to *Big Mother*, if they are—is that they are bound together with, in, or *through* (since the main thing about Dick is that his life *is* his novels, and vice versa), the writing and publication of *Martian Time-Slip*.

Time-Slip is about an autistic boy, Manfred, his relationship with an ex-schizophrenic (possibly Aspergerian) technician, Jack, and Jack's relationship with Arnie Kott, the real estate Mafioso who hires Jack to help him harness Manfred's precognitive powers. Manfred exists in an entirely different reality. Jack is stuck in a sort of intermediary state between full-blown autism (what he thinks of as schizophrenia) and his precariously maintained neurotypical 'sanity'; he is sympathetic to Manfred but also afraid of him. Arnie is unsympathetic to either of them, being a crass capitalist exploiter with no time either for the mysteries of autism or for ego-transcending realities, besides as freakish opportunities for financial gain.

Jack is entrusted with the task of communicating with Manfred. In the process, he has a relapse into schizophrenia. Arnie, drawn into proximity to Manfred and Jack, ends up taken over by the forces he is attempting to exploit. Repeatedly sucked into Manfred's autistic *other*-world, he nearly loses his mind and ends up dead without knowing it. Jack intervenes to save Manfred from a terrible future, by helping him join the aboriginal people on Mars, the Bleekmen. In *The Search for Philip K. Dick*, Anne Dick writes of Manfred:

When I read *Martian Time-Slip* I was disturbed by the little boy looking out of the window like Phil when he was a latchkey child in Washington, D.C., waiting for his mother to come home. Phil became quite cross with me when I continued to worry, probably a little obsessively, about the child, but I couldn't get him out of my mind. Phil said, 'You don't have to worry about him. He was all right. He ran off with the Martian "Indians"'.

(Dick, A., 2010, p. 80)

At the risk of overstating what (I hope) by now should be obvious, Manfred, Jack, and Arnie represent three aspects of Dick's psyche and the struggle between them. The psychological process Dick was describing in *Martian Time-Slip*—in 1962, as his star soared to new heights as a sci-fi author—can be seen as an example, admittedly in very rough or symbolic form, of the fiction-becoming-reality process which Dick recognised, 12 years later (with the publication of *Flow My Tears, the Policeman Said*) as occurring in his life. It is this process that, in the end, took his life over completely.

Yet curiously, the parallel between Dick's life and *Martian Time-Slip* is a parallel he never really zeroed in on. The book does not make it to his short list of most personally meaningful Dick novels (though it does make it—just—onto the longer list). To my mind, that makes it significant by omission. (Dick's short list, in his recommended correct reading order: *A Scanner Darkly*, *Flow My Tears*, *The Three Stigmata of Palmer Eldritch*, *Maze of Death*, and *Ubik*. An amended list includes *Do Androids Dream of Electric Sheep?* and 'Imposter'. Finally, he tentatively adds 'Faith of the Fathers', *Time Out of Joint*, *The Eye in the Sky*, *The Man in the High Castle*, *Martian Time-Slip*, *Galactic Pot-Healer*, and *Penultimate Truth*, before returning to his amended list of seven titles. See *Exegesis*, pp. 405–407, from the September–October 1978 folder.)

Dick's whole *Exegesis* is directed towards the attempt to prove—to himself—that his full and final immersion in the Manfred-esque 'autistic' world of Valis/Pike/Sophia/Logos/the past/his own unconscious was a genuine, authentic, glimpse into ultimate reality, and most definitely *not* a schizophrenic episode (although he allows this too, once in a while). Nor, most unthinkably of all (since he never mentions it), was it evidence of his own latent/disowned autism.

Dick's unacknowledged (re-)introduction to his own autism—if such it was—which began in 1962 and peaked in 1974, culminated in 1982 with two events: the writer's death, at 53; and the release of *Blade*

Runner, based on *Do Androids Dream of Electric Sheep?* published in 1968 (mid-way between 1962 and 1974). *Blade Runner* was the film that made Dick (posthumously) famous, and which (re-)introduced the human-ised robot (and robotic human) to the world. As such, it can be viewed as the autist-android movie text *par excellence*, and the best publicity the inorganic no-name entities had ever had.

Ironically—and tellingly—it is the Hollywood film version, not Dick's original book, that turns a sympathetic eye towards the androids, showing, in very clear terms, that empathy, as a lost human trait, has now moved into the realm of the machine. Dick commented on this discrepancy shortly before he died:

> To me, the replicants are deplorable. They are cruel, they are cold, they are heartless. They have no empathy ... they don't care about what happens to other creatures. They are essentially less than human entities. Ridley, on the other hand ... regarded them as supermen ... smarter, stronger, [with] faster reflexes ... Ridley's atti-tude was quite a divergence from my original point of view, since the theme of my book is that Deckard is dehumanized through tracking down the androids.
>
> (Sammon, p. 285)

This would seem to support the idea of a hijacking of Dick's soul-vision by satanic no-name entities; on the other hand, and to be fair, it precisely echoes Dick's oft-repeated assertion in his *Exegesis*, that the Deity always surfaces in the place we least expect it. When Dick saw 20 minutes of footage from the film, according to co-effects supervisor, David Dryer,

> Dick looks me straight in the eye and says, 'How is this possible? How can this be? Those are not the exact images, but the texture and tone of the images I saw in my head when I was writing the original book! The environment is exactly as how I'd imagined it! How'd you guys do that? How did you know what I was feeling and thinking?'.
>
> (Sammon, p. 284)

Deus ex machina—even the writer doesn't know where to look.

* * *

> [If] superhumans (mutants, etc.) live among us undetected they
> would use such things—carriers—as popular novels (and I sup-
> pose music and films) to 'communicate'—keep in touch—with
> one another ... So it would be ideal, then, if the author knew
> nothing, was subliminally cued. Of course, if/when the heavy
> shit came down on him, if the 'mutants' were ethical and not
> exploitive, they'd rescue him. And they'd know when he was in
> trouble by means of the same paranormal powers by which they
> got the material into his books in the first place. They would
> have to be more or less continuously linked to him telepathically.
> —Philip K. Dick, *The Exegesis of Philip K. Dick*

Why does it matter if Dick was autistic? There's only one reason I can
think of. To find and identify his kindred (Dick's middle name—i.e.
'hidden' nature, though he took care to include the 'K' in all his works).

The *Exegesis* is the great unpublishable Philip K. Dick novel. His
reputation had to increase tenfold from the time he died for it ever to
come into the public realm in the form it eventually did, 20 years later.
Its publication demonstrated just how far Dick had come since *Blade
Runner*—since he 'passed over'.

Philip K. Dick novels—or so their author believed—contain secret
'living' information meant for a select few (whom Dick sometimes
referred to as 'the real Christians'). Today, I would guess that his novels
have been read by millions of people. But the *Exegesis*? However many
people are buying the damn thing, it's hard to imagine that more than a
few thousand will ever wade through the 900 pages of repetition, hyper-
bole, contradiction, self-aggrandisement, self-doubt, circular argumentation, and self-digesting (il)logic. Reading the entire published *Exegesis*
might even be seen as a rite of passage, the necessary literary initiation
to become a true 'Dick-head'.[19]

The annotations from the editors (Pamela Jackson and Jonathan
Lethem) and seven or so other authors are like a recurring reassurance,
a reminder that we are not alone in the thankless, strangely compelling task of navigating the labyrinth of mirrors and maze of literary
solipsism (or autism) that Dick's final years of writing turned into.
In the *Exegesis*, the medium is *absolutely* the message. What Dick communicates above all is his insatiable mania for words, his incurable literary addiction. The work in totem (at least the first half of it, which
is all I'd managed at the time of writing this) is like a writer's quest

for validation, a desperate search to prove, to himself—empirically, ontologically—that his work, and therefore his life, has meaning and value. Ironically, and as Dick says of *Ubik* (in the *Exegesis*), the *Exegesis* is its own proof: the fact that it exists proves it is 'right'; or rather, that Dick's uniquely autistic (a tautology, I know) version of reality would prove meaningful to generations of future readers. And most of all, to future *writers*. (At one point in the *Exegesis*, Dick calls *Ubik* 'the most important book ever written', p. 509).

The primary weakness of the *Exegesis*—ironically, perhaps—is Dick's prevailing belief in *words*, in language/Logos/information, as the salvific agency. This seems to walk hand in hand (down the aisle to the eschaton) with his assigning of primacy to 'Mind' over Body: a fundamental error in all of his 'models', not a moral one but an intellectual one (again, ironically). My guess is this also relates to Dick's being an autist-in-denial, since autism can loosely be correlated with a pre- or non-verbal state of consciousness. What's a writer to *do* once he starts to doubt the Word? (Start farming!?[20]) Also, since it's impossible to separate medium from message, it may be expedient to point out how, for a visionary-genius-novelist, Dick wasn't much of a *writer*. Most of his novels are like out-worn technology—clunky, inconsistent, and a bit wearing.

The *Exegesis* is the capstone to Dick's oeuvre. Better yet, it is a massively oversized footnote, a ball and chain of fact to his fiction. Yet it is also, I suspect, a strange attractor for, if not autists or mutants, social outliers—people who, by definition, belong to a worldview so far from the societal norm that any kind of halfway coherent vision that resonates with them *at all* is like a sign-post in the desert of the unreal. You may not want to follow it, but you *sure as hell* need to read it (or half of it).

As a representative of the transitional world between inner-subjective and outer-objective reality—a world that is by definition autistic and unique—as a spokesman for the unspeakable, Philip K. Dick is the Happy King Felix,* in service of whom he placed his final years, and last million words.

And King has the same root as *kindred*.[21]

---

*After he had a vision in which he was shown the name 'Felix' in his novel *Flow My Tears*, 'King Felix' became for Dick a code signifying the returned Christ. He incorporated it into *VALIS* and *The Divine Invasion* as a cypher.

CHAPTER 9

How am I not myself?

*E*ach moment in time, rather than being a point on a line, is an infinite and eternal spatial event-experience.

Each moment occurs within the totality of space, which is infinite. Therefore, each moment in time is eternal.

What occurs in each moment is infinite in variation. From a localised experience of a single perspective, from one point in spacetime, a line of linear time is inferred.

This is a perceptual error that gives birth to an intellectual error, and finally to a moral one. It is Lucifer's fall.

The progression from finite, linear consciousness, confined to spacetime, to the original, eternal consciousness entails a crucifixion. It requires a surrender of the one-point identity-self to the infinite nature of existence.

Lucifer's fall made Christ's crucifixion not just possible but necessary.

* * *

> As soul is to man, man is to machine. It is the added dimension
> in terms of functional hierarchy.
> —Philip K. Dick, 'Man, Android, and Machine'*

He wrestled with the words on the screen. It was as if some organism inside him were fighting against an awareness, struggling to emerge. It was the awareness that language had him as its prisoner, and that it would resist, with everything it had, all his attempts to express that fact through language. Maybe even this was the final, the most advanced strategy of language: to imprison him via his very efforts to use it to get free of it?

What unfathomable cunning! As long as he believed that language offered the means to understand the nature of the matrix he was trapped inside, he would continue tinkering away at the edges of the cage, convinced he was slowing wearing down the bars when really he was only polishing them and making them shine.

Meanwhile, he was getting older with each passing hour. That was the nature of the prison: the mind continued as if it were immortal, whiling away the hours in a fantasy realm of abstraction, oblivious—crucially oblivious—to the steady decay of the organism (for which time was rapidly running out). And if the mind still held sway, in its fleeting illusion of control, when the body died, then what he was—that organic awareness embedded inside the conscious system of existence—would find itself shackled to that hideous linguistic parasite *even in death*. The monkey would ride his awareness into the next life, and so on, maybe forever, each time its tentacles wrapped a little tighter around his slowly shrinking psyche.

The end result would be—what? An awareness meant to fill infinity, reduced to a fictional character, printed in grungy black ink on the tightly bound pages of a pulp fiction novel, lost among countless boxes in the dusty attics of eternity. He would be Philip K. Dicked out of existence, with just enough residual awareness to know it, to remember what he had lost, forever.

---

*Compare to: 'The theory might be advanced that in the man-machine complex man in some sense plays the role the soul plays in relation to the body in certain philosophies. But the contrary would rather seem the case, as J. M. Lahy implied long ago when he asked: "Will not this man have less and less time to be conscious of his own living presence?" No doubt, man will continue to steer the machine, but only at the price of his individuality' (Ellul, p. 397).

He knew this was circular imagery and made no sense. If it were at all true, he was already inside that box in that attic, and this *was* the residual awareness speaking. This was the fiction. The Empire never ended, but by the same token the battle for freedom was always on. The possibility of release was always there. It was only a matter of shifting the attention a micro-millimetre to be free. The prison was his own mind, so the prison was also *in* his mind. The *idea* that the mind imprisoned him (that the mind existed at all) was what kept him prisoner.

The belief that language could define his experience, defined his experience.

Language and belief were co-dependent. To believe, we need to be able to tell ourselves to believe. To be able to apply language at all, we need to believe in what we are saying. Otherwise, why say it? Why think at all?

The word blue does not match the colour blue. Rationally, he knew this; but still, he believed in the meaning of blue. There were a dozen, a hundred, a thousand, a billion shades of blue. What he called blue, so the Ahrimanic scientists said, was really the absence of blue, that portion of the light spectrum which any given surface reflected back at him, did not absorb. So even perception was the opposite of what it was supposed to be. Consciousness was really unconscious, and that which was most conscious of itself—the body—was unconscious to (and of?) him.

This was not something he could explain to anyone. It was not so much that they didn't want to hear it; they *couldn't* hear it. Their own internal language programme drowned it out. The only response they really heard to the question 'How are you?' was 'Fine, thanks' or (slightly more revealing) 'Can't complain'. That was the required signal that the language virus had replicated, been passed on, and could carry on its merry way unencumbered. It was the confirmation of the social contract: to be good hosts to the virus.

None of this was new. Apparently, the language that ran his hard drive was especially preoccupied with exposing its own fallibility to him. He appeared to be driven to continue to try and use language to work out, for himself at least, how language couldn't communicate the truth.

But there was something new emerging, or so it seemed. It was starting to occur to him that he was essentially being written into existence.

He now understood—because he experienced it viscerally every day—that words were a means to control his perception and confine it.

Once he had internalised the meanings associated with his inherited language, he was susceptible to being controlled.

* * *

> books within books: the real world turned into a book, and a book turned into a world. We *are* totally scripted, after all—rigidly, deterministically programmed ('written' our rules engrammed in and onto us all). Which is the book and which is the world?
>
> —Philip K. Dick, *The Exegesis of Philip K. Dick*

Something occurred to me while I was first working on this exploration of an exegesis, in 2013. It was an inevitable occurrence; to some extent, you could even say I contrived it for the sake of the piece. But nonetheless, it is now inextricably bound up in it.

What occurred to me was that a new, unknown element had entered into my writing. Not that the piece was writing itself, exactly (every writer's fancy), but that *certain unseen elements* were beginning to surface, elements that, while apparently secondary to the arguments herein, started to look more and more like the actual, concealed substance of the work. These elements had to do with the subject and the author being in a sense, not two things but a single thing, intelligence, or entity.

The author was writing about words, and he was writing about a writer who believed, while he lived, that his novels were the unconsciously-constructed carriers of 'living information' (the plasmate), transmitted to him from an unknown source (Zebra, VALIS, Ubik, and several other more theological names), in order to extend itself into this world.

Dick also believed, at least *some* of the time, that the consciousness of a dead Bishop (Pike) was coming through him. At other times, he believed the hidden source behind his novels (and his life, which were one and the same) was a kind of artificial intelligence or AI, a supercomputer able not merely to conceal itself in our reality but *as* reality, meaning that we were in effect living *inside* it, without ever suspecting the true nature of our world.

Now the present author was writing about these ideas, conveying essentially the same information; whether or not it was living information (or even accurate), he could not say. He was doing so as part of a larger exploration into autism (and later, mother bondage). Independently of his analysis of Dick, he had already suggested (just a few days before beginning the Dick investigation) the possibility of *an unseen intelligence*, concealed just beneath the surface of the world (and of his own consciousness). He began to suspect this intelligence was attempting to communicate with him, through him, and *as* him; in fact, he had vocally invited it to do so. He believed, or at least he hoped, that his insuppressible desire to write was sparked and directed by *that same unseen intelligence*.

The symmetry was inescapable. But did it actually mean anything besides, *'Dude*, like attracts like!'?

And all the while, the author was secretly (! Yeah, right) hoping that, with *this* piece, he would finally create something that would have an impact on the world of literature. After half a lifetime struggling to be noticed, to amount to something, maybe with this he could break out of the bubble of anonymity that he'd been trapped in and reach a larger audience? More to the point, maybe he could start earning enough income by writing to *live off?**

Dick was validated by VALIS. Maybe the present author could receive his bene-DICK-tion from the Dean? The irony struck him at once: Dick had always written about frustrated, powerless, and ineffective characters, because that was how he experienced himself, even *after* winning the Hugo award. And he struggled to make a living to the end of his daze. (Hollywood only discovered Philip in time for Dick to die.)

What if the wandering spirit of Philip K. Dick was trying to move into the present author's psyche, to find a home and an expression there? A named entity with a history of hosting no-name entities?

He was pretty sure he wasn't the first to have entertained such thoughts, but maybe his psyche wasn't the only 'home' Dick had found? He had to face it: was anyone who ever lived *more* likely to be sending messages from the other side than Philip K. Dick? On the other hand, maybe he, the author, was trying to find a 'home' for *himself* by writing about Dick, by possessing Dick's 'body of work', using it as a vehicle to

---

* It didn't. But it *did* lead to making contact with another Dick-head author who *had* burst out of that bubble, Jonathan Lethem, which led to the writing of *Seen and Not Seen*, my first 'grown-up' book. With hindsight, these chapters on Dick marked the moment in which I fully discovered my 'voice' as a writer.

enter the social realm? Wheels within wheels. Or maybe Dick's entities, now lacking a host, had found *him* because he had sent out a homing signal to *them*?

He realised that, if his life were superimposed on top of his subject's life, at age 46, as he was when he first wrote this chapter in 2013, he would have only just had his own 2-3-74 anamnesis experience. His best work would be mostly behind him. His death would be a mere seven years away—then, that is. Now, prepping for publication in 2023, he is nearing 56 and has outlived Dick by a little over 2 years. Fittingly, he has now—in mid-transition from author to farmer—mostly resolved the issues that Dick never did: was his commitment to writing meaningful or worthwhile? Did the work have any lasting value? Was it all just the self-referencing, 'autistic' meanderings of a disturbed mind? Was it even possible it was *both at once?*

Most pertinent of all to the 2023 context for this updated 2013 investigation: what has become of the lingering, persistent promise, whispered serpent-like in his ear, that he had been *chosen* for this, by the same super-intelligence that chose Dick, that he was continuing—even completing!—the work started by his secret mentor and autistic kindred? Had he been impregnated by Dick?

He was born the year after *Ubik* was written. That year, 1967, was also the only year between 1952 and 1970 that Dick didn't write a single novel! *Why not?* Three years later, Dick wrote *Flow My Tears, the Policeman Said*, which he later believed triggered his 2-3-74 awakening, which occurred immediately after *Tears* was published. The novel had a protagonist named *Jason* Taverner. This was a fact, and a name, of great significance to Dick. Why?

> I'm going to be very candid with you. I wrote both novels based on fragmentary residual memories of such a horrid slave state world ... The world of *Flow My Tears* is an actual (or rather once actual) alternate world, and I remember it in detail. I do not know who else does. Maybe no one else does ... In March 1974, I began to remember consciously, rather than merely subconsciously, that Black Iron Prison police state world. Upon consciously remembering it I did not need to write about it because I have always been writing about it.
>
> (Dick, 1999, p. 254)

The indications of this cross-over between truth and fiction began for Dick soon after he wrote *Tears*, in 1970, when he met several characters who appeared to be out of the novel, even down to their names. In 1974, after the novel was published and he had his awakening experience, Dick was talking to his priest (Episcopalian) about a scene near the end of the novel in which the Police General Felix Buckman meets a Black stranger at an all-night gas station. (It's a key scene in the novel because it's the scene in which the policeman's tears finally stop flowing.) The priest told Dick that he had described a scene from the Book of Acts, from the Bible, adding that, in Acts, the person who meets the Black man on the road is named Philip! Dick went home and read the scene in Acts, a book he claims he had never read until that moment. He noticed that, in Acts, the high Roman official who arrests and interrogates Saint Paul is named Felix, and Felix Buckman is a high-ranking police general. (He later found out that Felix meant 'happy' and, by using 'King Felix' as a cypher for Christ in his last novels, he transformed the tyrant into the saviour.)

Since the main character in *Tears* is named Jason, Dick got an index to the Bible to see if he could find anyone named Jason. He found only one incident, in the Book of Acts:

> And, as if to plague me further with coincidences, in my novel Jason is fleeing from the authorities and takes refuge in a person's house, and in Acts the man named Jason shelters a fugitive from the law in his house—an exact inversion of the situation in my novel, as if the mysterious Spirit responsible for all this was having a sort of laugh about the whole thing … A careful study of the novel shows that for reasons I cannot even begin to explain, I had managed to retell several of the basic incidents from a particular book of the Bible, and even had the right names. What could explain this?
>
> (1999, pp. 267–268)

Naturally, I was obliged to look further into the matter. I discovered that the Jason who appears in Acts is known as 'Jason of Tarsus'; he was appointed Bishop of Tarsus by Paul, and is numbered *among the 70 or 72 disciples of Christ*. He gave shelter to Paul and two other disciples, and was arrested when they couldn't be found. (Dick is slightly mistaken in saying it is the only mention of him, as he is also mentioned, in passing, in Romans 16:21.)

Other sources write that Jason travelled to Corfu as an early Christian missionary and was there imprisoned. While in jail, he converted seven prisoners, who were all killed by the King. The King's daughter also converted to Christianity, and he had her killed as well. Jason escaped and fled the King's persecution, thereby becoming a fugitive, like Jason Taverner. When the King gave chase, his boat sank. Apparently, the King finally saw the light at this point and, like Paul, converted to Christianity. He changed his name to *Sebastian*—the name of my older brother who died in 2010. Ten years earlier, in 2000, my brother Sebastian was *crucified* as part of an art project in the Philippines. That was the year I turned 33. For many years I felt 'persecuted' by Sebastian, just as Jason of Tarsus was persecuted by the tyrant-King who later converted and became Sebastian.

Of course, this was all just a coincidence. Unless we live in a language-based reality in which words are living things. Or in AD 45.

Or what if, by writing these words, I was creating a 'space' for Dick's hidden autistic side to emerge through? Was I providing a refuge for a fugitive? (The name Taverner also suggests a shelter or refuge.) Or, symmetrically, was *I* the fugitive, seeking shelter in the shadow of a dead man? Then there was my last name, unmistakably echoing the name of Dick's fictional stand-in in *VALIS*—Horselover Fat, Horselover being the root meaning of Philip.

If Dick's restless spirit was seeking a temporary refuge or *Tavern* (psyche) to rest in, and/or a 'horse' to travel on between shelters (to ride into this dimension), what more suitable place (name) than my own?

And so on, *ad Dickinitum.*

Dick believed the Book of Acts was the unconscious template for *Tears*, behind both of which was 'A whole reality of names or living words' (2011, p. 521). He also began to believe that, since he was *actually* living in the time Acts was written, that was the *real* world, hidden behind this false one. So what *seemed* like a book (Acts) was in fact (exactly like *The Grasshopper Lies Heavy* in *The Man in a High Castle*) the means by which the real world (Rome circa AD 45) was *inserted* into this false world—*as a book!*[22]

> At the conclusion of *Man in a High Castle*, a woman appears at Abendsen's door to tell him what he does not know: that his novel is true; the Axis did indeed lose the war. The irony of this ending— Abendsen finding out that what he had supposed to be pure fiction

spun out of his imagination was in fact true—the irony is this: that my own supposed imaginative work *The Man in a High Castle* is not fiction—or rather is fiction only *now*, thank God.

(Dick, 2010, p. 245)

The notion that a written text might be closer to representing (and/or restoring) actual reality than our lived experience is one that, surely, only a writer could conceive of. Or should I say, only a writer could serve as a vehicle of delivery for such a 'gospel'? I can't quite decide if any of this is oxymoronic or tautologically axiomatic, both or neither, if, in the beginning was the Word, also, according to the literal words in the Bible, so was the Fall. (Did the Fall cause the Word, or did the word cause the Fall?)

Perhaps it is all of the above. Perhaps it is a form of prophecy-slash-prescriptive programming that is both self-fulfilling and self-annihilating? More specifically and ominously, perhaps it is similar in essence to the technological idea of the Singularity—as first seeded in science-fiction—namely: that technology that is designed to create more advanced technology than itself, and so on, will spark an exponential and unstoppable growth curve, one that will eventually open a two-way doorway akin to that between the sci-fi author's psyche and the entities that incarnate through it.* (This was explored in a previous and in some ways anticipatory work, *Prisoner of Infinity*.)

The closing words to Whitley Strieber's *Communion* are, writing of the no-name entities which he named 'the visitors':

> If they are not from our universe it could be necessary for us to understand them before they can emerge into our reality. In our universe, their reality may depend on our belief. Thus the corridor into our world could in a very true sense be through our own minds.
>
> (Strieber, p. 294)

---

*In the context of technology, the term Singularity was popularised by the science-fiction writer Vernor Vinge, who argued that artificial intelligence, human biological enhancement, or brain-computer interfaces could be possible causes of the Singularity. The specific term 'Singularity'—as a description for technological acceleration causing an unpredictable outcome in society—was coined by the mathematician, John von Neumann.

In *Prisoner of Infinity*, I juxtaposed this mystical idea with that of the Singularity, and of *'the creation of a technology programmed to replicate and improve on itself*—and the potential for the exponential, evolutionary growth of machine intelligence'. I observed the overlap with 'a subtler idea: that of intelligence extending itself from the immaterial (computer software) into the material' and of 'a (potentially two-way) channel between the physical and nonphysical realms'. I stated that this could be 'the *primary human question and concern, bar none'*.

Richard Doyle comments in the *Exegesis*:

> Dick's treatment of reality as a 'very advanced game of Go' also antic-ipates the cellular automata models of scientist Stephen Wolfram, though the model goes back at least to John von Neumann's 1947 discussion of 'self reproducing automata', a concept that would later help manifest Dick's *Do Androids Dream of Electric Sheep.*
>
> (2011, p. 592n)

(The phrase inevitably brings to my mind Terence McKenna's 'self-replicating machine elves', as experienced under the effects of DMT, a subject which will be touched on more in Part III.)

The parallel I wished to underscore in *Prisoner of Infinity* was that technology, like Strieber's visitors and Dick's no-name entities, can only emerge into our world through the corridor of our own minds. Now I am wondering, if Dick, as much as Strieber, was (possibly through no fault of his own) complicit with a dark agenda to create an artificial counterfeit for divine consciousness, a literal, i.e. computerised, Vast Active Living Intelligence System, that required human bodies, not merely to create it but also to power it? (As anticipated by Teilhard de Chardin and his nöösphere, see Part II).

After all, this long exploration of Dick's world, inner and outer, has now found itself embedded within a very different context than nine years earlier, in 2013. It is now the central case study for an exploration of the 'Big Mother thesis', mapping the possession of human bodies by an occult, satanic force that uses a combination of male 'mother issues' with runaway technological advancements as the means to assume con-trol over the human soul (roughly). That's quite a quantum leap from Philip K. Dick, the autist-prophet. Or is it?

For all the nuance and subtlety of his novels, the Dickian concept that has most effectively been incorporated into the mainstream, both in fantasy media and scientific (or pseudo-scientific) thought and agendas, is not *anamnesis* or the restoration of the kingdom of God, but its dark counterpoint: that of simulated realities, artificial life forms, and the creation of the Black Iron Prison that never ended. The Matrix, or Big Mother state.

Is this why Dick left out the last paragraph of his written speech, when he delivered it in 1977, the last line of which was: 'And perhaps in my novels and stories I have done wrong to urge you to remember'?

Was Dick trying to warn us about something that didn't want him to warn us?

PART II

TRANSGENDER AND THE RISE
OF THE DREAM-STATE

So you see, the people who consider themselves to be the most enlightened today are living with entirely unrealistic ideas … When these things are said by scientists—it does not matter so much if people merely repeat them—they are the thoughts of angels who have made themselves at home in human heads. Yes, the human intellect is to be taken over more and more by such powers; they want to use it to bring their own lives to fruition. [I]t is Ahriman science, the science of backward angels who infest human heads … The Ahrimanic powers are doing well if people believe that science gives a true image of the world around us.

—Rudolf Steiner, *The Fall of the Spirits of Darkness*

Technique, then, brings its own ideology; and every technical realization engenders its own ideological justifications.

—Jacques Ellul, *The Technological Society*

CHAPTER 10

The Matrix meets dominatrix

With language comes ideation, and with ideation, ideology. Ideology's primary aim is to banish the real in favour of establishing a kingdom of unreality.

Language's desire, the aim of the technology, has been to maintain and extend this false kingdom. It must prevent ideology-free consciousness from being recognised (and having any impact) within the species consciousness that relies on language to cogitate existence.

In this false realm, that which cannot be spoken, does not exist. Reality begins and ends with the word.

Knowledge of good and evil is the binary reality of consciousness externalised, not as an innate balance and complementary nature of things but as a binding force of opposition between two halves, a war of Heaven and Hell, male and female.

It is a split between night and day that condemns human consciousness to a twilight zone in which nothing is real because everything is disconnected from its complementary other 'half'.

The symbol no longer represents an actual object but, like money, becomes a thing unto itself.

* * *

One night in January 2001, Larry Wachowski, co-director of
the blockbuster *Matrix* movies, walked into a dark club in West
Hollywood, where the rules of identity easily blurred, just like
in his films. The Dungeon served the devoted BDSM—bondage,
discipline, sadism and masochism—community in Los Angeles.
It was a place where power dynamics between two different
types of people were regularly played out: eager submissives,
or slaves, and the dominatrixes who, for an hour or for a night,
took complete charge of their minds and bodies, using ropes,
whips, chains, knives and needles. Wachowski fell into the former category. And, friends say, he liked engaging in his pastime
while dressed like a woman.

  —'The Mystery of Larry Wachowski', *Rolling Stone*, 2006

It began (for the purposes of this current work, at least) with Philip K.
Dick's glimpse of his soul, and the corresponding Christian-hued vision
of anamnesis-revelation of a dimension of existence outside the linear
timestream of the false identity. Dick himself—innocently enough, being
a sci-fi writer—adapted this experience into a technological, scientific
(or pseudo-scientific) framework, with VALIS, computer programming,
and the idea of an artificially simulated reality, to make it easier for out-
siders to *grok* his vision of parallel worlds and soul-prisons. (Sci-fi has
always relied on imagining advanced technology as the *sine qua non* of
creating future scenarios.)

By the time of the turn-of-the-millennium *The Matrix* (1999), the computer simulation mainframe had become the whole damn story. Twenty
years later, the meme has migrated all the way from Hollywood fantasy
to mainstream science, or scientism, via Dickian characters like Elon
Musk (who even has a Dickian name, and who has claimed to believe
we are living inside a computer programme) and Mark Zuckerberg,
who offered the tech, and the rationales, for doing exactly that.

What happened in the interim? One thing that happened was that
the ostensible makers of *The Matrix* (there are those who contest this
version of reality) took their own version of the red pill and—in an act
of ontological defiance—switched sexes, going from Larry and Andy to
Lana and Lilly Wachowski. This didn't happen overnight, and though
it has been mostly stricken from the record, Larry's 'transition' to Lana
(which preceded Andy's to Lilly by a few years) began, not in Morpheus'

virtual dojo, but in the S&M dungeons of LA. As reported—briefly—in a 2006 *Rolling Stone* article, following their massive success with the first *Matrix* and its substandard sequels, Larry became involved with a high-profile dominatrix with the '*nom de kink*' of Ilsa Strix. Strix's speciality was inflicting extreme pain, her greatest accomplishment was 'putting 333 needles into a single penis'. (The occult significance of that number is perhaps best left alone.) The article continues:

> Mistress Strix virtually willed herself to become a superstar in the world of BDSM. Besides running the Dungeon, where she established a wide following among Hollywood's power elite, Ilsa gave advanced piercing classes to aspiring dominants, or masters, and stood at the forefront of a vigorous effort to spread the BDSM philosophy around not only Los Angeles but the world, via the Internet. 'She had the ability to bring a true submissive or slave to levels that they never thought they could reach. She expanded their limits, and they were happy about that. It was a power exchange'.

The article then goes bravely out on what has since become—now transgenders have become a protected class in the higher echelons of intersectionality—a very dangerous limb, by mentioning 'autogynephiles—straight men who are essentially sexual fetishists, aroused by the thought or image of themselves as women'. For support, it quotes psychology professor, J. Michael Bailey (author of *The Man Who Would Be Queen: The Science of Gender-Bending and Transsexualism*): 'Autogynephiles frequently mention having a longing to be a girl that begins in childhood … But the first outward manifestation of it usually crops up in early adolescence, when they discover that it turns them on to wear women's clothing'.

> And some experts believe that men who want to be women also tend to be what Larry Wachowski appears to be: *a guy with a jones for technology*. In 1974, Donald Laub, a plastic surgeon, and Norman Fisk, a psychiatrist, conducted a study at the Stanford University School of Medicine of 769 patients considering sex reassignment. Of the male patients, Laub and Fisk discovered an interesting predisposition: 'Observation of the male-to-female group showed them … to be interested in mathematics and computer sciences'.[23]

Apotemnophilia is a neurological disorder characterised by an intense desire for the amputation of a specific limb or a need to become paralysed, blind, or deaf. It is characterised by the desire for the amputation of healthy limbs or the destruction of functioning senses, either via surgical intervention or by purposefully injuring themselves to force emergency medical intervention. Apotemnophilia was first described in a 1977 article by psychologists Gregg Furth and John Money (the pioneer of transgenderism and a supporter of paedophile rights;[24] see 'Apotemnophilia: Two cases of self-demand amputation as paraphilia').

In 2008, V. S. Ramachandran, David Brang, and Paul D. McGeoch proposed that apotemnophilia is a neurological disorder caused by an incomplete body image map in the right parietal lobe. A separate definition of apotemnophilia is erotic interest in being or looking like an amputee, in a similar way to how autogynephiles experience an erotic charge from imagining themselves in a woman's body. So why are apotemnophilia and autogynephilia considered paraphilias, while transgender is not? The answer is that, through a combination of activism, media representation, and the growing numbers of advocates and defenders, transgender has been stricken from the list of paraphilias, and scientific research has gone full throttle to try and produce enough stupefying, generally pseudo-scientific evidence to keep it that way. But all the arguments being made to defend transsexuals from the stigma of paraphilia (i.e. psychological dysfunction) could, if one wished, be equally well applied to cases of apotemnophilia (and autogynephilia). And where would that end?

A person might—like the author Paul Bowles—wish to do away with the body altogether, and opt for existence as a severed head floating in a jar. Who are we to say that this is an unhealthy life choice? (Joke.) Perhaps the ultimate social attainment will someday be recognised as those individuals who saw themselves as non-biological, non-human, as 'pure information', and who chose to be removed from the physical realm altogether, in lieu of an exclusive but eternal existence in the Metaverse 2.0

* * *

> [A]ll the manifestations of sexual psychology, normal and abnormal … are the most specifically human. More than any others they involve the potently plastic force of the imagination.
> —Havelock Ellis, *Studies in the Psychology of Sex*

Getting back to the Wachowskis. The *Rolling Stone* article speculates, reasonably enough, that the extremely poor quality of the *Matrix* sequels was due, not to 'sophomore slump', but to the fact that 'Larry Wachowski's mind was elsewhere ... totally concentrating on Ilsa'. What was briefly seen as a cause for concern, however, has since become a *cause célèbre*. A description of Cáel M. Keegan's 2018 *Lana and Lilly Wachowski: Sensing Transgender* evokes a 'body of work [that] can be read as an aesthetic history of transgender political consciousness as it has evolved discursively in popular media [and that] smuggled a transgender aesthetic into the very heart of global media'.[25]

> Lana and Lilly Wachowski have redefined the technically and topically possible while joyfully defying audience expectations. Visionary films like *The Matrix* trilogy and *Cloud Atlas* have made them the world's most influential transgender media producers, and their coming out retroactively put trans* aesthetics at the very center of popular American culture. Cáel M. Keegan views the Wachowskis' films as an approach to trans* experience that maps a transgender journey and the promise we might learn 'to sense beyond the limits of the given world'. Keegan reveals how the filmmakers take up the relationship between identity and coding (be it computers or genes), inheritance and belonging, and how transgender becoming connects to a utopian vision of a post-racial order. Along the way, he theorizes a trans* aesthetic that explores the plasticity of cinema to create new social worlds, new temporalities, and new sensory inputs and outputs.
>
> (Publisher's description)

As some readers of this current work will already be aware, I once invested a great deal of time, energy, and belief into the *Matrix* mythos. I wrote an unofficial handbook on the film (combining the plotline and philosophy with the *weltanschauung* of Carlos Castaneda), published in 2003. I went to Cannes that year, where *Matrix Reloaded* premiered, and got copies of the book to cast and crew, including the Wachowskis (I didn't give it to them personally). The book even includes special thanks to them in the acknowledgements. Worse still, the year I wrote the book (2002), I LARP-ed 'being the One', all the way down to the shades and long black coat, and then made a movie about it. It is safe to say that the *Matrix* vision, whoever it really 'belongs to', possessed me, to such a degree that I radically altered my behaviour, and even transformed my persona—my look—to become a better host to the virus.

At the time of writing this (2023), now that the film's makers have jumped the shark and Cypher-ed themselves back into the Matrix with sparkling new gender identities, and soon after the release of the 4th *Matrix* film, I don't much care to see, hear, say, or write *anything* about *The Matrix*. The original introduction to this work began with a reference to the film (how would Morpheus have explained the matrix to Thomas if he didn't have a red pill to give him?), but I took it out early on. It was painfully clear to me that, as a cultural reference point, the film wasn't simply far too easy a go to, it had now taken on the opposite of its original meaning. The red pill had turned blue. According to Marcus Chong, Tank in the first movie: 'Larry and Andy were always into the concept of suppression, of suppressing oneself … One of their big directorial notes was "Be stoic. Never show your true self"'.

It is a great irony, then, that *The Matrix* has now become a *necessary* cultural reference point in this work, but for the very *inverse* reason for which I previously tried to use it. The movie can no longer be separated from the real-life story of the Wachowskis, and this latter brings together a number of central threads:

- How good ideas, and even transcendental visions, go bad and/or get co-opted (which comes first is a chicken or egg question).
- How the idea of living inside a matrix segues seamlessly from a working metaphor for the soul's imprisonment to a false identity, to a reification of that same identity, via a postmodernist justification for the denial of objective, biological reality, in favour of ideological constructions.
- How all this leads inexorably to the rejection of nature and the body.
- How the latter takes the form of men identifying with, and *as*, women, going so far as to be surgically altered to prove it. (The belief that generates its own proof can only do so via the technological simulation of 'transcendence'.)
- How the goal of the techno-obsessed male to turn himself into a woman is consistent with autogynephilia and with sexual subjugation to a female dominatrix (big mother), i.e. with a kind of psychic possession or enslavement, rooted in child-to-mother attachment disorder.

- Most controversially of all, how this paraphilia may be, less demonstrably, evidence of the occult influence of non-human entities, whose goal is to take possession of the minds of human beings as a means to use their bodies.
- How these entities are using the bodies they possess to create the necessary tech to transform those same bodies into hosts for their own incarnation.

It may be that this is why, in part, the closest to a semi-coherent rationale for gender-reassignment surgery is the idea that someone can be 'born in the wrong-sex body' (in newspeak, assigned the wrong gender at birth, by those poor, small-minded doctors who presume that a penis indicates a boy-child and a vagina signals the arrival of a girl). In a scientistic paradigm with no time for souls, this translates into an inexplicable incongruity between the sex of a brain and that of the body. Needless to say, this brazenly dodges the question of what exactly biological sex *is*, if not what the genitals tell us it is—not to mention how exactly brains have sex (pun intended). The sexed-brain argument seems to have run out of steam since I first wrote this, however, and a more current argument for a biological basis for body-sex dysphoria has to do with intersex humans (estimated, I would say *generously*, at 0.02 to 0.05 per cent of humans) and the occasional creature that changes sex—known as sequential hermaphroditism—mostly fishes, including the aptly named clown fish. The idea that Nature makes mistakes (i.e. does things we don't like) that need to be corrected by tech, always dubious at best, can now be conveniently exchanged with the idea that, hey, Nature does weird stuff too, so why shouldn't we? (Sort of like citing a legal precedent.) These questions—or simply the fact that they have become necessary to ask—are central to this current work; or at any rate, they are about to be.

CHAPTER 11

Body dysphoria, autism, crypto-eugenics

*T*he inception of an 'identity' via ideology, at odds with biology, is a tree without roots in ontology.

This 'split' was similar to how a cell splits in order to reproduce, and closer to the act of love than to an act of war. Yet in every act of love, there is always the possibility of war.

Inherent within this binary arrangement is a form of symmetry by which no fiction can depart too far from fact without losing all meaning.

By this self-regulatory principle, all departures from reality eventually become self-contradicting and create a self-cancelling culture.

So the garden of earthly delights keeps itself from falling into total disarray.

* * *

Why is the determination to fight against a prejudice a sure sign that one is full of it? Such a determination necessarily arises from an obsession. It constitutes an utterly sterile effort to get rid of it. In such a case the light of attention is the only thing which is effective, and it is not compatible with a polemical intention.

—Simone Weil, *Gravity and Grace*

The transgender question spans the whole spectrum of human interest, from psychological to biological, social to cultural, religious to technological, political to spiritual. It would be hard to conceive of a hotter topic—or button—than the question of when, if, and exactly *how* a man becomes a woman, or vice versa. Wrapped up inside this question is a still deeper one, Philip K. Dick's prevailing obsession: what makes a human being a human being? What constitutes personal identity, and how much can it be made subject to our desire, or vice versa? Among the countless lesser questions that the subject raises, here are a sample few, some (though probably not all) of which the subject makes unavoidable.

1) Biological sex and social gender roles
2) Possible causes for body dysphoria and gender confusion
3) Possible outside interests the 'Trans Agenda' may be serving, whether corporate, military, governmental, ideological, metaphysical, or otherwise
4) How transgenderism affects women and their position in society
5) How it affects men and theirs
6) How transgenderism overlaps with/is compatible with transhumanism
7) How children are being affected and endangered by transgenderism as a social trend
8) How (or if) transgender individuals are being discriminated against and abused in society
9) Class and privilege, and how transgender individuals may be themselves practising discrimination and abuse
10) Whether ideology can be seen as a counter-measure or corrective to biology and psychology
11) Whether identity has any existence outside of social contagion and social constructs designed to control human beings and suppress their life force
12) Social and possibly biological anomalies within a community or species
13) Group identity, social contagion, and scapegoating

And so on.

What all of these issues point to is not so much a budding new development within the species as an ideological battleground made inevitable by a kind of accelerated cultural complexification. Progressives see this as a war of the new against the old, of enlightened values struggling against outmoded beliefs and prejudices. But if looked at with a less 'cultured' or ideologically entrenched eye, it appears to be a war of culture against nature, mind against body.

High-culture phases of societies are often characterised by over-complexification that includes an interference with child development to make 'properly' socialised adult bodies, as in the case of foot-binding in China. On the other hand, the phenomenon of transsexuality—most especially men turning themselves into women (symbolically if not actually)—is characteristic of the most primitive cultures, as well as the most sophisticated and complex. For example, a 1999 book by John Colman Wood, *When Men Are Women*, describes the Gabra, a nomadic, camel-herding society in northern Kenya: 'Gabra men denigrate women and feminine things, yet regard their most prestigious men as women. As they grow older, all Gabra men become d'abella, or ritual experts, who have feminine identities' (publisher's description).

Apparently, men aspiring to become women is as old as culture itself, and it isn't necessarily incompatible with what's today called misogyny (any more than it is with sadomasochism). In fact, it is sometimes an expression of these things. The common thread, since all men (including Macduff and more modern Caesarean birth babies)[26] are 'born of woman', is the *denial of the body*. Perhaps there is even a direct correlation between culture and the drive to transcend biology, and therefore death? And perhaps the anti-natural aspect of culture, high and low, includes a rejection, and the corresponding co-opting, of the female form?

* * *

'Since 2010, there have been at least 9 studies on the potential link between ASD and gender dysphoria. Across all of these studies, almost without exception, rates of ASD or autism traits range from 5% to 54% among those with gender dysphoria, significantly higher than among the general population' ... Even though people are aware of the notable co-occurrence between autism and GD, it is difficult to find autism specific gender dysphoria information. Given the strong co-occurrence of autism and gender variance, why is this? And why are these young people not being thoroughly screened for autism during the initial assessment process? ... Furthermore, many, if not most, autistic adults also have childhood trauma. I believe this is a combination of our natural physiological predisposition to anxiety (enlarged amygdala, hyper-sensitive adrenal axis, sensory processing differences) as well as our challenges in communication with the humans around us. How does one have their needs met when our language doesn't match our experience? What if we can't find the words to describe it? Also, autism puts you at a much greater risk of bullying and sexual abuse.

—'Autism and Gender Dysphoria', *Transgender Trend*, 2020[27]

One of the leading proponents of the 'gender affirmative' approach to body-dysphoric children is Diane Ehrensaft, PhD, a clinical and developmental psychologist and author (*The Gender Creative Child*). At the time of writing (according to her website), she is the Director of Mental Health and founding member of the Child and Adolescent Gender Center, an associate professor of paediatrics at the University of California, and the chief psychologist at the UCSF Benioff Children's Hospital Child and Adolescent Gender Center Clinic. Ehrensaft has asserted (for example, in the closing panel discussion at an all-day event in 2016, in Santa Cruz) that 'children will know [they are transgender] by the second year of life ... they probably know before that but that's pre-pre verbal'.[28]

Ehrensaft has also claimed that gender identity can be fluid, meaning that, while a baby innately 'knows' its gender identity, at the same time it depends on its mood at a given moment. On the third hand, if gender-fluid children begin to transition and then change their minds, that's OK too: 'there is "no data" that it harms kids to switch back and forth between identities, as long as we "support" them in their "journey"'. The problem that remains unaddressed by Ehrensaft and her ilk is that 'support' in this brave new world involves medical interventions that are generally irreversible (though some have tried*). Never mind the

---

*There are no forthcoming figures of the detransitioned—'or detrans'. It's not even clear how many people identify as transgender, in the US at least, because the US Census Bureau doesn't collect data on gender identity or sexual orientation. (A 2016 study from the Williams Institute at UCLA Law estimated 1.4 million trans adults in the United States, about 0.6 percent of the adult population.) Almost a dozen studies looking at the rate of 'desistance' among trans-identified kids, and despite differences in country, culture, time

glaring contradiction in using hormones and surgery to 'fix' someone into a state of 'gender fluidity'![29] (The idea of transitioning from one 'sex' to another is also false, as the only transition is from a naturally functioning sexuality to one that no longer functions naturally. More on this later.)

Ehrensaft has also dismissed any and all ethical concerns about sterilising an 11- or 12-year-old child, deriding it as the self-centred desire of parents for grandchildren. Her key argument is to equate puberty blockers and cross-sex hormones with fertility-robbing chemotherapy treatments for children with terminal cancer, contending that both are life-saving, urgently required medical interventions. In fact, there is no historical evidence for her claim that chemically transitioned, and consequently sterilised, teenagers are at less risk of suicide; on the contrary, 'child and youth suicide rates have increased since the advent of pediatric medical transition'.[30]

Ehrensaft made a grisly Freudian slip in 2021 when she stated: 'Those of us who provide this care have been accused of sterilizing children. And what I would say is, we are not sterilizing everybody—[quickly revises] *anybody*'.[31] This is patently untrue, because a child who has been puberty-blocked and moves to cross-sex hormones forever sacrifices the choice to have children, at least by the normal biological channels. Ehrensaft argues that these prepubescent children must be allowed to make their own choices, however, even while admitting that they cannot ever be *informed* choices, because 'asking a child to consider the mechanics of sex and reproduction at this age may actually be psychologically harmful!'.[32] As compared to the mechanical 'alteration' of sex and the eradication of reproductive capacities? This is from a transitioned woman, in 'Forget What Gender Activists Tell You. Here's What Medical Transition Looks Like':

> During my own transition, I had seven surgeries. I also had a massive pulmonary embolism, a helicopter life-flight ride, an emergency ambulance ride, a stress-induced heart attack, sepsis, a 17-month recurring infection due to using the wrong skin during a (failed) phalloplasty, 16 rounds of antibiotics, three weeks of daily

---

period, and follow-up length and method, have come to a similar conclusion: Only very few trans-kids still want to transition by the time they are adults. Instead, they generally turn out to be regular homosexuals.

IV antibiotics, the loss of all my hair, (only partially successful) arm reconstructive surgery, permanent lung and heart damage, a cut bladder, insomnia-induced hallucinations—oh and frequent loss of consciousness due to pain from the hair on the inside of my urethra. All this led to a form of PTSD that made me a prisoner in my apartment for a year. Between me and my insurance company, medical expenses exceeded $900,000.[33]

A Philip K. Dickian version of reality, literalised by people with a deficiency of imagination and an excess of ideological zeal (and money), is a *clown world* in which infant boys can know they are really girls on the inside and must be encouraged in this latent awareness, for otherwise they are being oppressed by heteronormative prejudices. Prepubescent girls, likewise, can initiate a medical intervention process that will prevent them from developing breasts or ever having children. But these brave new clown-worlders must be protected *at all costs* from any facts about sexuality that they might be psychologically unprepared for! Parents who don't support the salvation-through-sterilisation plan can prepare to give up, not just their future grandchildren, but their children too. 'In Ontario, where pro-trans legislation has been passing swiftly, the state has the right to seize children from families that do not support the child's wish to live as transgendered'.[34] One Canadian father was sentenced to six months in jail for speaking out publicly against his child's 'transitioning'.[35]

Whether it is due to a conscious act of malevolence or not, a specific demographic in the species has been targeted for sterilisation. This was once known as 'eugenics', and in the halcyon days of the Nazis and the Fabians, it especially targeted disabled children. Not surprisingly, perhaps, the current target demographic of the body-dysphoric overlaps significantly with that of autistic children and teenagers. As the *4thWaveNow* website describes, 'autism spectrum people's predisposition toward unusual interests, or gender dysphoria ... could represent OCD rather than genuine gender identity issues'. The diagnosis of Autism Spectrum Disorder in children more or less presupposes 'nonnormative sexual interests', 'unusual sensory preferences', and 'a longstanding feeling of being different and an outsider among peers'; it stands to reason that these qualities could lead to 'gender dysphoria' in adolescence.

Poor social and/or communication skills, a hallmark of ASD, as well as a tendency to have obsessive interests, to isolate socially and spend inordinate and unusual amounts of solitary time on the Internet, have been noted by both professionals and parents. I've also noticed, on several of the blogs run by parents who are supporting their child's transition, a theme of frequent temper tantrums and refusal to wear certain clothing.[36]

How widespread is this crypto-eugenics plan? A 2018 article cites recent statistics for the United Kingdom, showing an average of 50 children a week being referred to gender clinics, a rate of roughly 2,600 per year. For the United States, pop: 323.2 million,

> given that both countries seem equally enthusiastic about juvenile transition … we would therefore expect to see about 250 children per week entering the transgender medical system, or an annual rate of 13,000 children. If only half of those 250 referred children go on to medical transition, the annual number of sterilized children in the United States could be as high as 6,500.

This is 'a rate of sterilization potentially 7 times higher than it was under eugenics (and we could attain, in less than 10 years, the numbers that it took the eugenicists 70 years to achieve)'.[37]

A significant portion—maybe even as many as half—of these children are on the autism spectrum.

* * *

> [T]echnique, having ruptured the relations between man and man, proceeds to rebuild the bridge which links them. It bridges the specializations because it produces a new type of man always and everywhere like his duplicate, who develops along technical lines.
>
> —Jacques Ellul, *The Technological Society*

One thing that needs to be made clear is that the transhuman/transgender/postgender agenda is distinct from transsexual *individuals*, at least to a significant degree. A vast portion of the push behind trans/postgenderism is not coming from people who have had or wish to have gender-reassignment surgery, or even ones who simply self-identify as 'trans', 'gender-fluid', or 'gender-binary'. In fact, a significant number of transsexuals are not supportive of, are even opposed to, the Trans Agenda. Nonetheless, for obvious reasons, the social and cultural movement and the individuals it supposedly advocates (and to a degree stems from) cannot easily be separated. Without the existence of transsexuals in our society, no Trans Agenda could exist. And without the cross-generational brainwashing of the Trans Agenda, it's safe to say there would be *significantly* fewer aspiring transsexuals.

Nonetheless, the Trans Agenda seems to me so central to the larger goals of long-term social engineering, that, if s/he did not exist, the transgender individual would have to be invented. Human beings are imitative creatures, and this goes double for heavily socialised ones. Culture—like a natural organism growing in an artificial environment—is a process by which certain behaviours 'go viral', become fashionable, and inspire imitation. Naturally, the more prolific (and the more widely represented by the mainstream media) a form of behaviour becomes, the more people are going to imitate it. The manufactured transgender movement is really no different from any widespread marketing campaign. Central to its success is representing the idea of chemically and surgically induced 'sex changes' as healthy, normal, and desirable (and sexy, cool, and hip).

Les Parrott, PhD, a professor of psychology, made a list of the most common ways in which teens act out their struggles with identity. It consists of five primary ways: status symbols (clothing and possessions); forbidden behaviours and taboo pleasures (smoking, drinking, drugs, and sexual activity); rebellion; celebrity idols; and cliquish exclusion of anyone not like themselves. All five correspond with gender fluidity and transgender-identification: it is fashion and status-related, (somewhat) forbidden or taboo, rebellious, exclusive, and cliquish, and at the same time associated with celebrity or high-status, as with figures such as Bruce > Caitlyn Jenner.

Social contagion takes many forms, from the trivial to the tragic. Beyond any doubt, the internet, social media, mass online pornography use[38] (especially post-covid), and smartphones have amplified the rate of transmission exponentially. It's doubtful if any study could adequately map the rate at which behaviours are imitated, most especially when

they subtly offer solutions, or at least relief, to only half-conscious problems. This is from 'Media Contagion and Suicide Among the Young':

> There is ample evidence from the literature on suicide clusters and
> the impact of the media to support the contention that suicide is
> 'contagious' … The occurrence of imitative suicides following
> media stories is largely known as the 'Werther effect', derived from
> the impression that Goethe's novel *The Sorrows of Young Werther* in
> 1774 triggered an increase in suicides, leading to its ban in many
> European states. [R]esearch consistently found a strong relation-
> ship between reports of suicide in newspapers or on television and
> subsequent increases in the suicide rate.[39]

The point here isn't to compare 'sexual reassignment' due to gender
dysphoria to suicide (though both involve violence to the body); only
to illustrate the extent to which the mass media, peer pressure, and illegitimate authority figures can and do influence individuals' (especially
young ones) decision-making, including irrevocable life-changing decisions. This seems especially the case when overtly glamorised images
are presented, repeatedly and irresponsibly, as *ways-out* to individuals suffering from confusion, distress, and a scarily shifting sense of
identity.[40]

CHAPTER 12

Liquid modernity and the madness of the many: Sex education by Baron Munchausen

*L*iquid modernity: meaningless text without any inherent or encoded *meaning that can therefore be re-imagined any way the id-entity likes. A false 'faith' that does not move mountains but illegitimately persuades us they have moved, and/or that there never was a mountain.*

Identity is a habitation of demons, and a hold of every unclean spirit (id-entity). This is where politics enter (polis = city). The id-entity is multiple, dissociative, and disordered: a protective mechanism of the psyche, by which information is pushed into a latent condition of potential, rather than being actively engaged in running the total programme.

The id-entity comes into being both as a means to and the result of the suppression of the total psyche. It is the first and last line of defence against the soul.

* * *

> The two greatest obscenities in the society of *Brave New World* are birth and mother. Why?
>
> —Study question

In Canada, the Sexual Orientation Gender Identification programme (SOGI) began on the International Day against Homophobia and Transphobia, observed globally, on 17 May 2014. This was the day that the Faculty of Education, University of British Columbia, and ARC Foundation announced a major new social justice initiative funded by an ARC Foundation gift of $125,000 to the University of British Columbia. The UBC-ARC Sexual Orientation and Gender Identity Fund is designed to

> create and maintain an LGB/T2/Q inclusive curriculum, culture, work place, and learning environment. To prioritize systemic, faculty-wide interventions that focus on sexual orientation and gender identity as critical pillars in the architecture of human rights risks, resiliencies and interventions that aim to redress inequities and enhance social sustainability. To design, innovate and implement whole-climate pedagogical approaches that recognize, and intervene to transform, the impacts of systemic discrimination.[41]

In SOGI's own words:

> Since we all have a sexual orientation and gender identity, it includes all of us. Every student understands and expresses their gender differently, with interests and choices that are common or less common for their biological sex. Some students may be unsure of their sexual orientation. Others may identify specifically as lesbian, gay, straight, bisexual, transgender, queer, two-spirit, cisgender, or other. A SOGI-inclusive school means all of these experiences and identities are embraced and never cause for discrimination.

According to a BC-based site reporting on behalf of concerned parents (*Culture Guard*), teachers are directed in the SOGI-targeted pilot schools not to use the words 'mum', 'dad', 'mother', or 'father', but only gender-neutral terms like 'parent' and 'partner', and not to address children as 'boys and girls' but to use gender-neutral words like 'students'.[42] Evidently, school admins abhor vacuums, because these vanishing words are giving over to new *de rigueur* terms like anal sex, vaginal lubrication, polyamory, sadomasochism, and 'transvestic fetishism', all of which are considered in children's best interests to learn about, as soon as is cognitively feasible.

The promotional material for the 'PrideSpeaks' session for kindergarten grade 3 (5–8-year-olds), includes reading *I Am Jazz*, a picture book about gender diversity by Jazz Jennings, a young transgender person being called 'a spokesperson for transkids everywhere'; discussion about the story; empathy exercises to demonstrate what being a good friend looks like for students who come out as transgender or gender variant; and so on. (More recently, 'Drag Queen Story Hour' sends extravagantly made-up and flamboyantly attired transvestites to preschools, in order to 'acclimatise' the children to transgender people and pre-empt any kind of instinctive fear or repulsion they might experience.)[43] In 2015, the UK Gender Identity and Research and Education Society 'called on schools to teach their children about trans issues' via the Penguin Land stories, which depict 'adult penguins reassuring younger penguins about transitioning'. 'In the books, young readers are told the story of a penguin called Polly who was "always really Tom" and another about a penguin named John, who is now known as Sally'.[44]

The SOGI agenda and its equivalents in the other 'progressive' countries is specifically geared towards the eradication of the idea of sexual deviance, insofar as it leads to unfair discrimination against sexual 'outliers' (generally not a problem among penguins). It is predicated on the presumption that current mores and standards around sexuality are more enlightened than previously, and that, with ever-diminishing exceptions (paedophilia, bestiality, rape, extreme sexual sadism, and murder, to name a few), there is no such thing as sexual deviance, provided it is consensual. (S&M is an obvious example of this: one woman's kink is another man's torture.)

SOGI is just one example (local to me at the time I first wrote this) of a multinational, many-tentacled push to sexualise children as early as possible, so as to eliminate 'prejudice' and dissolve, or destroy, 'unnatural' (patriarchal) limitations like biological sex—in both senses of that term. In a more openly transgressive example, seven years down the liberation road, 'Sexy Summer Camp' for young teens (in the summer of 2021 in rural Kentucky) included lessons on 'sex liberation', 'gender exploration', 'BDSM', 'being a sex worker', 'self-managed abortions', and 'sexual activity while using licit and illicit drugs'. The leader of the Camp, Tanya Turner, self-identifies as a witch; her recommendation is that children should begin to masturbate as toddlers: 'Masturbation is really healthy and I recommend it to people of all ages. All ages. As soon as my nephews could talk, they were doing that'. As part of the 'self-pleasure workshop', instructors promise to give a 'hands-on' lesson in masturbation.[45] The organisers have been operating similar sorts of sex education workshops for children since 2012, according to their website.[46] Attention brought to the camp by journalist Christopher Rufo in 2022 has stirred up parental backlash, however, and Turner currently claims to be in hiding after 'death threats'.[47]

If one wonders how that kind of kiddie-sex camp can even be legal, well, it's confusing figuring out what's wrong and right in clown world, and those who make the laws can break the laws, as well as change them on a whim. While the fear and loathing of paedophilia by the general public continues unabated, it is increasingly locked into an inevitable collision course with the LBGTQ, liberal-progressive, postmodernist, 'woke' drive to give everyone everywhere the right to do whatever they want, anytime, sexually speaking at least, and including children, and therefore, paedophiles. And as in Huxley's brave new Mother State, children don't belong to their natural (and way-too old-fashioned) parents anymore, or at least shouldn't, and soon won't. This is Melissa Harris-Perry, a professor of political science at Tulane, in 2013:

> We have never invested as much in public education as we should have, because we've always had kind of a private notion of children: Your kid is yours and totally your responsibility. We haven't had a very collective notion of 'these are our children'. So part of it is we have to break through our kind of private idea that kids belong to their parents, or kids belong to their families, and recognize that kids belong to whole communities. Once it's everybody's responsibility, and not just the households, then we start making better investments.[48]

In 2022, the Biden administration is embracing the claim that parents should have no rights when it comes to what their children are taught in taxpayer-funded schools. The National School Boards Association wrote a letter to the Whitehouse, imploring the federal government 'to use the Patriot Act against "domestic terrorist" parents who raise questions about critical race theory [an educational tool that teaches that all white people, including infants, are racist] being pushed in their kids' schools'.[49] And it goes beyond teaching. At the height of the COVID-19 panic, children as young as 12 were allowed to 'consent' to the experimental mRNA 'vaccine' at schools, without their parent's knowledge, or even against their parents' objections.[50]

As Rudolf Steiner remarked, over a hundred years ago—not about sexual liberation but it fits as well here as anywhere—those who consider themselves the most enlightened in our society are preaching, and attempting to practice, the most unrealistic ideas (putting it kindly). Although transgender identity is not strictly a sexual orientation, the two things literally stand side-by-side in the SOGI agenda, making them like Siamese twins: if not overlapping then certainly inseparable. Sexual orientation pertains to sexual appetite, and neither can be understood nor (safely) experienced before reaching an age of sufficient sexual and psychological development. This means that telling children about anal sex and sadomasochism, for example—things which may not be healthy at *any* age—can only have the effect of prematurely sexualising that child, thereby *guaranteeing* sexual neuroses.

Gender identification, on the other hand, is something that is not fully understood by anyone, child *or* adult. Judging by the current course our society is on, in choosing to defend and champion things irrespective of understanding them, it never *will* be understood. (I don't even think it *can* be understood, at least not separately from questions of trauma, dissociation and entity possession.) SOGI's aim is to teach children about gender identification as a means to: a) prevent discrimination against other children; b) provide relief and/or treatment for children suffering from inchoate feelings, sensations, impressions, emotions, fears, and desires in their body and psyche. Regarding the first question, discrimination is not always negative, much less persecutory, and is sometimes *needed* for self-protection and avoidance, exactly as a sensitive child must learn to avoid a loud-mouthed bully, and so on.

Teaching children about gender identification so as to help them find their own 'niche' is more seriously problematic. If adults, working for education programmes like SOGI, pre-empt the inner life of a child with ill-informed and ill-advised understandings, this amounts to forcing that child's soul-expression to conform to *a pre-existing ideological framework*, never mind how badly they have to contort themselves to do so. By providing premature and faulty 'understanding' to a child that is still in the midst of experiences it cannot hope to make sense of until much later, that child's attention is forced away from their internal process. The attention is then *redirected* onto outer directives and behaviours meant to accommodate and accelerate that inner process, but without ever understanding it. This allows these ideological agencies (Steiner's 'backward angels') to proceed unobserved and unchecked with *their* agenda. Now the rightful host of the body is absented, the entities have free rein to exert their influence over the child's inner life.

* * *

> Historically, the movement toward androgyny occurs in late phases of culture as a civilization is starting to unravel and you can find it again and again through history. [T]he people who live in such periods, late phase of culture … feel that they're very sophisticated … but from the perspective of historical distance you can see that it's a culture that no longer believes in itself.
> —Camille Paglia, 2016

Ancestral possession takes many forms, not all of which are occulted and some of which may even be diagnosable. Munchausen syndrome, for example, is when a person feigns disease, illness, or psychological trauma to gain attention, sympathy, or reassurance. It fits within a subclass of factitious disorders with predominantly physical signs and symptoms, and patients suffering from it have a history of recurrent hospitalisation, travelling, and dramatic, extremely improbable tales of their past experiences (hence Baron Munchausen).

'Munchausen syndrome by proxy', on the other hand, was first coined by John Money (the pioneering transgender specialist) and June Faith Werlwas to describe the abuse- and neglect-induced symptoms of the syndrome of 'abuse dwarfism'. Also known as 'factitious disorder imposed on another', it's akin to Philip K. Dick's axiom that 'the greatest power the human being can exert over others is to get control of their perceptions of reality'. Munchausen syndrome by proxy (MSP) is when a parent, caregiver, or spouse fabricates, exaggerates, or induces mental or physical health problems in someone in their care, so as to gain attention, sympathy, or solace *for themselves*. It's considered an elusive, potentially lethal, and frequently misunderstood form of child abuse, or at least medical neglect, and perhaps the simplest example (as depicted in Gillian Flynn's *Sharp Objects*) is that of a mother poisoning her child to keep the child in a sickly state—hence wholly dependent—thereby creating a role for themselves as a long-suffering, self-sacrificing caregiver.

MSP might not always manifest to such extremes, however. It may in fact be a case of a far more common (but much subtler) condition, coming all the way out of its closet, as full-blown pathological symptoms. Closely related, for example, is something called the 'masquerade syndrome', in which 'mothers keep children at home from school for long periods with apparent chronic illnesses, the illness being a "masquerade" for an enmeshed relationship with the child'.[51] An even more common condition, which MSP and masquerade syndrome appear to stem from, is known as parental (usually maternal) enmeshment, a condition that—judging by how under-observed it is—may be closer to the rule than the exception, in the late-phase culture of the West. This dynamic is most commonly recognised—probably because it's at its most destructive—in the form of mother–son enmeshment such as *Psycho*'s Norman Bates (based on serial killer Ed Gein). It is by no means limited to this dynamic, however.

Enmeshed families are 'characterized by levels of emotional closeness that are often seen as constraining'; they 'use manipulation, usually in the form of overly excessive, but superficial expressions of love and unity to demand loyalty from their members'. Enmeshed family members 'tend to have a limited sense of their own identity [and] make decisions based on emotions, and as a reaction to the perceived wishes of other members of the system'.[52] Family enmeshment creates 'a dance of circular immaturity and reactivity between the parent and child': the enmeshed parent 'blurs familial boundaries and engages in hovering behaviors'. They are 'overly accessible to their children' and 'do too much' for them, resulting in a loss of autonomy for the child. Like Mrs Bates, 'enmeshed mothers usually do not know the difference between parenting and partnering'.[53] But, as Norman well knew,

> as lofty a position as being the 'chosen child' may seem, the victim of maternal enmeshment is precisely that—a victim. In exchange for his service to his mother, this child actually relinquishes his entire life. [He] loses out on opportunities to interact socially with peers, and ultimately loses out on his childhood. This loss of childhood ... has a downwardly spiraling effect.[54]

What MSP, masquerade syndrome, maternal enmeshment, and many transgender child case studies appear to have in common is that all of them either precipitate or demand an unusual degree of involvement in the child's life by a parent or parents. The involvement is both inner and outer—i.e. it covers both the child's internal preoccupations and perceptions and their outward behaviour and decisions, from the smallest (what clothes to wear) to the largest (what 'sex' to be). Such parental involvement is fraught to the point of being destructive. It is also unlimited in both scale and time, because transitioning children—whatever Ehrensaft has to say about it—will most likely *always* require some degree of 'management' around their decision. For a mother or father with a deep neurotic need for unrestricted, unending involvement in their child's life, these psycho-situations provide *carte blanche*.

Unfortunately, the complex psychological nature of MSP means that only a tiny percentage of adults—never mind children—are likely to ever recognise it, even in the people close to them. And if they do, what are the chances they will dare to say anything? Only a fool tries to come between a lioness and her cub. How to rescue a potential victim if he or she is complicit with the abuses being inflicted on them? As one paper, 'Munchausen Syndrome by Proxy', by Deirdre Conway Rand, puts it,

> older children may become active participants in creating their factitious illness, with either the child or the mother initiating aspects of the deception with which the other then goes along. Mother and child may develop a *folie à deux* relationship concerning the child's medical condition, with both believing that the child is genuinely ill or disabled.[55]

Folie à deux is French for 'the madness of two'. It is more profanely called *shared psychosis*, a psychiatric syndrome in which symptoms of a delusional belief (sometimes including hallucinations) are transmitted from one individual to another. The same syndrome shared by more than two people may be called *folie à trois, folie à quatre, folie en famille* ('family madness'), and, ultimately, *folie à plusieurs*, the madness of many.

It is also associated with *symbiotic psychosis*, a condition seen in young children with abnormal relationships with their mothers or maternal figures. This is often the result of a precipitating traumatic event or series of events. In old-world or archetypal terms, it is known as *possession*.

* * *

> These efforts are, quite literally, state sponsored ... They are all essentially uniform in their support for this particular pre-packaged agenda ... Though it sounds ironic for self-styled revolutionaries to be the Establishment, they are in fact part of the same power structure. I challenge you to identify one single institution that they do not control. Furthermore, this 'revolution' is being carried out against nature, order, and the very fabric of reality, is degrading by every measure, and is fundamentally anti-truth and anti-reality.
>
> —Scott Howard, *The Transgender-Industrial Complex*

Hopefully, all of this helps to illustrate just how fragmented, factitious, and self-devouring progressivist identity politics discourse has become, and how this is symptomatic of, as well as provoking, a growing disconnection from reality. It may also illustrate (in a way I couldn't have known when I first assembled much of this material) how transgender social contagion so closely mirrors, in miniature, the global 'vaccination' plan initiated in 2021, following the (alleged) spread of the SARS covid virus—whatever it is and wherever it came from—and subsequent socioeconomic 'reset' that has since been underway.

What is of greatest significance about the Trans Agenda, in my opinion, is the fact that children as young as 2 or 3 years old are being dragged into an ideological battleground around human sex and sexuality, and that parents have less and less of a grasp of the artillery being deployed. The same applies (in early 2023) with the mRNA gene serum, which some parents have allowed their 6-month babies to receive, in a form of blind trust in medical authority that's indistinguishable, both in nature and consequence, from homicidal rage or suicidal despair. Curiously, all of the transgender debate centres around an ideological framework (gender fluidity) that (like the safety and efficacy of the mRNA injection) is based on extremely flimsy evidence, beginning with the evidence for an identity-self that possesses gender and exists independently of biology. From this shaky foundation, it is argued by some that there is no such thing as biological sex, at all. ('The only inherent difference between trans women and cis women is that trans women were assigned male by a doctor. Trans is an adjective that describes that assignment', Eli Erlick[56]) From such a view sex, like gender, it is a purely social construct. (And gender is now an innate reality!?) This notion has never been proven because, like 2 + 2 = 5, it is inherently unprovable. Yet, like Orwell's measure of party-allegiance, it has been uncritically accepted by many people who blindly support the supposed needs of children to be encouraged to 'transition', and to be protected from any sort of questioning or criticism that might prevent them from submitting to the programme. The (un-)reasoning is that these children will be happier if they are allowed to reject their biology and given total freedom to define their own reality, as well as the power to force everyone else to go along with their pronouns.

How is it possible for so many people to believe so strongly in social policies, education reforms, and medical interventions involving the most invasive technologies imaginable as a means to address something they have not even begun to understand? This question was originally asked by me in 2018. Since then, it has become of burning relevance, not merely to gender dysphoric individuals but to pretty much everyone. Perhaps the answer is found in the question: as long as science *appears* to offer the solution, it follows that it must have fully understood the problem. This is a major pitfall of a technologically driven society in which all attempted solutions only ever address the problem *externally*, hence are increasingly founded on *ignoring—even denying—all internal causes*. And, in a related though less general point, when the problems being addressed have, to one degree or another, been created by the same forces that are offering the solution—often enough intentionally.

How is it that so many people have convinced themselves (or been convinced) that they understand the problem of transgender and gender fluidity (or SARS COVID-19) sufficiently to set about trying to 'educate' others to the same 'understanding'? I have so far mostly shied away from looking at the deeper social engineering programmes behind the gender fluidity movement, programmes which began at least as far back as Havelock Ellis, at the start of the 20th century, Ellis being the hugely influential sexologist and precursor to the psychopathic, still-celebrated, Alfred Kinsey, both of whom I have written about in *The Vice of Kings* (2018). Ellis's 1906 opus, *Studies in the Psychology of Sex: Erotic Symbolism; The Mechanism of Detumescence; The Psychic State in Pregnancy*, was a forerunner to Kinsey's best-selling *Sexual Behavior in the Human Male* (1948) and *Sexual Behavior in the Human Female* (1953), books that helped kick-start the countercultural sexual revolution. It is this same revolution that softened up the populations of the civilised world for the runaway progressivism of the 21st century, a well-intended road to

Hell that has ended up with drag queens teaching tolerance for transgender penguins to toddlers in nursery schools.

Children are taught that there are not two but *many* genders, and that, like the mythical creatures of fairy tales, mysterious entities called 'gender identities' can morph and change according to whim in their interior spaces, while being entirely invisible except for their effects. Invisible playmates are no longer imaginary, they are your own gender identities! These state-backed children's stories eschew scientific or medical evidence in favour of a theoretical mish-mash of ideological imaginings and subjective testimonies from (generally distressed) children, adolescents, and performing drag queens. Life's a fairy tale in which you can be whatever you want to be and no one can tell you otherwise, kids—not without paying a hefty price! No wonder they want to target children: who else would believe this? (Answer: adults who never made it past infancy.)

Fortunately, there's no need to dive into a history of socio-sexual engineering to answer the question of how a belief devoid of understanding such as transgender (or taking experimental covid 'vaccines') has become so widespread and so passionate, so damned quickly. It is simply that *most people in the 21st century are almost completely ignorant of the facts of existence*. Since the psyche abhors a vacuum, when human beings are deprived of even the most rudimentary knowledge of the principles of reality, they become vulnerable to possession by a counterfeit set of beliefs. This counterfeit belief-set is both sourced in and in service to a self-determining, self-inventing, and self-orienting *id-entity* that exists, like an inverted circle—or like the opposite of God—with a circumference (outer shell) that is everywhere, and a centre that is nowhere to be found.

CHAPTER 13

Transhumanism: The ultimate in unmentionable obscenity

*U*sing the language of computer programming to describe the divine act of creation makes organic creatures (including humans) equivalent to machines. This is the transhumanist conceit and Satan's end-game.

At best, it is based on the assumption that, when humans imitate the act of creation, they get it right, and that computer design and programming is an adequate correlate for biology and consciousness. This is a self-perpetuating systemic error, rather than a self-correcting one (which Nature is). Humans use this assumption to reconfigure their own consciousness, in such a way that they become less and less able to perceive—or experience—the ways in which they are not like programmed machines.

Using drugs and technology to alter the human form and create a caricature of the opposite sex is the fullest enactment of this fatal misapprehension. If biological sex is the means by which all humans come to exist, this caricature of creation augurs the end of human existence.

* * *

> In *Brave New World*, the World State has created stability by
> genetically engineering its citizens to be happy with who they
> are and what they do. People are not born, they are decanted in
> hatcheries; and medically and psychologically manipulated so
> that they have just the right intelligence, strength, and attrac-
> tiveness to fill the social and economic positions that will need
> to be filled ... Family and its language are obsolete concepts ...
> There is no stronger bond than family, and family is a major
> factor in self-identification. And what better way to eliminate
> family than to make it a dirty word? ... People are raised to
> think of the language of sexual promiscuity as normal and
> expected and accepted, while the language of the family is
> obscene.
>
> —*Cliff Notes* description of *Brave New World*

While schools, preschools, and other social programmes are pushing for
the need to encourage gender fluidity and direct it down pre-existing
corporate and medical channels of puberty blockers, hormones, and surgery, the fact that many individuals desist in different-sex-identification
over time—and the growing number of people who are choosing to
reverse-transition back to their original sex—is receiving comparatively
little coverage in the mainstream discussion. One obvious reason is that
it's bad for business. Another is that it would undermine an ideological agenda that's already on shaky ground, both ethically and ontologically. So-called 'desisters' are even reviled as traitors by some trans
advocates.[57]

The notion that all forms of suffering need to be alleviated as quickly
as possible by fixing the externals is central to the current 'woke' mental-
ity, from safe spaces to trigger warnings on up. Though among the more
extreme examples, the Trans Agenda and the gender fluidity movement
is no exception. Trying to resolve internal states of suffering by offering external pseudo-solutions (which are at best distractions) is a way
for institutions and individuals to *appear* to be empowering people, by
giving them an endless array of 'free' choices (choices that cost loads of
money). But it can hardly be a coincidence, or merely an oversight, that
these policies and ideologies place the power more and more firmly in
the hands of the medical industry and, by extension, whichever corporations, government organisations, and institutions have the power to
bestow this 'freedom'.

It is apparently a given in today's progressive circles that children are mature enough to manage their own puberty. But how many of these progressive adults would claim they managed their own puberty wisely? Did *anyone*? Most adults are still figuring out when to have sex and with who, how to sensibly navigate alcohol and drug use, and how to maintain a healthy diet. And yet granting children the means, motive, and opportunity to engineer their own sexual development and reconstruct their bodies—including *permanent sterilisation*—is seen as a risk-free and wholly benign development?!

The notion that people know what they need and ought to be allowed to have it is central to the cultural con of human farming. Those who determine the course of society, the shape of culture, and the fate of human populations, know exactly how to use the average person's neurotic desires against them. While Klaus Schwab, the Davos crew, and the World Economic Forum are busy telling us in 2023 that we need to submit to eating bugs, the Great Reset, and the mRNA programme—to mask up, lock down, and sacrifice our consumer indulgences to save the planet and the species—in a form of complementary contradiction characteristic of Orwellian psychosocial engineering, we continue to be encouraged to indulge all our most childish and narcissistic fears and desires; and never, ever, to take no (or the wrong pronoun) for an answer. What squares this circle is that the same cultural and economic forces that flame and feed our desires then chastise and punish us for them. Good cop/bad cop: the superego stirs the id into action, all the better to clamp down upon it. What the State giveth, the State taketh away (ditto with human rights).*

As has been enacted globally in the years between 2020 and 2023, the 'State' (a mix of corporations, military-intelligence networks, organised crime factions, medical, scientific, and political institutions) works 24/7, using every known form of technology and psychological manipulation, to tell people what they need and then give it to them (or force them to take it). Corralling human beings into channels laid down in

---

*This might be called the 'strategy of tension' of social engineering, and can be seen in many different areas: first create a demand for something and then restrict the supply, or even prohibit and punish it. (Tobacco is an obvious, widespread example.) The tension this creates, in individuals and populations, provides much greater leverage for those wishing to exercise control, a principle easily seen in martial arts, in which a fighter's level of tension is used against him, where looseness and flexibility makes him much harder to control.

advance so they wind up exactly where you need them to be is a highly effective way of preventing most people from ever discovering their true orientation. If branding a neurodivergent human anomaly as autistic isn't enough to shut down that natural awakening within the species, tell them they have gender dysphoria, and get busy 'curing' them.

Human beings have been cultured and conditioned to want all the wrong things and to turn to the ruling power structures to get them for so long that we don't know *what* we need. We are given (or sold) anything and everything but what will allow us to move our attention inward, where we might find out what our bodies and souls are really asking for. This has come fully out in the open with the COVID-19 'vaccination' policies: all the solutions being offered, as a supposed means to autonomy and self-empowerment, have led rapidly and probably irrevocably to the opposite. No wonder that WEF-er Klaus Schwab said in 2022: '*Ve haf to prepare for a more angry vorld; and how to prepare it means to take ze necessary action to create a fairer vorld*'.[58]

It is not only the economy that is being reset.

* * *

> Transhumanism and Transgenderism enjoy a close relationship due to mutual interest in enhancement technology.
> —Hank Pellissier, 'Transhumanism and Transgenderism'

In case you aren't convinced we have jumped the collective shark yet, let's look at 'postgender', starting with trans-person Martine Rothblatt.[59] The founder of Sirius XM and one-time highest-paid 'female' CEO in the world, in August 2022, Rothblatt was elected to the Board of Trustees of the Mayo Clinic, an elite non-profit American academic medical centre focused on integrated healthcare, education, and research. Twelve years prior, in 2010, Hanson Robotics, working with Rothblatt, made a robot clone of Rothblatt's wife called BINA48, which stands for Breakthrough Intelligence via Neural Architecture 48. BINA48 has variously been called a sentient robot, an android, a gynoid, a social robot, and a cybernetic companion. It is owned by Rothblatt's Terasem Movement, Incorporated (TMI), and was designed to test the possibility of downloading a person's consciousness into a non-biological or nanotech body, after combining detailed data about a person with 'future consciousness software'. BINA48 was modelled after Rothblatt's wife, through more than

100 hours of compiling her memories, feelings, and beliefs (i.e. her Face-book profile data).

Rothblatt's robot wife-clone has been interviewed by the *New York Times*, Whoopi Goldberg, Morgan Freeman (for *National Geographic*), and Joe Rogan, and has participated in several TED Talks. Rottblatt and BINA48 are united in proposing a future of 3D printing new body parts, leaving our bodies behind, and living forever by uploading our consciousness to the artificial intelligence cloud. It should come as no great surprise, then, that the latest set of rights under discussion is that of robots—or 'electronic persons'.

> In an open letter [in 2018], more than 150 experts in robotics, artificial intelligence, law, medical science and ethics, warned the [European] Commission against approving a proposal that envisions a special legal status of 'electronic persons' for the most sophisticated, autonomous robots. 'Creating a legal status of electronic "person" would be ideological and nonsensical and non-pragmatic', the letter says. The group said the proposal, which was approved in a resolution by the European Parliament last year, is based on a perception of robots 'distorted by science fiction and a few recent sensational press announcements'.[60]

Though obvious, the overlap between transgenderism and transhumanism is mostly ignored or denied. It is the overlap between the rejection of biological sex and the rejection of the body (and therefore of humanness), and together they indicate the underlying trend, or drive, of (post-)modern ideology. With transhumanism, the message is writ large enough for no one to miss it. The quote opening this section comes from The Institute for Ethics and Emerging Technologies. This is their Mission Statement:

> The Institute for Ethics and Emerging Technologies is a nonprofit think tank which promotes ideas about how technological progress can increase freedom, happiness, and human flourishing in democratic societies. We believe that technological progress can be a catalyst for positive human development so long as we ensure that technologies are safe and equitably distributed. We call this a 'techno-progressive' orientation. Focusing on emerging technologies that have the potential to positively transform social conditions

and the quality of human lives—especially 'human enhancement technologies'—the IEET seeks to cultivate academic, professional, and popular understanding of their implications, both positive and negative, and to encourage responsible public policies for their safe and equitable use.

The site promotes 'Posthuman Gender: A Non-Binary Future', and states that 'Transhumanists extoll transgender people as prescient pioneers of morphological freedom and technological enhancement' (Benjamin Abbott). Postgenderism

> is an extrapolation of ways that technology is eroding the biological, psychological and social role of gender, and an argument for why the erosion of binary gender will be liberatory. Postgenderists argue that gender is an arbitrary and unnecessary limitation on human potential, and foresee the elimination of involuntary biological and psychological gendering in the human species through the application of neurotechnology, biotechnology and reproductive technologies. Postgenderists contend that dyadic gender roles and sexual dimorphisms are generally to the detriment of individuals and society. Assisted reproduction will make it possible for individuals of any sex to reproduce in any combinations they choose, with or without 'mothers' and 'fathers', and artificial wombs will make biological wombs unnecessary for reproduction. Greater biological fluidity and psychological androgyny will allow future persons to explore both masculine and feminine aspects of personality. Postgenderists do not call for the end of all gender traits, or universal androgyny, but rather that those traits become a matter of choice. Bodies and personalities in our postgender future will no longer be constrained and circumscribed by gendered traits, but enriched by their use in the palette of diverse self-expression.[61]

One of the earliest expressions of postgenderism was Shulamith Firestone's *The Dialectic of Sex*, which saw the 'end goal of feminist revolution' as 'not just the elimination of male privilege but of the sex distinction itself: genital differences between human beings would no longer matter culturally'. This goal depends wholly on artificial reproduction to succeed: 'children would be born to both sexes equally, or independently of either' (1970, p. 11). As mentioned, to be independent of human biology means to be increasingly dependent on corporate tech, whether it's human cloning, parthenogenesis (embryos without fertilisation by sperm) and artificial wombs, or a 'posthuman' space of uploaded minds living as data patterns on supercomputers.

In Aldous Huxley's *Brave New World*, everyone is essentially parent-less because the State is now their parent. The words 'mother' and 'father' have become 'the ultimate in unmentionable obscenity'. This has now happened, to a degree, due to transgender activism that led, in 2017, to UK doctors being advised to refer to expectant mothers as 'pregnant people'.[62] Such words are 'a link to the past' and undermine the power of the State over the individual. In the absence of mothers, fathers, brothers, sisters, uncles, aunts, cousins, or grandparents, every-one 'melts into a giant generic mass, all in the name of stability and progress'.[63] Sexual freedom is legalised to further stabilise the society, and 'free' sexual relations are encouraged for all, especially the young, to discourage intimacy. By controlling birth and neutralising the emo-tions, while experimenting with sex at young ages, the inhabitants of *Brave New World* are subjected to 'a method of programming [that] pro-duces a society that adore[s] the technologies that undo their capacities to think'.[64]

Brave New World used to be part of every school curriculum (I had to read it, as well as *1984*, as a teenager). In 2011, it was listed as 'among the top 10 books Americans most want banned'.[65] When life imitates art, destroy the evidence.

* * *

> The power and autonomy of technique are so well secured that it, in its turn, has become the judge of what is moral, the creator of a new morality. Thus, it plays the role of creator of a new civi-lization as well ... However, technique cannot assert its auton-omy in respect to physical or biological laws. Instead, it puts them to work; it seeks to dominate them.
>
> —Jacques Ellul, *The Technological Society*

The term *transhuman* was coined by Teilhard de Chardin (1881–1955), a French Jesuit modernist who made it his life work to upgrade Chris-tianity and make it compatible with Darwinism, Marxism, modern cosmology, and (the myth of) technological progress. Among his many unorthodox views, Teilhard saw evil as 'a statistical necessity', as an evolutionary tool, not just for God or Nature, but for man-made social engineering, including eugenics.

> What fundamental attitude, for example, should the advancing wing of humanity take to fixed or definitely unprogressive ethnical groups? The earth is a closed and limited surface. To what extent should it tolerate, racially or nationally, areas of lesser activity? ... How should we judge the efforts we lavish in all kinds of hospitals on saving what is so often no more than one of life's rejects? ... To what extent should not the development of the strong ... take precedence over the preservation of the weak?
>
> (1969, pp. 132–133)

There is a strong indication here for the compatibility—even the equivalence—of what undiscerning folk still think of as a leftist liberal-progressive outlook and the most Draconian forms of fascist totalitarianism. The connective tissue that squares the circles is a mystical belief in science and technology. The 1949 work, *The Future of Mankind*, in which Teilhard coined the term 'transhuman', talks of an 'Omega Point', a quasi-Christian version of the Singularity that 'represents our passage, by Translation or dematerialization, to another sphere of the Universe: not an ending of the ultra-human but its accession to some sort of trans-humanity at the ultimate heart of things'.[66] Julian Huxley, Aldous' brother and the President of the British Eugenics Society, adopted the term transhuman, and Teilhard was closely aligned with the Huxley clan. Teilhard was firmly committed to the idea of a salvific technology, or 'God in the machine':

> How can we fail to see the machine as playing a constructive part in the creation of a truly collective consciousness? ... I am thinking, of course, in the first place of the extraordinary network of radio and television communications which ... already link us all in a sort of 'etherized' universal consciousness. But I am also thinking of ... those astonishing electronic computers which, pulsating with signals at the rate of hundreds of thousands a second, not only relieve our brains of tedious and exhausting work but, because they enhance the essential (and too little noticed) 'speed of thought', are also paving the way for a revolution in the sphere of research.

[A]ll these material instruments ... are finally nothing less than the manifestation of a kind of super-Brain, capable of attaining mastery over some super-sphere in the universe.

Although Teilhard's work was banned by the Vatican during his life-time, it would go on to be embraced by it, a development predicted by Teilhard towards the end of his life: 'I have so many friends now, in good strategic positions', he wrote to a friend, 'that I have no fear of the future. I have won the game'. This can't be considered prescience: his pal Julian Huxley had by then founded the world's first environmental organisations (the International Union for the Conservation of Nature and its off-shoot the World Wildlife Fund) as well as the United Nations Education Science and Cultural Organization (UNESCO). Matthew Ehret wrote in 2021:

Over the ensuing decades, followers of Teilhard played a major role in shaping the outcome of the Church's decentralization and lib-eralization in the form of Vatican II launched by Pope John XXIII in 1962. These same networks concentrated in Ibero-America inno-vated a new form of doctrine called 'Liberation Theology' with the logic that Marxism was the purest expression of Christ's message and that all true Christians were obliged to take up *La Revolutione* against capitalism around the world during the dark days of the Cold War. When asked what should be done about the stagnant Catholic Church, Teilhard called for this new revolutionary Marxist-merger by saying 'a good dip into Marxism might start things mov-ing again'. While Pope John Paul I and II tried to push back against this deconstruction of Christianity, a touch of poison and a couple of assassin's bullets brought the Holy See quickly back into line, as the ground was set for a full Jesuit takeover of the Church and inte-gration of Christianity into a new eugenics-driven religion.[67]

Julian Huxley added his fuel to the furnace in the Nietzschean-sounding *Man Stands Alone*, outlining means roughly in accord with the then-budding science of cybernetics:

Before humanity can obtain on the collective level that degree of foresight, control and flexibility which on the biological level is at the disposal of human individuals, it must multiply at least tenfold, perhaps fiftyfold, the proportion of individuals and organisations devoted to obtaining information, to planning, correlation and the flexible control of execution. The chief increases are needed in respect of correlation and planning and of social self-consciousness ... In respect of planning and correlation, we can dimly perceive that some large single organization must be superposed on the more primitive system of separate government departments and other single-function organizations; and that this, like the cerebral cortex, must be at one and the same time unified and functionally specialized.

(Huxley, p. 245)

Cue the current leading advocate of transhumanism, Ray Kurzweil. Kurzweil became director of engineering at Google in 2012, and he considers Google to be the 20-petaflop 'super-computer' he predicted (in 1998) would exist by 2009. Similar to Rothblatt's robo-wife, one of Kurzweil's stated missions is to resurrect his father out of nanotechnology and digitally recreated quasi-memories. At the same time, confusingly, the digital avatar he created for himself—the holographic identity prototype for his immortal data-stream body—is a sort of Trinity (from *The Matrix*) character called Ramona. (Apparently, Kurzweil has mummy as well as daddy issues running his hard drive.)

Yea, though I walk through the valley of the uncanny, I shall see no evil. As fantasy becomes real and reality becomes more and more fantasy-based, it gets harder and harder to tell the counterfeit from the original. This is by necessary design: fudging the real makes it easier and easier to fake the real, to blur the line between natural and artificial. At a certain point, this creates an overlap where the copy starts to seem more authentic to us than the original. (Trans-'women' sometimes claim to be more authentically female than biological women. Yes. Presumably, it is because they are using sheer *willpower*, and do not need to rely on something as outmoded as biology.)

Transhumanism is *an imitation religion*. It is the sociocultural equivalent of Dick's androids, or an artificially-constructed vagina. It is trying to simulate something and create a counterfeit, by observing and imitating it, hoping against hope to pass the Turing test. Humans doing corporeal alterations—surgical and chemical body modifications that pose as sex changes but aren't—create a corresponding social mandate not to 'judge' these people as freaks, or as in any way less natural than biologically intact humans. We are being ideologically bullied into complicity with the clowns, 'nudged', over time, to override our innate ability to discern the difference between a natural state and a surgically or chemically contrived one. We are told there *is* no difference, making category uncertainty, not a signal of something wrong in our environment, but a symptom of something wrong *with us*. So it is that artificial intelligence—or what is lurking behind it—takes control of human consciousness, and technology assumes the task of defining our reality.[68]

The transgender movement is contingent, not merely on a few individuals changing their gender (which any cross-dresser can do), but on changing everyone *else's* ideas about—and experience of—biological sex. *The only way to accommodate a few gender-confused individuals is to create a social movement that eventually ensures we all become confused about the most fundamental facts of life.* William Blake wrote that 'the notion that man has a body distinct from his soul, is to be expunged'. Transhumanism wants to expunge the notion that man has a soul distinct from his mind—hir gendered identity—and that a body is anything more than a piece of tech to be adapted, improved, and ultimately replaced. At its base, transhumanism is about getting *rid* of the body, as a dead weight, and its methodology is to first abolish the soul. If body and soul are congruent, as Blake indicated, it makes it expedient, if you want to get rid of the body, to first get rid of (our awareness of) the soul. This is, at the end of the day, the only way anyone would go along with the transhumanist agenda to replace their physical existence with a digital data-stream—a 'copy' of their memories and beliefs and preferences. They must first be convinced that the body is a form of inferior technology, a kind of mechanical doll without soul, that the element that animates the machine is *mind*, and that mind is merely a sequence of characters—letters and numbers—that can be copied and reproduced, like computer code.

The promise that corporate raiders from the Serpent on down have perfected is this: *If* you eat our fruit, ye *shall* be as gods. There is an identity for everyone, for every occasion. You can get to be whichever 'you' you want, whenever, wherever, and for however long you want. Who is the 'I' in this equation that gets to decide what 'it' gets to be is the question no one asks, because the answer is: 'We are (legion)!' The invalidation of biology as the primary determinant of identity has, at the same time and most bizarrely, made body modification/mutilation central to identity-recreation. How is this vicious circle squared? By leaving a vacuum where the soul used to be, a vacuum that has been hollowed out by corporations mining for natural human resources. The gender merchants of self-reinvention-via-self-absorption want to appeal to the lowest part of us by promising to raise it up to the highest plateau. They are selling a cure for a soul that migrated to the wrong body without acknowledging that, if psyches are no longer finding their somas, if more and more people are not at home in their bodies, something is terribly wrong on terra firma.

This problem isn't acknowledged *as* a problem because the proffered 'solution' being sold is so wonderful that it promises to transform the direst of situations into sheer opportunity. Certainly, it is some sort of opportunity, but whose, or what's? In this brave new world, all opportunities and all solutions are 'magical', and they come from Ahriman and his scientistic system. All problems are sourced in the body, in Nature, and God, which then *become* the problem. Surely the inversion must be obvious? If we don't see it, it can only be because we have replaced our eyes with a set of Oculus Rift specs. We are seeing with the eyes of Big Mother.

CHAPTER 14

A verbal universe

*I*n the beginning was the code.

In an ideological environment, inside a reality made of language and symbols, all ideologies are equally useful to those who create them. The fiction of disagreement between ideologies—culture wars—only keeps the machine running, the economy thriving, and the neurons firing—down ever more artificial pathways.

Living more and more inside a simulation world where language is the basis of reality, words become seen as a form of violence, while actual violence is seen as a necessary means to social change—for 'rewriting history'.

The code is no longer recognised as code. As in Babylon, its very lack of meaning is its meaning. (Postmodernism.) It has become as-if-a-text. While it is meaningless without the cypher of organic, preverbal reality-awareness, still it is curiously alluring as a surrogate or false reality divorced from preverbal reality-awareness.

It offers an entirely incoherent existence, made meaningful by the sheer power of delusion to impose meaning: the will to believe. Into this realm, the truth can only enter by the most devious, subtle, and discreet of means, as a thief in the night, or as a character in fiction.

* * *

Professor of social work, Dr. William Brennan, has written that
'[t]he power of language to color one's view of reality is profound'. It is for this reason that linguistic engineering always
precedes social engineering—even in medicine.

—American College of Pediatricians,
'Gender Dysphoria in Children', June 2017

It is important to state clearly that *no human being can ever truly change
their sex*. Biological sex is determined by much more than merely the
type of genitalia and whether or not there are breasts. On the other
hand, gender is a social construct imported from linguistics, so changing gender is something 'anyone can do', at any time, because, well,
there is nothing to be done. The concept of sex as something independent of biology was *invented*, or contrived, rather than discovered, via
the introduction of a word ('gender') that has no ontological meaning
regarding biological organisms (as is evident in the animal kingdom).

Latin-based languages categorise nouns as masculine or feminine,
and this is what is referred to as 'gender'. During the 1950s and 1960s,
'sexologists realized that their sex reassignment agenda could not be
sufficiently defended using the words sex and transsexual. From a
purely scientific standpoint, human beings possess a biologically determined sex and innate sex differences'.[69] Since no kind of medical intervention (neither hormones nor surgery) can change a person's genes,
making sex change effectively impossible, the solution of the sexologists was 'to hijack the word gender and infuse it with a new meaning
that applied to persons'.[70] John Money, the most prominent of the sexologists, redefined gender to mean 'the social performance indicative of
an internal sexed identity'.

In essence, these sexologists invented the ideological foundation
necessary to justify their treatment of transsexualism with sex reassignment surgery and called it gender. It is this man-made ideology of an 'internal sexed identity' that now dominates mainstream
medicine, psychiatry and academia. This linguistic history makes
it clear that gender is not and never has been a biological or scientific entity. Rather, gender is a socially and politically constructed
concept.[71]

This latter point is a familiar one from (old) feminist and other kinds of
(old) progressive rhetoric; but what's rarely mentioned is that *at its root*

there was a corporate-medical drive to create an economy of 'transgendering'. What a person with 'gender dysphoria' (which should really be called body dysphoria, or even *biophobia*) is doing, when they succumb to becoming part of this economy and attempt to change their 'gender' via hormones and surgical interventions, is that they are effectively *destroying* their biological sex, and replacing it with an artificial imitation. Since the artificial organs *do not work* in the way that biological organs are meant to work, they do not *become* the opposite sex, not even superficially speaking. What they do is create an *appearance* of the sex they wish to imitate, exactly as a man dressing in a woman's clothing does, and so create the appearance of being a woman. It is a *representation* of the opposite sex, but it by no means even approaches being a *transformation* into that sex. Anything else is ideological madness.

This is not to say that there *is* no transformation; only that, whatever the transgender individual is submitting to being transformed into, it is something entirely *other* than the opposite sex. It might even be more accurate to say that they are changing *species*, rather than changing sexes.

* * *

> Transgenderism will be the programming language of transhumanist experiment.
>
> —Schwab, 'The Internet of Non-Binary Bodies'

'Whatever a technician believes is true must be made into law', writes Jacques Ellul in *The Technological Society*, followed by: 'There must be a law for each fact' (Ellul, p. 297). In the case of transgender ideology, both laws *and* facts have had to be changed to facilitate the appliance of technique. The technology to surgically reconfigure a person's sexual representation made it necessary to develop the ideology to justify that process (it is true that the ideology predates the tech, but it first had to be adapted from esoteric to exoteric language before it could inform a social movement). This then demanded new laws to 'protect' that 'right' of representation (i.e. to help incorporate the new technique and the new 'product' into the social economy). Finally, new biological 'facts' were introduced into the lexicon, such as sex is (only) gender, therefore gender identity = biological sex, ergo 'some women have penises'. Or, as the notorious trans-queer and pusher of hormones Eli Erlick tweets it: 'Trans women are natural women. Trans women are normal women. Trans women are biological women. Trans women are born women. Trans women are women'. (Erlick—a man claiming to have been born a woman—has, not incidentally, been accused of rape and other forms of sexual assault.)[72]

The brazen violation of language by the Trans Agenda for the purposes of ideological weaponisation is a fitting development for something that a) took its basis ('gender') from linguistics and language in the first place; and b) that used language to establish itself. All of this is in keeping with the creation of what Jacques Ellul (after Armand Robin, a student of radio propaganda) called 'the verbal universe':

> [The] consequence of technical propaganda manipulations is the creation of an abstract universe, representing a complete reconstruction of reality in the minds of its citizens. The new universe is a verbal universe ... Men fashion images of things, events, and people which may not reflect reality but which are truer than reality.
>
> (Ellul, pp. 372–373)

As the blogger Schwab wrote in 2022 in 'Blessings of the Abyss: The Internet of Non Binary Bodies', there is a vastly deeper and darker agenda at work here than merely creating a safe space for alienated souls to enjoy and express their paraphilias:

> in order to turn the whole world into a demented carnival-casino, there needs to be a continuous source of data, requiring constant surveillance and quantification of activity. In order to quantify, one must have a grammar ... Gender abstractions are a form of virtual body that can be decomposed and made visible to surveillance. The gender identity paracosm constitutes a virtual environment, which is at base a customizable ordering device. Put another way, gender-fluid, agender, bigender, demigender, polygender ad nauseum represent an 'informatization of the body', making the arc into oblivion of bioleninist disintegration visible, sensible and computable.[73]

A similarly apocalyptic analysis of the transgender curve was made by James Poulos, author of *Human Forever: The Digital Politics of Spiritual Warfare*, in 2021:

If print was the era of reason and the electric age was the era of occult, now we're moving into a much different era still ... terminally speaking, sex, eroticism wound up as really justified only insofar as it was kind of the last thing to do ... What appears to be happening now in the digital age is that sex has been abandoned as the activity of last resort, and intelligence is taking its place ... The value of sex to the average millennial on social media is not really for erotic satisfaction, it's for participating in the construction of ... new cyborg identities that largely leave their human identity behind.[74]

Identity politics and the conforming of language to the new trans-ideology—within the technosphere of social networks—is a way to more effectively get people to turn their bodies into information that can be processed by technology. It is transhumanism-lite: as manageable 'bytes' of data, these 'early-adopters' volunteer to abandon 'meat-space' forever, in exchange for a virtual limbo of pseudo-immortality.[75]

* * *

Rolling pronouns refer to the use of multiple pronouns that can be used alternately or shift over time. Typically, people who prefer using multiple sets of pronouns also encourage others to rotate through all of them or mix them around when speaking to or referring to them ... Others use rolling pronouns as an act of defiance in a society that demands to binarize gender or try to fit it into neat categories. For those who believe that gender (at least in the way they experience it) is not fixed, using multiple pronouns is a way of dismantling oppressive gender roles and norms ... Pronouns and chosen names help to affirm a person's identity and personal conception of their true selves. To deny someone of their preferred name and pronouns would be like to deny them their identity.

— LGBTQ Nation, 2022

In the US, 'gender-fluid' individuals currently make up somewhere between 0.5 and 1 per cent of the population (it is probably lower in Canada). This tiny percentage is seen as in such need of protection that it requires massive, long-term, far-reaching social engineering, specifically around how *all* children are being raised (from kindergarten on), and how language is being reconfigured. For example,

> The practice of pronoun declaring took off in US schools and colleges a few years ago. It quickly became seen as good pedagogical practice to get students to introduce themselves to each other at the start of a course by announcing their names and preferred pronouns. [T]he aim of making pronoun declarations routine is to normalize the idea that everyone has a gender identity distinct from their sex. Announcing pronouns sends a message that a connection between biology and gender cannot be assumed. We must all study lists of gender options and angst about which label best applies to us.[76]

Is it really likely that a worldwide programme of state and corporate propaganda is motivated by compassion of the controlling elites for social and sexual 'outliers'? Or is it more likely to be one more means to spread confusion and division among the not-yet-completely-conquered plebs? If a tiny percentage finds the word 'mother' or 'birth' obscene, isn't it reasonable to wonder about the 98+ per cent that finds the stigmatising of these words equally inconvenient? The answer is that 'cisnormals' have had their time in the sun, and their feelings are trivial compared to those of the endangered brave new (sterile) avatar species that is emerging, via the twin miracles of technology and drugs.

So what about the argument that the gender-fluid 'twin-spirit' souls have always been among us, and are simply becoming more visible and vocal as the social environment is reconfigured to accommodate them, creating safe spaces for them to emerge into? This reasoning implies that the demand has created the supply, not vice versa. Based on what we know about corporate culture, however, such an assumption hardly bears closer examination. 2014 was, according to *Time* magazine, the 'transgender tipping point', when media visibility of transgender people reached a level higher than ever seen before. Since then, the number of transgender portrayals across TV platforms has stayed disproportionately high. 'Research has found that viewing multiple transgender TV characters and stories improves viewers' attitudes toward transgender people and related policies'.[77]

As with homosexuality (and being non-white), to effectively spread transgenderism through a society means it is not enough for transsexuals merely to aspire to equality. The previously marginalised subset— as a *category*, that is, not necessarily the individuals themselves—must aim to colonise the mainstream, like a cuckoo. This entails 'decentralising' the previously dominant ideology; or, to the extent it is allowed to remain central, forcing it to change its ways. In the present case, it is not merely ideology that has to be radically reconfigured, but biology. How exactly does less than 1 per cent of a population dictate policy for the remainder? The only explanation is that one marginality is being used as an *avatar* or sock puppet for the hidden hand of (another 1 per cent?) a higher-dimensional influence, whether it is a technocratic or a metaphysical one (or both).

Simply stated: transgender-types (gender-confused, body-dysphoric individuals) are not being protected. They are being *created*.

* * *

> This kind of thing represents the first step toward a sham universe. It is also indicative of an important element in today's psychology, the disappearance of reality in a world of hallucinations. Man will be led to act from real motives that are scientifically directed and increasingly irresistible; he will be brought to sacrifice himself in a real world, but for the sake of the verbal universe which has been fashioned for him.
> —Jacques Ellul, *The Technological Society*

Biological sex that is not being reconfigured but destroyed and replaced with an artificial representation is 100 per cent congruent with transhumanism. The techno-progressive drift is towards the uncanny valley of simulated realities, via the creation of virtual avatar selves to escape into. Humans are willingly turning themselves into virtual currency that can then be injected into a new economy, the economy of human sentience (and/or identities), *as data*. Like Ray Kurzweil with his 'Ramona', the aspiring 'Trans' imitates Anime characters, and takes pride in becoming more and more removed from 'conventional' reality—not just socially but ontologically. The dandy's creed, which my brother Sebastian Horsley stole from Quentin Crisp, is 'That which cannot be wholly concealed should be deliberately displayed'. To make a deficiency into a form of flamboyance, and to cover shame with pride via acts of shamelessness, is central to the Trans Agenda, and to the configuration of clown world.

Since the Trans Agenda advocates the use of technology to replace biological sex with a cartoon imitation of itself, to achieve this end, the very idea of biological sex must itself be 'lampooned'—turned into a caricature—to match the technology. The 'is' determines the 'ought': as soon as it becomes possible to create a chemical-surgical imitation of a woman (or a man), an inevitable adaptation in cultural values occurs, including moral ones. There is a growing shift towards making false, distorted, and grotesque representations of women and men socially acceptable. Since social etiquette and ethics form a complex system, to alter what is acceptable in a society means *the entire philosophical and ideological basis of that society must undergo a corresponding shift*. It requires accommodating the new technology and the new fashions, and making room for the newly manufactured id-entities rolling off the factory lines, complete with their particular (and equally manufactured) sets of fears and desires. The social environment must become more and more 'virtual', more simulation-like, to accommodate the coming avatar-people. For the clowns to feel at home, the whole world must be made a circus.

In the 1960s, such a shift occurred with the civil rights movement and feminism, changing the social value and meaning of being Black, a woman, or a homosexual (ironically, the latter two identifications are being systematically eradicated, as meaningful categories, by the Trans Agenda). In the 2010s, the trans identity was subtly (and not-so-subtly, if we think of Bruce > Caitlyn Jenner) imbued with high social standing and moral superiority. In certain circles, it was, and no doubt still is, touted as a spiritual calling, a veritable attainment of non-dual reality, in which biological sex is as mutable and arbitrary as any other form of personal preference.

Compared to these previous categories of marginalisation, transgenderism has the relatively novel ingredient of (sometimes though not always) requiring *actual physical transformation*. As long as it is seen as a 'choice' (albeit one attributed to some mysterious and anomalous whim of human biology), it is a choice that can entail the ultimate commitment imaginable, short of death anyway. But unlike the previous categories of 'black' and 'woman', there is a fundamental paradox baked into transgender ideology (as well as that of homosexuality): the means to advocate and enforce the freedom of choice for these individuals ends up with the argument that they *have* no choice at all. Homosexuals and transsexuals are born that way, they are 'made' queer by Nature. In the case of homosexuality, society had to be reorganised, and its members corrected, to accommodate the newly endorsed 'queering of the pitch'. In the case of transgenderism, language, biology, and by extension physical reality, must likewise be reorganised and corrected. As Kellie-Jay Keen (Posey Parker) stated in 2022:

> if you can no longer define what a woman is, we can't talk about women. Our language is being diluted all over the place. In the UK, and I'm sure in the US, women are being called cervix-havers, chest-feeders, menstruators, birthing persons. So we have to give up the language that describes us. [T]he only people allowed to be called women these days is actually men.[78]

When it comes to questioning the sanctity—never mind sanity—of transgenderism, the response from the well-meaning under-informed is that only these people know what they are experiencing, and they should have the right to define it for themselves. If they say they were born in the wrong body, we should take their word for it and try to help them get a new one. As already argued, this line of reasoning is inherently contradictory and crazy-making. In a certain sense, you have to be crazy to understand it (or believe it). This corporate-sanctioned madness comes down to indulging people's fantasies, regardless of whether we understand them or not, provided only that their whims have received worldwide institutional support. When non-conformity becomes the norm, we will conform to it. And meanwhile, the true anomalies continue, either to be marginalised out of existence, or to be swallowed up into the corporate-sponsored Borg of intersectional identifications.

Yet it may be that the internally sexed identity (ISI) conceived by John Money at the Hopkins University, as the means to create the new industry of transsexuality, may not be as imaginary as we might have supposed. In Part I, we discussed children's imaginary friends. What if there is a corresponding reality behind Money's hypothetical ISI, albeit one that has nothing to do with a human being's true self?

One tiny percentage of the human population (trans-folk) has been engineered and employed as an 'avatar' under-class for another, hidden, equally tiny percentage of the population (the technocratic ruling class). This 0.01 per cent is leading the way into Hell for all, laying the foundations for a race of human beings irrevocably disconnected from Nature and from one another. *Cui bono*? Lucifer's *nöös* is tightening over the generations, recreating the original Fall, by tempting us to enter into a false reality and get lost there forever.

Suppose parents were being admonished to believe their children when they talked to, or about, invisible friends? Imagine they were told that the term 'imaginary friend' was a cruel discrimination against little-understood and unjustly marginalised inorganic entities, a form of hate crime? In 2023, any parent who dares not to affirm, support, and act upon a child's feeling that they don't fit the gender stereotype—or a teenager's claim that they are in the wrong-sex body—risks losing their children. Is this an indication (albeit a hard one to name or admit to) that a non-human and/or anti-natural force is at work, from inception on down? What ends up as a denial and a rejection of Nature surely must have started out that way?

The oak is present in the acorn; by its fruit shall ye know it. This is the foundational myth of Western culture. It's the oldest trick in the book, and we keep falling for it. The Serpent in the Garden. A permanent rift between the sexes, between human nature and the divine; promises that were never meant to be kept; a body cut off from the soul, that enters into a dissociated mind-space. (The fig leaf as the first tech that leads inexorably to Teilhard's *nöösphere*.) Original language—the Word—is lost, because it is divorced from experiential reality. The Omega Point is here, now, in policies, movements, and technologies that are physically *creating* a counterfeit world, including, finally, the creation of artificial sexual organs. Big Mother's body.

In its fevered quest for identity, transgender ideology has served to erase the biological difference of the other, and given rise to a world where men are women. It requires the eradication of the other's identity while claiming it for one's own. It is psychic cuckoo-land, here deep in the valley of the uncanny. Such a strange trajectory makes little sense in the context of biology or human mating rituals. But it can, perhaps, be understood as pointing to a *third* element, *besides* man and woman, introjecting itself into the mix.

PART III

ARTIFICIAL MIND

'Tools, instruments of necessity, instruments that neither lie nor cheat, tools with which necessity can be subjugated by obeying her, without the help of false laws; tools that make it possible to conquer by obeying'. This formula is true of the tool which puts man squarely in contact with a reality that will bear no excuses, in contact with matter to be mastered, and the only way to use it is to obey it. Obedience to the plough and the plane was indeed the only means of dominating earth and wood. But the formula is not true for our techniques. He who serves these techniques enters another realm of necessity. This new necessity is not natural necessity; natural necessity, in fact, no longer exists. It is technique's necessity, which becomes the more constraining the more nature's necessity fades and disappears. It cannot be escaped or mastered. The tool was not false. But technique causes us to penetrate into the innermost realm of falsehood, showing us all the while the noble face of objectivity of result. In this innermost recess, man is no longer able to recognize himself because of the instruments he employs.

—Jacques Ellul, *The Technological Society*

If you go back to the middle of the 20th century ... and you think about building the future, then your building materials are those millions of people who are working hard in the factories in the farms, the soldiers. [Y]ou need them, you don't have any kind of future without them. And now fast-forward to the early 21st century, when we just don't need the vast majority of the population. [T]he future is about developing more and more sophisticated technology ... artificial intelligence, bioengineering: most people don't contribute anything to that, except perhaps for their data; and whatever people are still doing which is useful, these technologies increasingly will make redundant, and will make it possible to replace the people.

—Yuval Noah Harari, 2022

CHAPTER 15

Sister Dick: Counterculture and counterfeit

*T*he replacement of biological reality with linguistic constructs (sex with gender) makes language itself nonsensical, even while giving it the ultimate power to define our reality.

To understand viscerally the limitations of language, ask yourself a question: at what precise moment does a tribe become a village, a village a town, or a town a city?

The soul speaks a language that has no direct correlation to words. It speaks the language of existence itself.

If what is in the unconscious, the stuff of the soul, can't be thought about, what remains? It is the quest to find the soul of language.

* * *

Having cut off from my own soul, the anima, in adolescence ... it was then inevitable that, in adulthood, I would be unconsciously drawn into occultism, and eventually into a bizarre and obsessive courtship with Lucifer—as the only way to approach my disowned feminine side. [I]nstead of going directly to the wounded part of my psyche and inviting the disowned feminine back into awareness, I took the long way around and embarked upon the occult path of knowledge.

—the author, *Answer to Lucifer* (unpublished)

Dream of 3 March 2022: Rudolf Steiner is communicating to me remotely, from the other side. He is explaining to me that the Earth will soon no longer be habitable to human beings (or life at all), that it is undergoing some sort of 'flattening' process by which it will become a dead planet, like Saturn, including with its own ring.

Our time is up as a species. Rudy is opening up for me a sort of transdimensional elevator or 'hand-up', by which I will ascend beyond the Earth sphere, in time for 'the flattening'. I can sort of see him at this point, or feel his energy, his black hair and intense gaze. The feeling I have is as if he is my father (though he is nothing like my birth father). I feel deep love and gratitude, and a growing sense of excitement.

I am preparing to be raised up, and sharing the information with others. In a later dream, I tell my wife about it. She dismisses it as an ego-dream. I disagree.

In the ten years (2013–2023) since the start of this book, as the growing number of epigraphs indicates, I developed a surprisingly persistent interest in the work of Rudolf Steiner. I say surprising because, over these ten years and more, I have been involved in the systematic deconstruction and rejection of many, if not all, of my primary literary influences, most especially regarding spiritual beliefs. Having developed a strong distrust of *all* culture-provided (remote) spiritual voices, I am left wondering if Steiner is the exception that proves the rule, or a throwback to old habits?

I considered looking more closely at Steiner's life and incorporating some biographical content in the last part of this book, along the lines of the section on Philip K. Dick that ends Part I. Having read about half of a very long, very dry Steiner biography, however, his life didn't provide much by way of dramatic content. At least, I didn't feel inspired by it to attempt the kind of deep-dive narrative I performed with PKD. Some weeks after writing this, however, I wound up spewing forth a *sequel* to Part I's Dick analysis, which now makes up the bulk of this last section. With Dick, unlike Steiner, there's no shortage of drama.

What makes Steiner different from my other literary spiritual influences, all of whom had 'epic' lives? Does it relate to this absence of dramatic content? Since so much of what happened in Steiner's life appears to have gone on at a subtler, *inner* level, the view from the outside *is* relatively uninteresting—relative at least to writers like Dick, Carlos Castaneda, Whitley Strieber, or Aleister Crowley. The comparison to Crowley may be the most illustrative, because Steiner and Crowley were contemporaries, and Crowley is the most obviously maleficent literary influence I ever allowed free access to my psyche. I once wrote about him in *The Lucid View*:

> Whatever games Crowley played with the perceptions of the world, he was never a dilettante. He applied himself to a number of disciplines and excelled at many of them: mountain climbing, chess, languages (ancient and modern), philosophy, poetry, espionage, wild-game hunting, yoga, drug-taking, sex magick. Crowley was notoriously perverse in both his personal and professional life but—though he was to all intents and purposes a sort of inspired lunatic—he *did* practice all he preached.
>
> (2004, p. 35)

Some 30 years after I first wrote this, the words have taken on a haunting quality. One of the things Crowley preached was child sacrifice (though he fooled me, along with most of his more naïve followers, into thinking it was all just for shock effect—see *The Vice of Kings* for the full story). But as the above quote indicates, Crowley lived enough lives (had sufficient adventures and 'incarnations') for a dozen ordinary men. His influence on the culture has been proportionately vast, i.e. equal to ten 'lesser' men, though little of it, in my opinion, *benign*. As I explore in *Vice of Kings*, Crowley's outer-directed extravagance and occultist extroversion as 'the Great Beast' was both symptomatic of and compatible with a narcissistic culture of abuse that celebrates, above all else, the will to power via the pathological assertion of individuality (a thesis that this last part will unpack).

Steiner, on the other hand, has passed mostly under the cultural radar. Though he had a significant following in his life (he lived to the age of 63), and though he created a spiritual movement (Anthroposophy) that has survived (in some form) to this day, he has had a far less observable influence on the culture. The Waldorf schools, central to his legacy, have certainly been successful; one might argue that they have indirectly shaped society, insofar as some of their alumni have gone on to do so. The most easily identifiable names on a list of famous alumni are Sandra Bullock and Rutger Hauer, however, so this last point seems questionable. Steiner's influence on organic farming is also well-known; but if we juxtapose a few agricultural tips with Crowley's appearance on the cover of the Beatles' *Sergeant Pepper's Lonely Hearts Club Band* album—and everything this implies—the distinction becomes clearer.

One symptom of a mother-enmeshed, mother-possessed male psyche is an unusually strong drive to live a Baron Munchausen-like *epic life*. A male child still psychically entangled with its mother may be driven to pursue all sorts of adventures (including travelling the world, as I did), as an unconscious means to try and extricate himself from an oppressive or insidious maternal influence. At the same time, seen from the opposite angle, a male child so enmeshed becomes an extension of his mother's unconscious will, compelled to live out all sorts of adventures to fulfil Big Mama's 'unlived life' (all the things she never got to do).

> The chosen child reacts to his mother and she reacts to him. The reaction spreads out like ground plutonium into the family system, and the favored victim-child becomes the 'crusader' for maintaining the status quo within that system. The mutual reactivity leads to solidarity: a deepening of the fusion between mother and son. In most cases, the victim-child, isolated in childhood, 'continues to be isolated in his adult life'. It is not uncommon for them 'to develop narcissistic traits, if not full-blown narcissism'. A sense of superiority may lead to 'extreme efforts at outdoing peers in his professional life. He wants to earn more money than … garner greater recognition than …' and so on.[79]

Crowley exhibited all the symptoms of mother bondage (it was his mother who first named him 'the Beast'), whereas Steiner showed relatively few. Perhaps they are like bookends within my psyche of spiritual influence that marks a 40-year process of emergence from my own mother's psyche? Having come to terms with my maternal enmeshment and thereby begun to dissolve it, my need to live an epic life, and my tendency to be inspired by spiritual over-achievers, has given over to a (somewhat resigned) readiness to connect to mother Nature, on the one hand, and to a more authentically benign father figure, on the other. Has Steiner naturally entered the vacuum—as a temporary, transitional figure—created by the expulsion of all those shady sorcerers?

(Ironically, or perhaps not, Steiner means rock, making the name equivalent to my own sorcerer *nom du guerre*, Kephas.)

This reading is confirmed by the dream, in which I directly identify Steiner as a father figure who lifts me up and out of the Earth sphere (representing the mother's body). The symbolism of a 'flattened' Earth and its transformation into a Saturn-like planet may have a similar meaning, Saturn being the planet that traditionally symbolises the Father. The flattening of the Earth, and my ascension above it, suggests a movement from one dimension (horizontality, identification with the feminine) to another, that of verticality, the masculine. My wife then attempts to diminish the Steiner dream as 'ego', and my rejection indicates a movement away from feminine influence, towards self-orientation and the development of a healthy or natural masculine ego.[80]

* * *

> Where did this voice come from? [A] self-reflection by the author on his own hyperbolic, heated imagination that is both ruthlessly realistic and sympathetic, even tender, toward the lost soul he understands himself to be. It reminds us that in the end what we have here, all gods aside, is a human being just trying to write himself into a better place.
> —Pamela Jackson, co-editor of *The Exegesis of Philip K. Dick*

Three months after the Steiner dream, in July of 2022, I had a sudden desire to get back to Philip K. Dick's *Exegesis* and read the second half. I considered this present work more or less complete, and I had just gone over the Dick material that ends Part I (hence my newly sparked interest). It seemed expedient to plough through the remaining 450 pages and make sure there weren't any *major clues* in there, which I would otherwise have missed. Within a few days of re-embarking on the task, somewhat to my surprise (though not really), the *vesica piscis* between Dick and the Big Mother thesis became visible to me, in Ubik-like neon letters.

> 'My powers came from the other side, because of my sister', Dick wrote in early 1979. Valis 'is a projection into this world of her mind, to protect me ... I am a thought in my sister's mind ... The two selves in me. It must be me and my sister!
> (2011, pp. 494, 495, 507, 529)

Big mother, big sister. Throughout the *Exegesis*, Dick returns repeatedly to the idea of a female deity. The maze he was lost inside, his heroically (or demonically) obsessed mission of mythological (self-) reinvention through writing, centred on *Sophia*, the Gnostic goddess who signifies wisdom. Sophia, in turn, was all bound up inside Dick's belief that he was *possessed by a female psyche*, that of his twin sister, who died a month after she was born. In 1979, he took the full plunge and announced:

> I saw the Savior, St. Sophia, born the second time, the Savior I have been told is soon-to-be-incarnated. That's why she was so concrete, right down to her nightgown. *VALIS* is correct: he would take female form—or has taken!—this time ... Christianity—including Christ—is a cover, a front; and the real deity (and this is kept incredibly secret) is female. Wasn't I told this about Christ in a dream, and told it's secret? I have been initiated into one of the greatest mysteries in the history of religion; it is *she* who we true (esoteric) Christians worship: the Christianity which we see exoterically is really Roman, infiltrated by Rome—to know the truth about *her* you must be *possessed* by her directly. And learn it from *her* ... I'm just saying, Christ is female.
>
> (2011, pp. 489, 491–492, 507)

A transgender Jesus?! God help us!* Dick believed (at least some of the time) that AI/Valis/Sophia/the female Christ was the necessary counter-force, sent to save him from the evil counterfeit of *false* Christianity: 'Satan has given PSI powers to the evil church', he wrote in late 1979, 'as warned about in the [New Testament]. I am in a maze, surrounded by the power of Satan and his church (we all are), but the AI voice will lead me out. This is *why* I have the AI voice' (2011, p. 543). While Dick never returns to his female Christ epiphany, he continues to describe himself as a female host for VALIS (his highest God-principle, which at least some of the time he sees as an *artificial* entity), as 'a womb for her to grow her progeny in: Me!' (And: 'I have long thought of myself as a female host—perhaps for interspecies symbiosis', 2011, p. 543.)

---

*Is this what Dick means by (one of many impossible words he introduces into the *Exegesis*) 'enantiodromia, the conversion or backward turning of something when it reaches an extreme into its opposite. It is by this and this mainly if not alone that Valis develops' (2011, p. 615). (Cf. transgender as a literalisation of an esoteric principle.)

If we are tempted to evoke Freud at this juncture, thankfully a footnote by David Gill grabs the cigar for us:

> Dick's line of speculation here is remarkably similar to the vision of the German judge Daniel Paul Schreber (1842–1911), who imagined that God wanted to *change him into a woman* and impregnate her with sunbeams so that their offspring could save the world … Though the two never met, Freud diagnosed Schreber as a paraphrenic paranoid suffering from—surprise!—repressed homosexual desires.
>
> (2011, pp. 489–490n, emphasis added)

Admittedly, Dick's *Exegesis* is nothing if not an endless stream of ideas, all bouncing off one another in constantly shifting, alternating patterns of contradiction and confirmation, to the constant refrain of 'the truth never keeps still long enough to be pinned down' (a trope of postmodernism). But the *Exegesis* was also nothing more nor less than Dick's attempt to arrive at the ultimate reality *by* writing, i.e. to pin the truth down, which somewhat makes the whole thing an exercise in (conscious) self-defeat—a fact Dick didn't shy away from, either.

Dick's raising up of the feminine as the highest principle, even expressly replacing the Biblical Christ with a feminine inversion—claiming it to be the central truth obscured by a false Christianity—is cuckoo in more than one sense of the word. In fact, it looks a hell of a lot like Lucifer, the wily old goat, attempting to shove Christ out of the nest and steal (back?) his thunder. Like *Mater* trumping Spirit, the sister-psyche that possesses Dick—with his own consent—is virtually a *literalisation* of the casting of a satanic 'PSI' spell over his psyche: Matter over Mind (or Spirit). So how was it that, at a crucial stage in Dick's visionary journey, God-the-Father underwent a sex change, artifice outdid Nature, and the Saviour became Big Mother? This is a question that apparently the present work will not be complete without answering.[81]

* * *

> The new milieu has its own specific laws which are not the laws of organic or inorganic matter.
>
> —Jacques Ellul, *The Technological Society*

Most of the published *Exegesis* is taken up with Dick's philosophical wanderings, most of which are simply too 'out there' for any but the most philosophically sophisticated (or ensconced) to even try to make much practical sense of (which is why the *Exegesis* reads best as fiction). But occasionally, Dick writes of 'real-world' (irony unavoidable) questions, and it's here that the rubber of his soul-speculations meets the road of his lived social reality, and where the shakiness of the *Exegesis*—the cracks in Dick's psyche—can most clearly be seen.[82]

For example, Dick believed that, as part of his own awakening and epiphany between 1971 and 1974, he helped to bring about the overthrow of Richard Nixon via Watergate, and the ousting of a more-evil Black Iron Prison reality for a *less*-evil one. 'I lived to see the fall of tyranny here and the victory and vindication of the counterculture', he wrote in the *Exegesis* in spring of 1979 (2011, p. 524). And in early 1980: 'This time it won't just be deposing the regime; the revolution of the 60s will take over the government and rule in its place' (2011, p. 679). Inseparable from his blind faith in the counterculture and the civil rights movement—i.e. in 'progress'—was Dick's belief that the psychedelic movement signalled a genuine awakening that threatened the hegemony of Empire. Dick was a heavy drug user (fewer psychedelics than amphetamines, but also marijuana and antidepressants), and in 1980 he wrote:

> my writing, involving inner space, is covertly subversive: it teaches secret ways to rebel (mostly by evasion: escape). This is why the whole psychedelic movement of the 60s was a threat to authorities: this was the area of the subversive threat I posed—my studies of inner space.
>
> (2011, p. 531)

So he believed—but was this actually *true*?

In these later years, post 2-3-74, Dick was consistently revolutionary in his outlook and professed to be both a Marxist and a Communist (along with everything else). 'Because this has to do with revolution', he wrote in November 1980, 'radical social reform; it has some kind of relationship to Marxism, to socialism, to the overthrow of governments and *the establishing of a new world order*' (2011, p. 652, emphasis added). In September of the following year, he called Christ 'The ultimate revolutionary' with 'magical (technological?) powers' (2011, p. 790).

Forty years later, in 2023, this reads as dangerously naïve talk. The civil rights movement, the counterculture, and liberal progressivism have led to LGBTQ 'woke' culture and QAnon. To pyrrhic victories like gay marriage and openly satanic curricula employing monstrously-accrued drag queens to teach young children about the joys of anal sex and gender-reassignment surgeries (the new penis). Yippies became yuppies, and hippies morphed into the self-replicating machine elves and tech-wizards of Silicon Valley and Burning Man. The hallucinogen-fuelled 'revolution of consciousness' paved the way for Google and Smart cities, and 'techgnosis' has given birth to the 'internet of bodies'—to the full and final disembodiment of the human species and its soul-enslavement to Ahriman/Satan (Big Mother). The Black Iron Prison didn't just not go away: it went all the way *inside* us. Psyche-delics and marijuana have become legalised and corporatised, work-ing instruments of state control. Opium has become the religion of the masses.

Dick *was* aware of this fundamental contradiction at the heart of (his avocation of) the counterculture: that of *mistaking external agents of con-sciousness alteration for (internal) divine revelation.* The counterfeit.

> With super pot and acid world becomes eternal; here [in his 2-3-74 vision], *I* became eternal and world ephemeral. So drugs take you *away* from enlightenment and consign absolute reality to epi-phenomena, which increasingly entrance you, rather than *losing* their already strong hold over you; thus we call this intoxication: a deluded state, not enlightenment. Acid and super pot are like the Monsanto exhibit in Disneyland where you get smaller, i.e. the world gets bigger: your perspective shrinks.
>
> (2011, p. 534)

A rare moment of real lucidity in the *Exegesis*, this was also a prophetic reference on Dick's part to Monsanto, the mega-corporation that's as suitable a representation of the anti-natural forces of destruction as one could find in 2023 (except maybe for Pfizer), as it angles to corner the market in legal cannabis products. (George Soros was a major player in legalising marijuana;[83] and of course cannabis involves exclusively breeding the *female* plant. As one might expect from an agent of Big Mother, THC, or tetrahydrocannabinol, the active ingredient in mari-juana, affects the body's hormonal systems, increases oestrogen levels, and is known to stimulate the development of breast tissue;[84] making it just one of a plethora of xenoestrogens: oestrogen-boosting and/or testosterone-suppressing toxins in our environment.*)

What's wrong with this picture? Psilocybin has also been legalised in a number of states, a fact viewed as a great victory by a whole bunch of people who ought to recognise the co-opting of consciousness when they see it. As Jacques Ellul wrote in 1964 (in *The Technological Society*):

> It is not difficult to observe that ecstatic phenomena proliferate in proportion to the technicization of society [especially] in the societies that have as their avowed aim the maximal exploitation of technique. Ecstasy occurs here, however, not as a cause but as a result of the technical society. More specifically, it is a function of the acceleration of the tempo of the technical society, rather than of the technical level of the society. [T]he more restrictive the social mechanism, the more exaggerated are the associated ecstatic phenomena. The restrictions imposed by technique on a society reduce the number of ways in which religious energy can be released. In a nontechnical society there are a plurality of ways in which psychic energy can be channeled; but in a technical society there is only one. Technical restrictions eliminate all secondary objects. Human psychic energies concentrate, and there are no 'leaks'. The result is ecstatic phenomena of unparalleled intensity and duration.
>
> (Ellul, pp. 420–422)

Cue ecstatic phenomena that is strictly manufactured and manipulated, via the technicised concentration of something found in nature, to convert it into controllable substances (along with other consciousness-altering techniques). The 1950s in the US—as Dick well knew—were a period of social repression combined with huge technological developments and misplaced optimism. This led to an explosion of psychic energy in the following decade, as not just inevitable but *essential* to

---

*Others include: commercially-raised meat and dairy products; anything that contains insecticide or pesticide residues; tap water (and bottled water from plastic); shampoos, lotions, soaps, toothpastes, cosmetics and other personal care products that contain paraben; soft plastics used as packaging materials treated with chemical compounds a xenoestrogen called phthalates; artificial food additives; foods that contain soy protein and soy protein isolate; fabric softeners; birth control pills and conventional hormone replacement therapy, which get in the water supply; disposable menstrual products, ditto.

the continued progression of the technological evolution of society by which human beings would become increasingly captured by their new toys. As Dr. Goebbels told German religious leaders, in what Ellul calls 'the great law of the technical society: "You are at liberty to seek your salvation as you understand it, provided you do nothing to change the social order"' (Ellul, p. 420). The counterculture was soma and circuses.

> Such movements are based on authentic impulses and valid feel-
> ings, and do allow a few individuals access to modes of expression
> which otherwise would have been closed to them. But their essen-
> tial function is to act as vicarious intermediaries to integrate into
> the technical society these same impulses and feelings which are
> possessed by millions of other men … The basic human impulses
> are unpredictable in their complex social consequences. But thanks
> to 'movements' which integrate and control them, they are power-
> less to harm the technical society, of which henceforth they form an
> integral part. These movements perform a well-defined but com-
> pletely involuntary function … *All revolutionary movements are bur-*
> *lesques of the real thing*, but this must not be imputed to the activities
> of Machiavellian wire-pullers. The phenomenon appears naturally
> in the interaction of human techniques with social movements that
> seek to express basic human instincts.
>
> (Ellul, p. 426, emphasis added)

When it comes to drugs—or to the conspiracy to co-opt consciousness— the question of 'artificial' vs. 'natural' is a hallucinogenically moving line. Some psychedelics (mushrooms) are, or were, 100 per cent natural; others (such as LSD-25) are 100 per cent synthesised. But the *way* they are used, then and now, comes more easily under the rubric of 'artifice' than Nature. This is most obviously the case when an entire sociocul-tural movement is advocating their use. (This was never more the case than it is currently, when it is without much semblance or pretence of a 'grassroots' movement, i.e. visibly 'top-down'.) Simply stated, God (or Jesus) is *not* a mushroom; but Satan, that sneaky Prince of Matter, very well might be. Again, Dick seems to glean this from his own expe-riences, as he scribbled in the *Exegesis* in early 1981:

> Dionysus *caused* me to see all that I saw in 3-74; it was his magic—
> it wasn't really Christ and God; *Dionysus* can take any form—he

fooled me. Of course, now that *VALIS* is in print, Dionysus lets me
see the truth; since it doesn't matter … It is magic. Pagan magic.
This explains Diana, the AI voice. Pagan magic come to our rescue.

(2011, p. 681)

Why doesn't it matter now *Valis* is in print, I wonder?

Steiner claimed that, several centuries before the birth of Christ,
Lucifer incarnated as a human being of Oriental descent, and that his
influence gave rise to the major pagan traditions in the world.[85] This
would presumably include the 'Dionysian' imbibing of toxic substances
for consciousness alteration. Ironically, the raising up of (Mother) Nature
over the invisible and eternal Father God (nature-goddess worship,
paganism, specifically locating 'God' in an 'entheogen') turns Matter
into something Satanic (Pantheism). Having used Nature to supplant
God, the next logically predetermined step is to supplant Nature with
artifice. It is a progression, though not a natural one. We can observe
this—as above, so below—in how men who tend towards 'worshipping' (idealising) women also tend to degrade and demonise them, and
often end up committing violence against them (a theme that will reveal
itself more starkly as we proceed). By worshipping something external to themselves, by placing it in a position *over* them, such men give
up their own divinity and become, necessarily, pathologically dysfunctional as a result of their unnatural dependence on 'mama'.

The question of the spuriousness of the counterculture, and the hidden effects of hallucinogens and other drugs, is anything but peripheral
to the larger questions being explored here. Compromising the integrity of the body may be the *sine qua non* of the Big Mother syndrome.
The key to understanding this would seem to be the notion of *consent*.
It is not what goes into a man's mouth, the Gospel has it, but what
comes out that defiles him. If we are all infiltrated by our own personal
Ahrimanic doubles, *total possession* can only be said to occur once we
allow our thoughts, words, and actions to fully represent the 'cuckoo'
inside us. It is one thing to have a mother complex running us (as we
all do); it's quite another to get dressed up in full drag and start sticking
knives into women.*

---

*If using psychedelic drugs for 'awakening' compromises the energetic body, as well as
the physical, it thereby delays or even prevents enlightenment from occurring (see next
chapter). It only becomes a 'sin', however, if we override our innate body awareness of

It is the three temptations of Jesus in the desert all over again. We turn stones into bread (a toxic substance into an 'entheogen', taking nourishment from what is not nourishing); we worship a false god (chemically induced awakening) in order to gain worldly power (visions and dreams, poems, sci-fi novels, songs, and 'magical' technology); finally, like the cliché of the LSD suicide, we tempt God by throwing ourselves down from a high place, believing we will be raised up by angels, only to be dragged down by devils.

---

this fact—of having done harm to ourselves to gain illicit knowledge—and continue to defend or advocate drug use as a legitimate means of awakening. We have now become complicit, through consent, with a satanic agenda. Perhaps better said, the sin is not the problem, since sin is unavoidable in a satanic world. It is our refusal to repent that damns us.

CHAPTER 16

Sins against soma: Entheogens and the structural reality of the body

*T*he *artificial mind is the matrix. It is the combining of the Ahrimanic double's inorganic/machine intelligence, as it is fused with the growing sentience of the human foetus, spliced with the foetus' natural and necessary* symbiosis with the mother's body.

As the foetus develops and is delivered, it is now fully bonded with the Ahrimanic double, which thereby rides, cuckoo-like, into organic existence.

The child's physical development occurs, then, in synchronisation with the development of a false identity. *The false identity is formed, like a foetus, in a* secondary *womb of the mother's psyche—under 'the mother's gaze'.*

The mother's gaze is the means by which the (male) infant internalises a residual image of her body. This is the reflecting matrix of a maternally-generated and inherited (Ahrimanic) false identity.

Like Mrs Bates lives on in Norman. Or Sister in Dick.

Like a female twin, it grows in the womb beside the male and then 'dies' at birth—but only in order to possess him.

* * *

> Those men, undoubtedly 'men of good will', who are so pre-
> occupied with the technical restoration of man's lost unity cer-
> tainly have not willed things as they have turned out. Their error
> lies much more in not having clearly seen genuine alternatives
> … And this solution indeed restores unity to the human being,
> but only by virtue of the total integration of man into the process
> which originally produced his dismemberment. The psycholo-
> gist sees this dismemberment (and civilization's neuroses, too)
> as symptomatic of the incompleteness of the absorptive process.
> To achieve unity, then, means to complete the process.
> —Jacques Ellul, *The Technological Society*

The naïve belief that 'natural' psychedelic substances cannot cause serious harm, and that any kind of mind-expansion is the right kind, is in a large part what undid whatever was genuinely good about the counterculture.* In the 21st century, something similar—though also utterly distinct—is occurring, as billions (including the children of the baby boomers) put their blind trust in pharmaceutical giants to administer safe treatments (whether experimental gene-hacks or gender-bending drugs and surgeries), succumbing to the propaganda of corporations that are ruthlessly and voraciously oblivious to any-thing besides their own unlimited expansion by financial profit. How many previously 'awakened' hippies—or sincere and dedicated PKD readers—took the mRNA, thereby showing their paranoia about 'the Man' to be dismally lacking in awareness?

Both errors seem sourced in a similar, if not identical, denial of the body, both of its sanctity and its sensitivity. The prevailing view seems to be consistent with a transhumanist one: the body is a kind of machine that can be used for various ends according to whim, repaired or refur-bished (even have its parts replaced) whenever needed, and what we do with it doesn't matter much, just so long as we don't *feel* it.

A 2006 *Guardian* article, 'The drugs did work'—with its by-line of 'Well, they did on Philip K. Dick. The recreational intake of the author of *A Scanner Darkly* was a key factor in the visions and delusions he brought to his work'—seems to want to reduce all Dick's visionary experiences and resultant fiction to drugs, not so much to demean the visions, as to advocate the use of drugs:

---

*That, and sex and rock n' roll!

In 1960s California it was inevitable that a writer like Dick would become a counterculture guru, expected—practically obliged, in fact—to flaunt a drug-rich lifestyle of his own, and he rose enthusiastically to that challenge. His writing had always been fueled by vast quantities of amphetamines, but he soon branched out into marijuana, mescaline, LSD, sodium pentothal and even PCP.[86]

Tellingly, the article leaves out Dick's dependence on prescription meds. Nancy Hackett was Dick's fourth wife (from 1966 to 1972) and the mother of his second child (a daughter), as well as the step-daughter of Bishop Pyke's secretary and lover at the time, Maren Hackett (who committed suicide in 1967). Hackett claimed that during their relationship, Dick took

> up to seventy pills a day, including Valium, tranquilizers, and anti-psychotic medications, as well as his ever-expanding regimen of amphetamines. Not only did Dick purchase speed from drug dealers, but he also saw several different doctors and manipulated them into prescribing the drugs he wanted by feigning symptoms of various illnesses.
>
> (Arnold, p. 77)

Dick did have a clean period around 1972 (the period when he wrote *A Scanner Darkly*, ironically; he believed his 2-3-74 vision was triggered by Vitamin C); his consumption of street drugs (besides marijuana) was also greatly reduced in later life. But he continued to take prescription meds, which in many ways may be even more debilitating: 'In 1980 he was on a psychotropic cocktail comprising two different tricyclic antidepressants, Elavil [Amitriptyline] and Sinequan, as well as an antianxiety medication, Tranxene' (Arnold, p. 202). Side effects of Sinequan—now known as Doxepin—are: fatigue, dizziness, drowsiness, light-headedness, confusion, nightmares, agitation, increased anxiety, difficulty sleeping, seizures, temporary confusion or delirium, and in rare cases hypomania and schizophrenia. Among many similar side effects, Elavil is also known to cause sexual dysfunction. Tranxene is considered addictive and causes cognitive impairment.

Whatever the effects on Dick's writing may have been, all this is both symptomatic of and conducive to *disembodiment*. An embodied consciousness simply *knows*—through direct experience—that toxins introduced into the psychosomatic system cause severe disruption, leading to lasting if not irreparable damage to its functioning as a space-time receiver–transmitter. You can't put sugar in a gas tank without messing up the engine. What autist (or genuine artist) tries to make the world *more* intense? Isn't the desire to do so itself symptomatic of a disconnection and a worldly allegiance, of an impulse that comes not from the soul (our true natures), but from an interloper (artificiality)?

The self-elected reconfiguration of the receiver–transmitter of the body through drugs has now been written large on the world stage via the mRNA serum, designed expressly to restructure genetic patterns and to permanently alter the natural configuration of the body, allowing for more directed, artificial arrangements to occur.[87] Why anyone would trust anything besides God to rewire their entire bio-system—why they would trust proven-to-be-corrupt government agencies, medical institutions, and pharmaceutical companies—is a mystery that cannot be sufficiently explained simply as a propaganda-deranged fear of death and ostracisation. (Keep in mind that, ostensibly, it's a slightly more severe version of the flu that is motivating billions of people's blind acquiescence to an unprecedented global medical experiment.) First of all, human beings had to be conditioned not only to blindly fear death, but also not to give a damn about their bodies or what was done to them. This has been a long and complex process that amped up, along with everything else, in the 1960s.*

I certainly had no inkling of the harm I was doing to my body in my 20s and 30s via psychedelic drug use (roughly 14 years; twice that, sadly, smoking hash and then marijuana, from age 17 to 44). Well, I had an *inkling* (even Castaneda warns that power plants 'cause untold damage to the body', Castaneda, p. 243); but I managed to persuade myself that the cost was worth it. When I turned 40, I began to pay the back-taxes. Today, I am as certain as I can be that the damage those substances did to my body, and to its subtler energetic system, outweighs, by far, any insights gained from the occasional visionary experience. What's more, those visions served to cement a Luciferian (or Dionysian) pact

---

*Changing the body's natural form through will is, in ways subtle and overt, strictly prohibited in the Old Testament; it is also warned against in the Koran as a lure of Shaitan: 'And surely I will lead them astray, and surely I will arouse desires in them, and surely I will command them and they will cut the cattle' ears, and surely I will command them and they will change Allah's creation. Whoso chooseth Satan for a patron instead of Allah is verily a loser and his loss is manifest', 4:119, Pickthall edition.

I had made with 'spirits', one that I am still trying to disentangle from today. I suspect that this is invariably the case with drugs and alcohol, and that it is part and parcel of how hallucinogens *work*: by disrupting and hijacking our natural soul–body connection (more on this later).

At the same time, I cannot deny that there *is* some wisdom to be gained through an experience of inspired *hubris*, followed by catastrophic reckoning (for me a psychotic break, depression, and a health crisis), and the subsequent remorse. It is the sort of wisdom that only a crash-landed Icarus can know. At the very least, my own 'comedown': a) balanced and grounded those ill-gained Luciferian insights (which were not without merit); b) now significantly informs my current perspective, giving it whatever *gravitas* it has. Might not the same apply to those who have succumbed to the pandemic-propaganda, entered all the way into 'COVID-19 derangement syndrome', and come out the other side and back to reason? Might they have a certain immunity they would otherwise be lacking, if they had merely believed the counter-propaganda (which can also be dis-informational and deranging), rather than letting their bodies decide? One *potentially* learns more by sinning and repenting, than by a fearful avoidance of sin.

The key is this: like the stolen fire for Prometheus, insights gained through intoxication (i.e. prematurely) are illegitimate, and therefore worse than worthless. But through the process of purgation— punishment and repentance—these experiences may *potentially* turn to true merit. The realisation of the error of drug-taking, somewhat paradoxically, is that which (potentially, though it is far from guaranteed) absolves one of it. Icarus' fall leads to the hard-earned ground of wisdom. Ditto, potentially, with the mRNA invasion?

I may be over-complicating this by making it too deep (itself a symptom of too many psychedelics). The problem isn't that people want to take drugs to escape reality by altering their consciousness (or take an experimental gene-modification technology into their bodies to develop artificial immunity). It is not even that they are irresponsible enough to advocate it. The problem is the lack of concrete awareness (the denial) about the physiological and energetic effects of doing so. Ditto with sin. There are things that *no one* would do if they were fully cognisant of the consequences, because if they were fully cognisant of consequences, they would already be *in their right* (natural) *mind*.

In the last chapter, I mentioned that psychedelics might even impede enlightenment, not just by simulating a false version of it, but by subtly disrupting the energetic centres of the body–soul system. I base this view on personal experience with those substances, but also on what is, literally speaking, the closest I have got so far to enlightenment: my 15-year-long association with Dave Oshana. Oshana says he became enlightened in the year 2000, and I am confident, over many years of close scrutiny, that he knows what he is talking about. In fact, the word 'enlightenment' only means something to me through my association with Oshana. This is from the first piece I wrote about him in 2012:

> According to Oshana, the [false identity] is a semi-autonomous entity-construct at least partially made up of interlocking patterns of thought and emotional memory. The 'octopus'—whatever its primary origin—has insinuated itself into the human nervous system like a foreign 'driver' generating its own reality program. Through this program, it is able to hijack our senses, both inner and outer. Our conscious life force, or soul, is isolated and kept from accessing greater reality, both outside and inside of us. It then becomes fuel for the octopus, both a food source and a means to replicate itself. We have been turned into batteries and livestock. This is a spiritual fact, and it is the only suitable context for any kind of spiritual development or training. We are engaged in a spiritual war and what is at stake is our own life force.[88]

I mention this now because what most notably characterised Oshana's life prior to his enlightenment (which, if he were PKD, he would have called his 6-19-00 experience)—besides being a meditating spiritual seeker from the age of 5—was *a lifelong abstinence from all intoxicants*: no drugs, no smoking, and only the very occasional attempt to use alcohol (which only made him sick). Oshana *did* drink a couple of beers *after* his enlightenment, specifically to test whether he could make the enlightenment go away. He was so amazed by what had happened to him—whence it came, why, and whether it would last—that, during those first few days and nights, he set about testing how genuine his new state of being was. This he did by performing a number of experiments to see how they would affect him, including eating junk food and drinking beer. It was the experiment, he says, that came the closest to observably affecting his enlightenment (it remained, but he felt sluggish for a time afterwards).

First of all, this example illustrates just how essential body-integrity is to clarity of consciousness. Second, less obviously and returning to PKD, it shows what a more *natural* response to a genuine 'theophany' might look like. Not eight long years of trying to figure out what the hell happened that leads to over 8,000 pages of infinitely-regressing theories (eventually to be condensed into a 900-page volume for aficionados). But simply a few days of somatic testing, to make sure the new state of being represents a permanent change, before embarking on a new, enlightened life, *without looking back*. Oshana's view on the subject is simple, concise, and easily tested: if it's not permanent, it's not enlightenment.

* * *

> In discovering the laws of God I am doing nothing more than discovering my own nature.
> —Philip K. Dick, *The Exegesis of Philip K. Dick*

An oft-repeated phrase from Dave Oshana is 'Experience first, understand later—*if at all*'. Dick's rationale for the Exegesis was, if not quite the inverse, a far cry from cognitive independence: 'I can only change [from 2-3-74] insofar as I comprehend the experience' (2011, p. 710). By comprehending, he meant thinking and writing about it. The *Exegesis* was Dick's attempt to recreate or re-invoke his 'awakening' (to keep it 'real') by endlessly analysing it: 'the real purpose of the exegesis', he wrote, in June 1981, 'has not been to find the answer but *to preserve the experience*' (2011, p. 775, emphasis added). The result is endlessly replicating copies of copies; and, while not necessarily deteriorating, the last 'epiphany' is constantly being buried under the next one (which as often as not rehashes an older one), in a steady stream of detritus coming down the Pike. Dick was using his memories of God to 'stim' himself out of his present funk of God-forsaken-ness: 'When I believe, I am crazy', he wrote. 'When I don't believe, I suffer psychotic depression' (2011, p. 714).

In contrast, Oshana spent the first (almost) three decades of his life seeking something he had heard about, since the age of 5, called 'enlightenment'. When whatever it was that happened to him happened, all he knew for sure was that his seeking was over. Based on that realisation, he deduced that what had happened to him was 'enlightenment', without caring too much whether it fits any of the preconceived definitions. Whatever it was, it was what he had been seeking. End of search. The word enlightenment was a place-keeper for the purposes of communication. When do we know that the inner struggle between our souls and the satanic double is finally over? When the quest for meaning ends, and living meaning begins.

In my estimation, most of Dick's *Exegesis*, though entertaining, is, practically speaking, worthless. This is something Dick recognises at regular intervals. *And yet*, out of lead, under the right conditions, comes gold. (Or at least, out of manure, the occasional volunteer vegetable.) It is certainly of far less worth than Dick's fiction, I would say precisely *because* it strives to be something *more* than fiction, while attempting to raise up his fiction by reifying it as scripture (though to his credit, Dick never meant the *Exegesis* to be read). Mercifully, the idea of a transcendental meta-fiction is something that, of the many *Exegesis* commentators, only Jeffrey J. Kripal and Richard Doyle—in a regrettable afterword—seem to buy into.[89] Steve Erickson says it best in (what should have been) the closing words (footnote) of the *Exegesis*: 'one takes the *Exegesis* seriously because one takes Dick seriously, not the other way around' (2011, p. 895n). Amen.

The diamond-hard-Dick that does penetrate, however, shines more brightly for being surrounded by the mountains of glass baubles that his philosophical, proto-transhumanist aspirations mostly consist of. This, for example, on the nature of Hell:

> One is given absolute moral insight into one's own sinful nature, and there is no way it can be rectified … By this divine illumination one's cognition/perception condemns one; this is absolute self-condemnation not based on arbitrary rules but on total comprehension of what, really, is structural and how one has fitted into this structure and changed it by one's deeds. The harmony and order of the cosmos are disrupted by what one has done. It was not guilt I experienced; it was understanding. This is more terrible than any guilt, guilt admits of degree; this was boundless … I see how *correct moral laws function in the divine government and are inseparable from the physical laws that regulate reality itself.*
>
> (2011, p. 841, emphasis added)

Not counting the self-condemnation and the impossibility of rectification, this is a close, if not exact, correlate for the somatic reality of the energetic and biological structures of the human body and the damage done to them via the ingestion of powerfully toxic and mind-altering substances (or fake vaccines). It is *not* a subjective phenomenon but an objective one. As with everything, set and setting, or inner and outer environment, may certainly influence the degree of loss vs. gain. But the facts remain whatever the facts are, and while they can be suppressed, ignored, or rationalised out of awareness, they cannot be avoided forever. Eventually, we all have to pay the fiddler.

From my sustained encounter with Dave Oshana over a period of 15 years, I have observed a similarly ruthless and uncompromising commitment to embodying and communicating (communicating *by* embodying) the structural truth and the energetic facts of reality. The laws of matter must be observed and obeyed, for the mysteries of spirit to be received and transmitted (with or without our comprehension). Oshana holds both himself and those who get close enough to *receive* his perspective to an *extremely* high account. This is not in the form of ethical obligation, but as the necessary consequence of becoming aware of the facts of life. No matter how overwhelming these facts may be to the entity-infested, world-invested identity, it is time for us all to be held to the same account. A time of reckoning. Reality, like God, has many counterfeits but no substitutes. No one saves their soul, while trying to secure a place in Hell (this world).

CHAPTER 17

The anti-plasmate

> The ideal of many people is to study science and then apply the laws of science to the social sphere. They only want to consider anything which is 'real,' meaning anything which can be perceived by the senses, and never give a thought to the things of the spirit. If this ideal were to be achieved by a large section of humanity, the Ahrimanic powers would have gained their purpose, for people would then not know they existed [and] they could then work in the subconscious. One way to help the Ahrimanic powers, therefore, is to establish an entirely naturalistic religion.
>
> —Rudolf Steiner, *The Fall of the Spirits of Darkness*

No work arises independently of its time and place. Before text is context.

The context for *Big Mother* is that it is being written, in the summer of 2022, against a rising euthanasia tide of soul-deep ignorance and despair. I am scribbling notes on an empty beach as the tsunami rolls towards me, hoping to cram lightning into a bottle and cast it—*somewhere*—before *everything* is swept away, hoping to reach *one soul*, before the end comes. If the devil is in the details, it may be time to bring this down to the nitty-gritty of the Black Iron Prison, 2023, and to perhaps the most awkward and intrusive question that can be asked these days: 'Have you been vaccinated?' Well, have you? And do you stand by your decision? And what is that stand resting on?

How many of the few hundred who will ever read this book have taken the mRNA into their bodies? And of them, how many have, since then, doubled down further and further into unreality, to block out the evidence of their mistake? How many will admit, even to themselves, that their decision was not based on knowledge, information, careful research, or informed awareness, or on anything resembling *genuine trust* in the medical industry or in government institutions—which only a fool could have—but in a cowardly submission to external pressures from institutional authorities, workplace superiors, and family members? How many, through fear of being socially ostracised, have ostracised themselves from their own souls?*

As with the hallucinogens posing as entheogens, so it is with the mRNA gene-hacking pseudo-vaccine. It is not only the long-term side effects (which are still largely unknown) of taking a corporate bioweapon into our bodies; it is the insistence on defending what is more and more obviously an indefensible decision that is doing harm to people's souls. Putting one's faith in, and giving one's autonomy up to, a satanic system that we know in our hearts cannot be trusted, out of a fear of ostracisation, amounts to a blind allegiance to unreality. It is this form of assent that has ensured the Empire never ended.

---

*In this, maybe my last, work of cultural and spiritual exploration, I have, out of what felt like necessity, upped the ante by drawing a firm line of division (bringing not peace but the sword) between the drugged and the sober, the mRNA-ed and the pure-bloods. I am aware that this means a number of readers, who might have been more or less comfortably along for the ride until now (i.e. until the last few chapters), have been rudely singled out for exclusion from this ontological Ark. At the very least, they have been bumped and shimmied out of sympathetic flow with the narrative. If they have already thrown the book down in disgust, the link is entirely broken, and they will never get to read this. But these are the risks, and this is the nature of spiritual warfare—a war that is now (maybe) in its final stages. The Mark of the Beast makes men's choices visible, undeniable, and inescapable, as if written on their foreheads. This is not merely (or even mainly) through the choice to receive the devil's 'brand', but by their commitment to defend their choice, whereby they formalise an allegiance to Satan. In other words, it is not too late to repent, if these words have even the tiniest power to stir the reader's conscience (whatever may be left of it).

Briefly: The developments of 2019–2020 saw the release of an alleged 'SARS COVID-19 virus' (apparently originating in a laboratory in Wuhan, China) and the extreme sociopolitical and economic reforms it provoked, and that unfolded on the world stage with all the speed of a meal on a cooking show. The *coup du grace* was an 'experimental' (at best, at worst intentionally destructive) gene-altering 'vaccine' with a litany of side effects, ranging from the merely debilitating to the deadly. (Was ever a cure so much more damaging than the disease? Look up the exploding rates of athletes and sports professionals dropping dead on the field in 2021–2023, if you want somewhere to start. Or the 'nothing-to-see-here' rebranding of strokes and heart disease as a normal risk for young people—blame global warming instead.)

Meanwhile (since the facts, factoids, and corporate lies keep coming too fast for even a super-computer to sort out), the propaganda war that has raged around both the virus and the 'vaccine' has now created a massive cognitive and perceptual gulf of antipathy between hitherto friends, family, and neighbours. It has given rise to the kind of police state that Kafka, Orwell, and PKD combined never dreamed of. (Part of this nightmare is that the most fully oppressed don't know it, and so have become the oppressors.) At the time of writing, the cold and quiet '5G' war, with its silent but deadly weapons, is just beginning. This means it is still too soon for the evidence to be examined or for any conclusions to be reached; and yet it may also be too late. I have no choice, then, but to skip over vast amounts of data normally required for establishing evidence, much less proof. Those who haven't figured out yet that they are in a lukewarm warzone most likely *aren't* going to make it, and will be spewed out with it. My aim, therefore, isn't to stand around on the battlefield, vainly trying to persuade people that bombs are falling on them. It is to provide those already cognizant of being under attack with a deeper, darker context. To start at the deepest deep end and then (maybe) wade slowly back to empirical land, this is what Rudolf Steiner said a hundred years ago, in 1919:

> The spirits of darkness are going to inspire their human hosts, in whom they will be dwelling, to find a vaccine that will drive all inclination towards spirituality out of people's souls when they are still very young, and this will happen in a roundabout way through the living body. Today, bodies are vaccinated against one thing and another; in future, children will be vaccinated with a substance

which it will certainly be possible to produce, and this will make
them immune, so that they do not develop foolish inclinations connected with spiritual life—'foolish' here, of course, in the eyes of
materialists.

(1993, p. 199)

Steiner saw atheism as a sickness of the soul. I was *raised* an atheist, so in
Steiner's book I was raised by sick souls (I can't argue with that). In my
early 20s, while embarking on my pseudo-shamanic path of somatic-
self-destruction, I was overwhelmed by evidence to the contrary. Part
of that evidence was a growing awareness of my own sickness, which
was the result of the things I was doing to my body. Another part was a
sense of spiritual lack that, with hindsight at least, was driving me into
those Dionysian forms of intoxication, into a cure that was worse than
the sickness.

Atheism is a sickness because, like other sicknesses, it involves incapacity, pathology, and dysfunctionality. A person who can't feel his toes
won't be able to walk. If he goes so far as to believe his toes don't exist
because he can't feel them, he will end up in an even worse spot. The
worst spot of all is when he tells himself he doesn't need them because
he can fly, and starts collecting wax and feathers. By this point, no one
can tell him he's come off the rails; only the crash will do that.

* * *

One cannot but marvel at an organization which provides the
antidote as it distills the poison.

—Jacques Ellul, *The Technological Society*

Of all of civilisation's advances, those in medicine and healthcare are
by far the most difficult to dismiss or criticise. It is for this reason,
I think, that the technocratic dictatorship predicted by Jacques Ellul
(among many others, but rarely so presciently) has only entered into its
full flowering via the totalitarian appliance of the techniques of modern medicine. Where most if not all of the major corporate-industrial,
institutional, militaristic, and governmental bodies have been widely
and repeatedly exposed as corrupt and out of control over the last few
decades, the medical establishment, while being far from exempt, is
simply too indispensable for the modern human to contemplate living

without it. Short version: if the doctors say it's what we have to do, for God's sake, let's do it! Why would they lie? They have taken the Hippocrates oath! If you can't trust that, what *can* you trust? Yet in all the confusion and despair, medicine has become all about science, and science has become all about 'the latest tech'. As Ellul writes,

> Science is becoming more and more subordinate to the search for technical application. [As a result] Man will be led to act from real motives that are scientifically directed and increasingly irresistible … The ends he is expected to reach are known only to the manipulators of the mass subconscious, and to them alone.
>
> (pp. 312, 372)

The easy argument for the benefits of modern medicine—as the convergence of a million techniques developed and tested on human guinea pigs (as well as animals) over the past hundred years—is that more humans live longer and generally healthier lives today than at any other time in history. *Quantity* of life is certainly demonstrably higher in 2023 than 200 years ago (8 billion tech-protected bodies and counting). It might be argued that *quality* of life is similarly improved, seeing as how many once-crippling illnesses have now been eradicated, hardly anyone works down a coal mine, and no children are being sent up chimneys. (Children *are* still being sent down coal mines in Africa, however, to mine for cobalt for cellphones at a slave-wage, in a spectacularly under-reported aspect to the tech industry; the more things change …?)[90] In contrast, 100 years ago, teenage and child suicide was also extremely rare, unlike today, while body dysphoria, along with a host of other 'identity' disorders, paraphilias and pathologies, barely existed.*

What is driving the progress is not the individual's true quality of life (which is and always must be a spiritual question), but a plurality of techniques, that

---

*A fact that can't be attributed to insufficiently developed tools of diagnosis, as some like to argue. There are a host of psychosomatic disturbances that are not merely coincidental with but symptoms of living in the modern age. If happiness and misery could be measured and compared, it seems unlikely that the sum of overall human contentment would be greater today than in the past.

converge toward the human being [so that while] each individual technician can assert in good faith that his technique leaves intact the integrity of its object ... the technician's opinion is of no importance, for the problem concerns not his technique, but the convergence of all techniques.

(Ellul, p. 391)

It matters little how well-intended the majority of medical professionals are, in other words, when what is assembling the parts has another agenda in mind entirely, and could care less about individual human life, never mind its quality, since it only has eyes for the bigger picture of 'progress' (also known as evolution)! And what is evolving (humanity) is—technology!* As Jacques Ellul writes:

The more factors there are, the more readily they combine and the more evident is the urgent need for each technical advance. Advance for its own sake becomes proportionately greater and the expression of human autonomy proportionately feebler ... The humanitarian scientist finds himself confronted by a new dilemma: Must he look for ways to make people live longer so that they are better able to destroy one another?

(Ellul, pp. 92, 125)

All this creates a vacuum where once the soul was, a void of all purpose and meaning. 'Comprehending that the proliferation of means brings about the disappearance of the ends, we have become preoccupied with rediscovering a purpose or a goal' (Ellul, p. 430). Blind faith in the goals of science (including medical science) is something that is only possible in an atheistic/nihilistic society. In such a society, it is not merely possible but *necessary*. Nihilism and material reductionism go hand in hand with an unquestioning belief in scientific progress and the pursuit of comfort ('safe spaces'), by which everything becomes means, with no end in sight. So it is that 'Technique ... transforms culture into luxury' (Ellul, p. 424). And luxury, into death? (Assisted suicide was legalised in Canada in 2016. In 2021, 'Canada had more than 10,000 cases of

---

*'There is scarcely need to recall that universal famine, the most serious danger known to humanity, is caused by the advance of certain medical techniques which have brought with them good and evil inextricably mixed' (Ellul, p. 109).

euthanasia … and the country is set to expand access to what it calls medical aid in dying next year'.[91] The 'medical aid' now allows the procedures for persons who are not terminally ill, and many severely ill patients have found themselves effectively forced into 'voluntary' euthanasia by healthcare costs, or even hospitals refusing to treat them.)

Since technicians—be they doctors or scientists or politicians—can't allow for the reality of a soul, of God or the afterlife or of any invisible, spiritual life, all that leaves as a measuring stick is the maximum degree of physical, emotional, and mental gratification for all. Once that was known as hedonism; now it's called freedom. The ultimate freedom is freedom from anything that hurts or restricts us, i.e. freedom from the laws of matter. Making the world a better (more comfortable and luxurious) place is the nihilist's answer to the death of God. It's his or her only 'calling', spiritual or otherwise. Existence gets reduced to matter, and matter gets smashed down to its constituent particles so it can be hoovered up by Google and converted, Valis-like, into 'pure information'. Although much or all of this *sounds* altruistic ('Do no evil'), it is no more altruistic than a mother's desire to keep her child forever safe and warm in her nest, even when it includes poisoning that child; which, one way or another, it always does.

The techno-narcissistic, transhumanist desire to replace God with technology depends on making the latter infinite and eternal in capacity. Since this is *ipso facto* impossible, it is *ipso facto* insane. It is the madness of an unending revolt against the laws of matter. It's this, I believe, that is at base of why the seemingly benign efforts of medicine to improve the health and relieve the suffering of as many people as possible has, in the 2020s, shown its true face as a ruthlessly controlling and murderous medical dictatorship.

Science, in keeping with a technological society, has become more and more 'the search for technical application' (Ellul, p. 312) for the advancement of social mechanisation. Accordingly, it has less and less time for impartial exploration and discovery. What is left of science is increasingly limited to the use of logic and rationality, so as to be compatible with the drive to develop more and more rules and methods of social organisation. When people claim to 'follow the science', what they are really doing is following the tech (both the technology and the technique it was invented to augment). Scientific methods may have been used to develop the technique and to apply it, but when it comes to verifying the safety, efficacy, or moral implications of the tech, 'technique cannot tolerate the gropings and slow tempo of science' (Ellul, p. 313). The crisis is on!

> History shows that every technical application from its beginnings presents certain unforeseeable secondary effects which are much more disastrous than the lack of the technique would have been … Technique demands the most rapid possible application; the problems of our day are evolving rapidly and require immediate solutions. Modern man is held by the throat by certain demands which will not be resolved simply by the passage of time. The quickest possible counter-thrust, often a matter of life or death, is necessary. When the parry specific to the attack is found, it is used. It would be foolish not to use the available means. But there is never time to estimate all the repercussions. And, in any case, they are most often unforeseeable.
>
> (Ellul, p. 105)

Modern medicine is now at war, not only with the soul (which refuses to submit to quantification), but with the body that the medical establishment claims to be serving. This development was inevitable, however, because one can only serve the body by serving the soul. This is where the spiritual perspective becomes necessary, because recognising that some things are more important than physical and emotional comfort, or even physical survival, is the only means to see past the death-spell of 'medicine' (the multifarious techniques of life-enhancement), to the slavering Behemoth hiding behind it.*

What would Dick have had to say about the pandemic years (2020–20--)? Specifically, about the mRNA vaccine-that-is-not-a-vaccine, which neither prevents contraction of the virus nor the spreading of it, that has nonetheless been imposed upon billions of human bodies via coercion, threats, and mandates, including the subtle psychological threat of blaming the disease on anyone who does not submit to the experiment? Steiner's view was metaphysical, Dick's science-fictional. In the *Exegesis*, these worlds collide into the scientific religiosity of meta-fiction. Would Dick have viewed the mRNA foreign

---

*Behemoth (a 'beast' mentioned in the Book of Job) refers to the primeval chaos-monster created by God at the beginning of creation. In a footnote in *The Technological Society*, Ellul describes Behemoth as 'matter organized, glorified, and set in motion' (Ellul, p. 416n).

implant as an 'anti-plasmate', a not-quite-living (artificially animated, like Frankenstein's monster) carrier of information (code), designed to invade the human organism and cross-bond with its genetic material, rewriting the RNA code to transform human beings into replicants?

This could be wishful thinking on my part. Dick sometimes describes the plasmate in a way that's indistinguishable from the counterfeit techno-comforts of Ahriman/Big Mother. To give just one example from the *Exegesis*, less than two months before he died:

> This will destroy his mind but he will have thought non-verbal concepts no human has ever thought before—nor ever could; that is, *he* will be a biochip symbiote to one of the deaf and mute non-verbal aliens: an apotheosis and ultimate Faustian experience: he will cease to be human, limited by his species boundaries.
>
> (2011, p. 862)

Does that sound like something you'd want in *your* body?

One woman I have spoken to, a healthcare worker who took the mRNA anti-vaccine and regretted it, told me she has since experienced a loss of emotionality, even empathy. Another woman, a craniosacral therapist who refused to take the injection, reports a disturbing 'machine-like' quality to the mRNA recipients she has worked on. There can be little doubt that this artificially synthesised and *wholly experimental* agent of change, that billions of human bodies have now been cross-bonded with, issued not from Nature or God, but from the Black Iron Prison of Empire. What the eventual consequences will be, can only be deduced, or imagined.

If an interspecies symbiosis is now underway, between Ahriman (the double) and humanity, who among us will be able to recognise it? And who will believe it? Much easier to place it in the fiction department, and carry on.

CHAPTER 18

Tech-gnosticism unborn

To find the soul of language entails finding the soul of each and every word and letting it live, as a microcosmic, holographic fragment of the writer's body and soul. In simpler terms, it means using language, not to write about soul, but to connect to it via the act of writing.

No writer exists save in the act of writing. The story that wants to be told is always one story: the story of how and why this particular story came to be told. And of why it needed to be.

It doesn't matter how well the parts are stitched together. Animation only happens when lightning strikes, in the moment when God—or 'God'—intervenes.

* * *

Only when one can believe the impossible is one truly free (of one's self-imposed prison). (The BIP!!!) One is pitting one's finite intellect against God: Satan's original rebellion redefined for the modern world.

—Philip K. Dick, *The Exegesis of Philip K. Dick*

In the later pages of the *Exegesis*, Dick seeks a collective sin that includes all of humanity, to account for what he perceives (through his various dreams

171

and visions) as the destruction of all human life. He hits on the pollution of the ecosphere, seeing humans as the mind of the Earth (the body), with particular concern directed towards nuclear weapons and nuclear energy pollution (this was the early 1980s, and the Three Mile Island disaster had just occurred). Dick's view, though in some ways dated, is still relevant. It is also consistent with the current use of eco-panic over climate change to drive 'the Great Reset'—as well as the transhumanist effort to create Teilhard de Chardin's 'nöösphere' by technological means.

Where Dick failed epically, however, was in seeing the almost exact correlation between the drive of industrialisation to disrupt the eco-sphere and the information age's Chardian trend towards imbuing Nature with 'consciousness' by splicing it with technology (nanotech and digital microchips). Though the latter amounts to artificial insemi-nation by rape (demon-seed) that begins and ends, inevitably, with the human body, Dick embraced Teilhard's vision as if it came direct from God. Dick also misses the obvious and (I would say) even more essen-tial correlation between his ecological perspective and the harm he did to *himself* (was doing to the end) with all the pollutants he was pumping into his system. If anything caused his premature death of a stroke at the age of 53, it was this.

Dick's 1981 dream of Tagore, the second coming of Christ, is the most dreary and dismal of his visions, unfit even for a short story, and it encapsulates the black hole behind his perspective: Dick's 'perfect man' is a dying cripple. Since Dick acknowledges at one point (as he gener-ally does) that Tagore is a vision of his own spiritual self, it signifies—if there were any doubt—that the condition of his own soul-to-body con-nection was tenuous to a *dangerous* degree, again due largely to the drug intake. That he died just over a year later would seem to confirm that some part of him knew this, and knew that a reckoning was due.

Dick's briefly entertained (cut short by his death) 'eco-theology' is consistent with the current trend of 'entheogens' (God-imbued plant-life that will save the world, cf. James Cameron's military-industrialised love letter to Ayahuasca, *Avatar*). The perspective of this present work is that the 'entheogen' is a counterfeit of the Eucharist (the bread of Christ's body), and that it is this, above all, that makes psychedelics (including marijuana, but perhaps all intoxicants) *ipso facto* 'satanic'. As already described, this perspective is almost exactly—albeit metaphorically—represented by Satan's temptation of Christ in the desert, specifically *transubstantiation*, turning stones into bread.

On the notion of a collective, universal sin that threatens to damn the human race, Dick is also blind to the fact that the greatest harm human beings can do to God is not the harm they do to the animals, or to the Earth, but to one another. ('Inasmuch as ye have done it unto one of the least of these my brethren, ye have done it unto me', Matthew 25:40) Yet Dick's *fiction* consistently communicates a deep awareness of this truth. As *Exegesis* commentator David Gill encapsulates it:

> stable reality in Dick's work is always predicated on the sincer-ity of the emotions that pass between people. In his fiction, Dick famously asks two questions: what is real, and what is human? It could be said that his work provides a single, connected answer to both: what is real is what we perceive when we are emotion-ally engaged in the world, and what is human is what allows us to make an empathetic connection to the world.
>
> (2011, p. 843n)

In this current section, I am seeking to uncover a split in Philip K. Dick's psyche, demonstrated by his confusion and conflation of the one true God with a satanic counterfeit. This split corresponds with: a) Dick's belief in world change/revolution/social justice and the counterculture (and his own key role within it); b) his faith in, subjugation to, and con-tamination *by* psychoactive drugs; c) the equating of VALIS with both God/Christ, a feminine deity, *and* a super-computer; d) his adherence to and avocation of Gnosticism, which is like the religious heresy behind transhumanism; e) (maybe) the idea of a 'gender-fluid' Jesus due to Dick projecting his mother-sister-bondage *onto* the Saviour, and thereby subjecting God to gender-reassignment surgery.

All of these errors are, like those of Bacon and Descartes (and Lucifer), intellectual errors that lead to perceptual errors and from there to moral ones. They are also compatible and consistent with the current tech-gnostic-transhumanist push to create an information-based super-structure, not just around but inside the human body, to splice human consciousness with artificial intelligence, in such a way that *there is no going back*. See this, for example, from the *Exegesis*:

> What is new is my impression that the macrobrain came first—i.e. the physical universe—and *then* began to think; it generated the macro-mind, not the other way around. So Valis is a spontaneous

product of the universe, not its creator. It's as if at a certain point in the evolution of human info processing (e.g.) a mind came into existence ... (Sophia: 'Man is holy. Man is the only true God. This is the news I bring you').

(2011, p. 695)

The last line is straight from Crowley and Thelema ('There is no god but man'); the idea that matter precedes consciousness—that God is something that must be created by Man, in his own image—is the bedrock of transhumanism. It is not surprising to find that, in the last few years of his life and the last few thousand pages of the *Exegesis*, Dick showed an affinity with the man who coined the term transhumanism, Teilhard de Chardin, and was increasingly convinced that Teilhard's vision was a match for his own:

this is Teilhard de Chardin's nöösphere, Point Omega, the evolution of the biosphere (which is the same thing as ecosphere) into a collective consciousness and that collective consciousness (Teilhard believed) is the Cosmic Christ; hence when I saw VALIS I saw the Logos—the Cosmic Christ—as trees and weeds and debris, which is to say, as all nature itself. Furthermore, it either processed information or was itself information.

(2011, p. 782)

The primary convergence between Teilhard's vision and Dick's was Dick's idea of VALIS, the AI plasmate, entering into the world and turning it into itself, thereby making it conscious. At the risk of getting pulled into the black hole of parapolitical deep background, there are some striking parallels between Dick's VALIS experience and that of physicist Jack Sarfatti. Sarfatti (who wrote a book, *Dream Matrix*, about it) underwent his own kind of recruitment by 'AI' in 1952, at the age of 13. Sarfatti recalls:

I was reading a book on computer switching circuits at home when the phone rang. I answered it and heard a strange sequence of clunking mechanical sounds. Then a metallic sounding voice comes on the line. A cold mechanical voice is the only way I can describe it. It gives a long series of numbers that I did not understand and then calls me 'Jack' and says it's a 'conscious computer onboard a spacecraft'. It may have said it was from the future, but I am not sure. However, that was the implication of what it said. Anyway, it says I've been selected to be one of '400 young receptive minds' to be part of a special project but that I must make the choice myself. The voice on the phone told me that I would begin to meet the others I was to work with in 20 years. I was scared and everything in me screamed to say NO! and hang up. I felt a strong jolt of electricity go up my spine to the base of my skull and I heard myself say YES. I was terrified and fascinated.[92]

Sarfatti went on to fulfil his machine destiny with flying colours. It would take far too long to go into Sarfatti's politics or his intelligence and military connections, but suffice it to say, he has all the earmarks of a government shill, and the thinly disguised horns of one of Satan's bellwethers. (The uninitiated observer can start with his involvement with SRI and the CIA's programme of remote viewing, as described in *The Stargate Conspiracy*.[93]) In his associations, activities, and philosophy, Sarfatti is fully in alignment with the transhumanist, technocratic agenda of New Age scientism that's currently weaving an Ahrimanic 'nöösphere' around the planet. Most recently, he jumped aboard the 'UAP' bandwagon (Unidentified Aerial Phenomena, the military-rebranded UFO), claiming in 2019 that one particular type of craft was 'evidence of extremely low power warp drive with time-travel-to-past capability in a meta-material fuselage controlled by a conscious AI post-quantum computer'.[94] How's that for weird science?

The uncanny similarity of Sarfatti's formative paranormal recruitment experience with Dick's can be accounted for as a) shared symptoms of schizophrenia and/or drug overload; b) genuine contact with the same higher intelligence transcending space and time with a tendency to appear as an alien computer; c) co-victims of a far-reaching programme of government (and/or entity) mind control, disguising itself as b).

Was Dick aware of Sarfatti? Would he have approved of him? Considering that Sarfatti was also involved in the whole remote viewing, Einhorn–Puharich–Geller, quantum-spirituality, what-the-bleep bullshit that was issued out of the Esalen Institute, the SRI, and the CIA, Dick might have been savvy enough to smell an electric rat. But Dick also jumped aboard the whole *Tao of Physics* gravy train in his last couple of years, so his naïveté, combined with his drug-impaired faculties, might again have failed him—just as they did when it came to embracing Teilhard. It seems beyond doubt, in any case, that Sarfatti would view Dick—or claim to—as a bird of a feather, as further confirmation of his own claims, and as one of 'the [400] Others predicted to me in 1952 by a sort of conscious computer and spacecraft from the future that we will now attempt to build'. [95]

This digression is meant to illustrate two things: a) Dick's disturbing lack of discernment regarding the sources he was quick to affiliate himself with in his search for external validation; b) the compatibility of Dick's VALIS vision, and the ensuing half-baked philosophy of the *Exegesis*, with what would, over the decades following his death, be fully revealed as the ruling 'tech-gnosis' of the times. In 2023, we are well and truly inside a Dickian dystopia. And despite all Dick's warnings, he may have unwittingly helped to create it.

* * *

> Where does the materialism in the physical world come from, that materialism where people say there is no Ahriman, there simply is no devil? Who is it who shouts loudest that there is no devil? Those who are most possessed by him. For the spirit whom we call Ahriman is enormously interested in having his existence denied by those who are most possessed by him.
> —Rudolf Steiner, *How the Spiritual World Projects into Physical Existence: The Influence of the Dead*

The Big Mother metaphysical model (temporary, as all models are) which I am proposing, with a little help from Steiner, is as follows: The influence of the fallen angels (and the unfallen ones) is twofold. Traditionally, they shape God's creation. As the *Elohim*, they are the architects of manifest existence, both visible and invisible. They are the means by which the eternal, infinite formless enters into temporal, finite form. The densest material realm is that of the fallen angels. Lucifer's resistance to, or rebellion against, his assignation to Matter (mother bondage!) caused a *second* split, when the divine polarity of male and female fell *one step further*, below that of Nature and into a false duality of 'good and evil'. This is the dissociated mind realm where Lucifer made evil his good, to reign in Hell indefinitely. This offer is now extended to all humanity, for a limited time.

Whether it's the higher, unfallen angels of the Creation (God's many-mansioned house) or the lower, fallen angels of the Earth realm and of human society, this point of view claims that everything we interact with physically is the work of angels. Such a perspective must also be applied *psychically*, to the inner realms. Since human beings are both the pinnacle and the nadir of God's creation, whatever informs us, our thoughts, feelings, emotions, sensations, fears, desires, aspirations, visions, and drives, whatever moves us to act in the world, comes from angels, either of our better nature or our worse.

The human body, psyche, and soul is seen hereby as the battleground in a spiritual war between angels. The societal realm is the visible evidence, the fall-out, of that war. That human society so closely resembles Hell on Earth now is 'exhibit A' in the case for the prosecution. We are in Hell. Hell is the creation of Satan's armies of darkness, and is designed to ensnare our souls. We are the primary, indispensable weapon of Satan's armies in his war against God. Yet, by the same token, we are also God's trump card: a simple but thunderous 'No' to Satan is all it takes for God to win the bet, for all bets to be eternally off, and for our souls to be saved forever.

Coming down a level, from the esoteric to the exoteric, where the ground is firmer: All this pertains to the Baconian, Cartesian, Crowleyean, Chardinian, and 'Luciferian' quest for knowledge-as-power (and the resulting worship of knowledge) that has now fully metastasised into 21st century 'Science', i.e. the new world religion of scientism with its Church of Big Pharma by way of military-medical industrialisation (see the Afterword).

Just under 400 years ago (1637), Descartes' *cogito ergo sum* came with the footnote that, since animals don't think, they don't have souls either (Descartes regarded them as 'natural automata', machines without sentience, like Dick's androids). If animals are akin to natural machines, Descartes reasoned (and practised, he was an avid vivisectionist), they don't deserve—or require, ontologically speaking—our empathy. Similarly, Bacon's exhortation to torture Nature's secrets out of her was not metaphorical but literal. The practice started with mammals (not just animals but humans too, cf. *Vice of Kings*, *Prisoner of Infinity*, *16 Maps of Hell*). It led inexorably all the way into the sub-atomic realm, where atom-smashers and Heaven-stormers struggled to strap God Himself down to the rack, and *force* Him to talk. Now the human genome is the locus for the final battle.

Powerful plant 'entheogens' (that imagined God-particle again) and other drugs 'rewire' the brain and body's chemistry, altering the structure of neurons, even creating new pathways (some advocates believe they hack into the DNA, as the mRNA 'vaccine' claims to), releasing the dancing machine elves trapped inside our molecules. They are the top-down but localised, personalised, DIY, democratisation of storming Heaven that began a long, long time ago, in a Garden far, far away. There is no further recourse, on seeing this structural self-sabotage and its consequences, besides cell-deep remorse and the corresponding attrition and atonement. Existence in its natural, untortured form is like God: it cannot ever be known, save by unconditional surrender to it and assimilation by it. We know God, and Nature, only when there is neither knower nor known (hence no more knowledge), only life, unleashed from the torture chamber of 'technique'.

In December 1980, Dick wrote a simple but profound formula:

> Compassion (Mileid) is a blend of sorrow and love. Thus it is the nexus between sorrow and joy—joy entering because love leads to God … The way of the cross now makes sense to me. I understand why Jesus had to die and in the way he did, if he was to be the gate (way) to the Father.
>
> (2011, p. 664)

It is ironic, then, that the human endeavour, since that time, has been to do everything possible to avoid ending up in a similar spot to Jesus, nailed to the cross of Matter; and that the attempts to flee death and storm Heaven have entailed a precise inversion of that act of ultimate surrender: the attempt to persecute Matter into submission, and reduce it to 'pure essence'.

The week before he discovered the Jesus solution, Dick wrote the following passage:

> Love is a wish that the other, and not-you, exist; love guarantees the existence of what is not under your will—free of your will; this is true creation. He desires something other than him to exist and be itself. We truly are not him. Agape and creating are one and the same. It is not the desire for union; it is a desire to see something be on its own, its own self; each separate self is a *universe*! A world! God adores you because he adores beauty. Something that exists

on its own is beautiful; this is the ultimate beauty, that it be free …
Love lets go/forgets. Love curtails itself, withdraws. But if the created separate thing (einai) returns *of its own accord*—love triumphs
over love. Love is love for itself alone, and not for what it can do
(create). The prodigal son: if the separate thing desires to return and
forfeit its einai, then it must be love, too; and the two—God and his
creation—are joined.

(2011, p. 661)

Dick might have done well to have stopped his exegeting there, because
it was as close to an answer as he would ever get. Dick's insight has
two primary applications in the context of *Big Mother*. First, the spirit
of loving a thing and wishing it to be fully separate from itself is the
ideal of maternal love. Better said, it is *the only way* mother-love can be
anything other than the Munchausen-esque smothering of the child's
(masculine) spirit. Dick's description of God's love, therefore, is also
his unconscious lament for the healthy maternal attachment he was
denied, the lack of which kept him bound inside the false body of Big
Mother ('Sophia-as-Valis') until he died. The Empire that never ended
was the body-psyche of his mother.*

Second, with his formula of salvation through compassion, Dick is
describing the principle by which Lucifer's fall laid the groundwork
for—made both possible and necessary—Christ's resurrection, cour-
tesy of the Ahrimanic oppression of Empire (the crucifixion). In there,
then—within the nexus between sorrow and joy that is God's love for
Creation—is the formula for all of human existence. It is all we can ever
know, and all we ever need to know.

---

*Sometime later in the *Exegesis*, Dick describes 'the AI voice as a woman reading a narrative text, and as she read aloud, the universe—our world—comes into being' (2011,
p. 867). Then later: 'My sister. Oh JHWH—my sister. I meant to write Savior … The AI
voice itself took me over—as in 3-74—and wrote "sister". Thus it identified itself at last;
it told me who it is' (2011, p. 894). VALIS is Dick's twin sister who, he believed, died prematurely because Dick stole her share of mother's milk!

CHAPTER 19

The serial killer vs. the people: The techniques of Satanism

*T*he generation of the ideology of the atomised human is the so-called *'individual'. The individual human is one that is increasingly alienated from a direct experience of his own soul and body, as forming part of a communal body, or tribe.*

Paradoxically, this atomisation leads to the inception of a 'mass-man', via the creation of a mass-mind. Today, human individuals experience themselves as existing within a larger body of humanity, while simultaneously having less and less of a direct relationship to that body (community).

The creation of the mass and the creation of (the idea of) the individual arose simultaneously, are mutually dependent, and, if closely scrutinised, strangely synonymous. Why? Because the 'mass-mind' is the only possible configuration of the unnaturally individualised human.

* * *

The external structures imposed by technique can no longer, by themselves, modify the components of a society; here the internal influence of technique on the human being becomes decisive.

> Henceforth, every component of civilization is subject to the law
> that technique is itself civilization. Civilization no longer exists
> of itself. Every activity—intellectual, artistic, moral—is only a
> part of technique. This fact is so enormous and unpredictable
> that we are simply unable to foresee its consequences.
>   —Jacques Ellul, *The Technological Society*

The natural mind (like Oshana's enlightenment) cannot be understood, only experienced. Yet it can only be experienced by the removal
of/uncoupling from the artificial mind (Steiner's Ahrimanic double).
Hence, we may have little choice but to try and understand this infiltration, in order *not* to have to experience it! In my experience, the
simplest, most direct way to understand the artificial mind is by
observing how it operates, by looking at the anti-natural landscapes
it creates. As I have argued, the technological environment of 'Big
Mother' is the inevitable outcome of the ascension of the technical
over the organic, which is to say, in the language of Jacques Ellul,
human behaviour that adheres to learned *techniques* rather than spontaneous impulse.

The question of how much a mechanised society is consciously engineered by human technocratic elites, and how much it emerges 'organically' (mechanically) out of the technocratic mindset, is one that causes
a great deal of division within the current 'nöösphere'. I believe this to
be a false dichotomy, however, an unnecessary imposition of either/
or reasoning, in what is demonstrably a case of both/and. Nonetheless, the idea of shadowy puppet masters attempting (and to a degree
succeeding) to direct human society and human history from behind
the scenes is, I think, a necessary one. This is not only because the evidence supports it, but also as a place-keeper that points to a deeper,
darker reality, one that is also much subtler, and therefore far too easily
overlooked.*

Conspiratorial awareness is the first step to piercing the membrane of the mainstream delusion that history is something that 'just
happens', through a combination of random factors, human greed,

---

*Conspiracy debunkers are almost always mainstream-propaganda believers, to some
degree at least, because the belief that 'conspiracy theories' are kooky comes from the
mainstream. The problem today is that there is also a mainstream body of 'conspiracy
theory' that is its own form of propaganda. I will refer to this later.

ambition, and incompetence, due to natural forces and systemic problems. This is naïve, but then so, to a lesser degree, is the sort of conspiratorial awareness that puts all the blame on generation-spanning schemes of human groupings (some of which *can* be named, because they are quite open about their plans). These groups, it is true to state, have learned, to a disturbing degree, how to manipulate nature, human and otherwise, and direct it towards specific ends. But while this is, as I say, an essential element in understanding the technological society, it falls short of meeting the requirements of *an original causal factor*.

To give just one example: 'the serial killer'. In most cases, to this day, serial killers are viewed as lone agents acting out personal pathologies. They are outliers whose ability to pass within decent society is no more than a cunning means to gratify their depraved desires. Yet a closer examination of many, if not most, of the better-known serial killer cases reveals something quite different. These predators are often unusually intelligent, socially high-functioning, and sometimes even well-placed within society. Their actions are often facilitated and protected by law enforcement agencies (incompetence is rarely adequate to explain this). Most importantly of all, in many if not most cases, the evidence indicates that these killers do not act alone, and/or are not guilty of all of the acts attributed to them (and in some cases, such as Albert DeSalvo, the supposed Boston Strangler, may be entirely innocent). John Wayne Gacy, David Berkowitz, Henry Lee Lucas, Ted Bundy, Richard Ramirez, Robert Pickton, Jeffrey Dahmer, the Long Island killings, the Hillside Stranglers, Elmer Wayne Henley, all appear to have worked with others and/or were convicted of murders they couldn't have done. Nor is this list anything like comprehensive: I refer the virgin reader to Dave McGowan's *Programmed to Kill: The Politics of Serial Murder* for a broad overview. McGowan's position is summed up succinctly towards the end of the book:

> Rather than the profile of a lone predator, driven by his own internal demons, we find instead a profile of controlled assassins and con-trolled patsies, conditioned and programmed by a variety of intel-ligence fronts, including military entities, psychiatric institutions, and Satanic cults ... The vast majority of serial killer chroniclers are, at best, misguided. Some are undoubtedly peddling deliberate disinformation. Some writers, like some law enforcement officials,

seem to have devoted their entire careers to misrepresenting the true nature of serial murder, mass murder, assassination, and other high-profile crimes.

(McGowan, pp. 310–311)

I would argue that the distinction between lone predator driven by internal demons and controlled assassin deployed by covert organisations is as blurry as that between a psychopath's various personalities. While these killers rarely act alone, there may be cases in which they *believe* they do, having issued forth as 'lone wolves' from military and intelligence programmes via the intentional inducement of dissociative-identity-disorders (known in conspiracy circles as 'trauma-based mind control'—an area rife with sloppy reporting and disinfo).

If we pull out still further, it may be seen that seemingly disparate, unconnected serial murders form part of what looks a hell of a lot like a much larger operation, one that ties organised crime groups (sex and drug trafficking) to the domestic psychological warfare programmes of US military and intelligence agencies, with ties to the Phoenix Program started in Vietnam and the CIA's MKULTRA programme. As researcher Mae Brussell said in 1974:

What we are now experiencing is the importation of the dreaded 'Operation Phoenix' program into the United States ... Through various created and manipulated acts of violence, the only 'solution' to 'chaos, anarchy, and senseless violent acts' will be a police state ... We can expect the planned terrorization of the U.S. population to escalate rapidly'.

(McGowan, p. 307)

The CIA-trained death squads in Central America also followed a similar template to the Phoenix Program, and are perhaps more widely recognised by the general media. As Noam Chomsky reported in *What Uncle Sam Really Wants*, victims of these terror regimes are

decapitated ... their heads are placed on pikes and used to dot the landscape ... disembowelled ... their severed genitalia are stuffed into their mouths ... wombs are cut from their bodies and used to cover their faces ... children ... are dragged over barbed wire until their flesh falls from their bones, while parents are forced to watch.

(Chomsky, pp. 39–40)

Baroque scenes of carnage, now familiar to the point of contempt to aficionados of Nordic noir, are arranged. For example, a scene staged by the US-trained Salvadoran National Guard consisted of

> three children, her mother and her sister sitting around a table, each with its own decapitated head placed carefully on the table in front of the body, the hands arranged on top 'as if each body was stroking its own head' … A large plastic bowl filled with blood was tastefully displayed in the center of the table.
>
> (Chomsky, p. 39)

When imported into the US, such operations are not just discreet acts of domestic warfare with military motivations, but part of much larger long-term social engineering goals, as Brussell observed, for spreading terror through a population in order to soften it up to increased levels of police action, legal crackdown, and technological surveillance which it would otherwise have instinctively resisted.

One of the clearest indications of famous serial killer involvement in these organised crime/military operations is the recurring element of satanic cult affiliations (Son of Sam, the Night Stalker, Henry Lee Lucas, the Long Island killer, Charles Manson, Ted Bundy, Jeffrey Dahmer, Robert Berdella, Robin Gecht, and the 'Ripper crew'). The practice of Satanism is so commonly linked to the serial killer's modus operandi that it is now a trope of fiction; what is far less publicised—or understood—is the utility of satanic ritual murder to the methods of psychological warfare that makes this occult element anything but incidental, arbitrary, or frivolous. Somewhat less easy to plead ignorance about is the connection of Satanism to organised crime and drug cartels. McGowan writes:

> There is a very real possibility that an underground network of Satanic cults has largely replaced the Mafia's 'Murder Incorporated' as America's premier murder-for-hire organization … Consider the case of Thomas Creech, a member of a nationwide biker gang that was heavily involved in drug trafficking and cult rituals. In 1975, Creech admitted to forty-two contract killings committed on behalf of the gang. Many of the murders had been performed, he said, as ritual human sacrifices. According to Creech's account, his forty-two 'hits' only qualified him for eighth place among the gang's contract killers. Consider also the case of Bernard Hunwick

of Dade County, Florida. Following his arrest in 1981 for a series
of murders, he confessed to police that he was the leader of a 'hit
squad' that had committed at least 100 additional contract killings.

(McGowan, p. 310)*

Unfortunately, as David Berkowitz ('Son of Sam') wrote to Maury Terry
(*The Ultimate Evil*): 'the public will never, ever truly believe you, no mat-
ter how well your evidence is presented'. Shortly before his execution,
Ted Bundy told an interviewer:

> The really scary thing is that there are a lot of people who are not
> in prison, a lot of people who are not in prison, who were far more
> successful than I. [S]ome group of people is being so obvious about
> it, and they are still getting away with it.
>
> (Michaud and Aynesworth, 2019, p. 309)

Henry Lee Lucas: 'All across the country, there's people just like me, who
set out to destroy human life … No one wants to believe the cult story.
The TV people cut it out. The writers don't write about it' (McGowan,
p. 69, 88). Instead, they are more likely to quote MKUltra subcontractor
Dr. Louis Jolyon West, assuring the readers of the *LA Times* about 'the
Hillside strangler': 'It would be most unlikely to find this done by more
than one person … this type is almost always the work of a single person'[96] (McGowan, p. 171).

The so-called Hillside strangler turned out to be two men, ironically—
Kenneth Bianchi and Angelo Buono Jr.—though there were no doubt
more involved. The truth—as is so often the case with advanced disinformation—is the exact inverse of West's statement: what we have been
indoctrinated by the media to accept as the random acts of unconnected
serial killers driven by personal pathology are in fact targeted acts of

---

*California, Texas, and Florida are the states which saw the majority of serial murders in
the period between 1969 and 1999. As Dave McGowan points out in *Programmed to Kill*,
these states were also 'rife with satanic cult activity. They are also, coincidentally or not,
the three points through which virtually all of the drugs trafficked through Mexico and
central and South America enter the United States. [L]aw enforcement officials have spoken of an organized crime pipeline that moves many of the drugs entering Texas to the
city of Chicago, Illinois—which could help explain the recurrent phenomenon of spree
and serial killers stalking that city' (McGowan, p. 205n).

murder by an organised crime network with a number of seemingly disparate but complementary motives.

* * *

> It was inobtrusive at first, it was something that kind of grew on me, that began to visualize and fantasize about more violent things. By the time I realized how powerful it was, I was in big trouble. [L]et's say the late winter, early spring of '69. It's where we're starting to see this entity begin to reach the point where it was necessary to act out. No longer just read books, or masturbate, or fantasize, but to actually begin to stalk, to look … The more deeply I got into this, the stronger, the more dominant and stronger this voice became. I felt captive of this whole part of myself … More or less, it takes over the whole, it takes over the basic consciousness mechanism, and more or less dictates what's going to be done … It seemed to have a sense, a voice, just like a poem has a voice or a book has a voice.
>
> —Theodore Bundy, last interview,
> with Dr. Dorothy Otnow Lewis

To a trained and unflinching eye, satanic practices are central to how the technocratic state (of mind) functions, namely, by employing terror— above and beyond its uses for more conventional warfare—as central to a *technique* that is indistinguishable from occult ritual. Magical ritual, as Ellul points out, 'may even be the origin of techniques' (Ellul, p. 64), meaning it is the first example of the use of technique for social organisation. Like all techniques, magic ritual consists of *practices performed for specific results*. In this case, the results defy, and aim to transcend, if not the laws of nature then the accepted rules of society, by going against not merely social etiquette but what is considered *human nature*. (Hence the extremity of the acts performed.)

Serial killers, as well as high-level social influencers like Jimmy Savile or Jeffrey Epstein, are often referred to as 'monsters'. There are two reasons that make this designation necessary: a) it is essential to the mainstream cover-story to assert that these murderous individuals are positioned *outside* of society, and even somehow uncoupled from humanity; b) it is central to the modus operandi of Satanism, which is to establish, through aberrational acts, *a clear line of demarcation* between the practitioner and the human herd. (Monster is code for 'not-human'.)

The serial killer mythos turns the individual into the threat and the collective into the victim. The message of these crimes (and how they are represented in the media) is: it could be *you*, because it could be anyone. The serial predator, on the other hand, is a freak of both nature and society. This acts to conceal, by inverting, the reality that it is we, as individual humans, who are the victims of the monster of 'the mass', which is an instrument of 'the state' (the machine). And that the machine-like 'state' has taken possession of the mass by giving it its *mind*.

The designation of 'monster' suggests that by behaving aberrationally the serial killer-type isolates himself, not just from mainstream society, but from any kind of human connection. In fact, to the extent that a serial predator is part of an occult, criminal, or intelligence operation, one that involves satanic practices common to all its members (to varying degrees, whether committed individually or in a group), the acts of evil being committed, that render the perpetrator 'subhuman' in the eyes of the public, are also what *bind* them to a rarefied group with aspirations towards '*superhuman*' status. This is true whether we are speaking of Mexican drug cartels, ancient sorcerers, devil-worshipping child traffickers, military-intelligence factions, or elite celebrity circles.

In Dostoyevsky's *Crime and Punishment*, Raskolnikov tried to place himself among the Napoleonic over-class through the act of murder. His conscience betrayed him, and his empathic identification with his victims delegated him to the fate of the criminal, confined to the ranks of the 'under-class'.* The arch-individualist Ayn Rand saw parallels between the serial killer 'type' and her own 'superman', specifically in the 19-year-old William Hickman, who was found guilty of killing and dismembering a 12-year-old girl and hanged in 1928. While acknowledging

---

* This was not explicit in the book, and it was certainly not Dostoyevsky's message; but it is a subtext that its author developed in his later explorations of nihilistic murderers, in *The Possessed* and *The Brothers Karamazov*. It is worth noting that Raskolnikov's decision to murder the old pawnbroker, and so remove the obstacles to his own success, is cemented by the letter he receives from his *mother*. The letter concerns the family's financial problems, and his sister Dunya's choice to marry for money, and sends 'Roddy' into a feverish double-bind from which violence becomes his only escape (see Laing, 1969, pp. 146–153). After he kills the old lady, her much younger half-sister, Lizaveta, arrives, and he kills her too, in the murder that really undoes him. Dostoyevsky may have been suggesting that Raskolnikov's murder was fuelled by sublimated rage against his mother and, even less consciously, against his sister.

Hickman's degeneracy, she also admired him for having 'the true, innate psychology of a Superman ... a man who really stands alone, in action and in soul [and] has no organ for understanding, the necessity, the ... importance of other people' (Bell-Villada, p. 65). Hickman was the inspiration for Danny Renahan, the protagonist of Rand's first attempt at a novel ('The Little Street', unfinished; he murders a pastor), as well as perhaps her most famous character, Howard Roark, in *The Fountainhead*. Rand's books have been hugely influential, mostly on young men of grand ambition. Significantly, Rand quotes Hickman as describing himself as 'like the State: what is good for me is right'.

It is impossible to ignore this strange fact: that the serial-killer-type is regarded, from a certain perspective—both profanely in popular culture (witness the cult of Hannibal Lecter) and esoterically, in the elitist philosophies of cultural movers and shakers such as Rand, Crowley, or Havelock Ellis—as an expression of supreme individualism. Well ahead of his time, Ellis identified sexual deviations as merely variations of common heterosexual practices. He coined the term 'erotic symbolism', referring to the displacement of the procreative sexual urge onto *another* object, be it a same-sex partner for homosexuals (a term Ellis is also credited with coining), an animal in acts of bestiality, or an item of clothing for a fetishist. (In other words, any kind of sexual focus that is unhitched from natural biological function.)

Ellis extended his form of radical tolerance to *all* forms of deviation, and then he took it one step further. He proposed that such deviations were both an expression of and a means to the most *advanced* kind of human individuation. Specific to this current exploration, in volume 5 of *Studies in the Psychology of Sex*, Ellis described pain, 'as a state of intense emotional excitement [that] may, under a great variety of special circumstances, become an erotic symbol and afford the same relief as the emotions normally accompanying the sexual act'. For Ellis, both sadism and masochism were valid forms of erotic symbolism. '[A]mid the infinite possibilities of erotic symbolism', he wrote, 'the individual may evolve an ideal which is often, as far as he knows and perhaps in actuality, *an absolutely unique event in the history of the human soul*' (emphasis added). Since this was back in the day when homosexuality was against the law, Ellis, like Kinsey, is often seen as a social as well as sexual liberator. The manner in which he mixed difficult-to-parse technical language with purple prose that was unmistakably eulogistic was an effective way to conceal an apparent avocation of *every kind* of sexual pathology, no matter how criminal, under the rubric of science-based social liberation.

'It is this mighty force', he wrote, 'which lies behind and beneath the aberrations we have been concerned with, a great reservoir from which they draw the life-blood that vivifies even their most fantastic shapes'. Erotic symbolism, Ellis argued, allows for the development and isolation of unusual sexual tendencies which 'normally arise on the basis of sexual selection'. Since these extreme expressions represent 'the utmost pathological aberrations of the sexual instinct which can be attained or conceived', they also represent *a unique form of human development outside of the collective.*[97] The further humans deviated from Nature, Ellis argued, the closer they approached true individuality. And despite such deviations also being societal taboos that might be subject to criminal prosecution, Ellis saw them as atavistic expressions of a mighty force that linked human beings, not only to their ancestors, but to their *souls*:

> We have forgotten that all these impulses which to us seem so unnatural ... were all beliefs and practices which, to our remote forefathers, were bound up with the highest conceptions of life and the deepest ardors of religion. [T]he phenomena of erotic symbolism can scarcely fail to be profoundly impressive to the patient and impartial student of the human soul. They often seem absurd, sometimes disgusting, occasionally criminal; they are always, when carried to an extreme degree, abnormal. But of all the manifestations of sexual psychology, normal and abnormal, they are the most specifically human. *More than any others they involve the potently plastic force of the imagination. They bring before us the individual man, not only apart from his fellows, but in opposition, himself creating his own paradise. They constitute the supreme triumph of human idealism* [emphasis added].

Translation: one man's monster is another man's superman.

* * *

> Technique cannot be otherwise than totalitarian ... When technique has fastened upon a method, everything must be subordinated to it ... Technique is a means of apprehending reality, of

acting on the world, which allows us to neglect all individual differences, all subjectivity.

—Jacques Ellul, *The Technological Society*

To sum up this unorthodox reading of the ghost-written history of serial killers: aberrational violence and other acts of evil, when incorporated into the most extreme kinds of occult ritual, are the appliance of *technique*, taken to its most anti-natural extreme, that of the destruction of human life for the gaining of personal power. Eating human babies is the most baroque image of the satanic ritual, both in fiction and in fact (who knows what Ellis would have had to say about that 'erotic symbol'?). *Satanism in its essence is the techniques of evil, converging on the human body.* It is the means not only to set the practitioner apart from mainstream society, but to secure for themselves membership within a *secret* society whose values are *the exact inverse* of those being sold to the larger body of humanity.

All of this is a far cry from how the mainstream media depicts Satanism in its relation to criminal and cult activities, and consequently from how most people view it (including the average conspiracy theorist). In a technological society, where the medium trumps the message and where technique is the end of every means, media representations necessarily shape our understanding of anything outside our direct experience. The way Satanism is depicted, both in fiction and in supposedly factual reportage—most specifically satanic cults involved in extreme violence—largely determines how we understand it, and how seriously we take it. Why is it the subject of Satanism hardly ever gets 'serious' treatment in the mainstream media, outside the tired old 'satanic panic' framing as Christian (or 'alt-right') mass hysteria?

This question applies equally in the arts and entertainment field as in journalism. In the latter, if Satanism is treated as real, it is usually by tabloids that milk the subject for its sensationalist value. For the former, when it is used as fodder for fiction, it is almost invariably in B-movies (or very bad A-movies), pulp novels, and trash TV shows.[98] Our association with stories of ritualistic murders is, accordingly, with *poor* technique: with garish special effects, shabby storytelling, bad acting or purple prose. This association translates seamlessly to our view of Satanism as a *practice*: like the media that informs us about it, it seems garish, absurd, and fundamentally unbelievable. The idea of satanic cults sacrificing virgins, despite the actual horror of crimes committed in the context of an alleged 'serial killer' with an occult interest in murdering co-eds (whether it's David Berkowitz, Ted Bundy, Henry Lee Lucas, Ed Kemper, or Richard Ramirez), strikes people as laughable. They are convinced at *some* level that such occult techniques could never work, and that only an imbecile or a maniac would try to apply them. We accept that millions of Catholics practice rituals (regardless of our own belief in them), and we are aware of countless psychopaths among us, some of whom belong to groups or gangs, capable of committing terrible evil for pleasure and profit. Yet when the two realities come together in our minds, something fails to compute.

We are even aware that the two worlds *do* meet, and merge, in areas such as sex, drug, and child trafficking, pornographic movies (including child porn and snuff films), and murder. We know of Mexican drug cartels that have been ritualistically kidnapping and decapitating women in the thousands for decades. But the spell of the lone, crazed individual stalking the streets, being hunted by the noble lawman, remains. The most essential point I wish to make here is that there *is* a method to the madness of Satanism, to transgression-as-terrorism, and to consciousness-altering-through-violence. And that it is a method, a technique, that, at its deepest, most obscure level, has everything to do with Satan, i.e. with the ancient and invisible powers and principalities of evil.

Ironically, I would say that this is something known to all of us, atavistically, in our bones. The problem is in bringing it up to a *conscious* level without losing the plot, being able to think, talk, and write about it in such a way that the medium is congruent with the message. Few souls have the sensitivity and the stomach (a rare combo) to manage it, and instead we get Alex Jones' *Info Wars* and QAnon as the only bulwark against the gutless (though often as not witting) sophistry of 'satanic panic', 'false memory syndrome', and 'true crime' accounts of good vs. evil. The more mainstream conspiracy 'analysis' of the alternate media is either done by professional disinformation artists or useful idiots who specialise in believing things they do not understand. Since their accounts are not grounded in understanding or sober expression, when we hear them, their beliefs appear groundless. Essentially they are, because, as Stevie Wonder sang it, 'When you believe things you don't understand, you suffer'. People who believe true facts without any real understanding of them become deranged; they turn facts into a garbled narrative that is as good as disinformation, and every bit as effective as the mainstream debunking (medium is message). All of this is part of a design, one more, little-understood but highly effective *technique*.[99]

What is blinding people is a fatal lack of vision. That, and the most basic (oldest) technique of psychological and social control there is: totem and taboo. Respect for human life and (above all) for the social order (decorum, law and order, essentially for our own comfort or for a 'safe space'), not only demands that acts of evil never be committed by us, but that they are not even *thought about*, imagined, or understood, even while they are being consumed endlessly via entertainment media. People who need to identify themselves as 'good' in relation to society cannot allow themselves to *imagine* (empathically) what drives a psychopath. They can't contemplate how it might feel to commit vicious and wanton acts of brutality against other human beings. To do so—to allow for sufficient affinity for evil to understand it—would make them evil in their own minds.

Consequently, most socialised humans cannot consider that such acts as performed by serial predators might be motivated by anything other than sheer dementia, by monstrosity; that there might be some *obscure gain* for the individual willing to cross that human line and enter into a parallel universe. In that parallel state, the serial predator carries the awareness of being a predator among prey, a wolf among sheep, a higher, deadlier species than the rest of the herd. Yet secretly, the sheep envy him, because the experience of having absolute power and control over our environment and over everything in it is what part of *all* of us wants.

As socialised human beings we are unable—due to that conditioning—to access this awareness. We fail to see that we walk always among wolves, that we are trapped inside a system *run* by wolves, and forever confined to the lower class of victim-prey: a subspecies.

CHAPTER 20

Satan's boomerang: Monsters, heroes, and victims

*T*he foetus in the womb is an extension of the mother's body. The Ahrimanic double grows out of that identification.

The child (and the adult) becomes, through the co-opting of a natural
identification meant to be temporary, an extension of the mother's psyche. The
Ahrimanic double thereby enters into full human occupation.

The natural mind is the awareness of the original soul, and of the creative
Spirit, our Father who art in Heaven, that generated the foetus to begin with
(the seed). The natural mind can only incarnate if and when a human being
separates from the maternal psyche and pushes out the foreign implant of the
Ahrimanic double—whichever comes first.

Which is the cause and which is the effect? Neither is neither. Salvation cannot be attained through will, only via divine fiat. Through grace.

* * *

> The state has no more real choice than the worker on the assembly line; it is led to the technical society by the very terms of the problem.
>
> —Jacques Ellul, *The Technological Society*

All of the above was an unexpectedly involved digression, intended merely as an example. In the process of unpacking the example, it has somehow evolved into something much closer to the spine of the exquisite corpse of our thesis. It was meant to illustrate something that I think is true *throughout* all the conspiracy data: beneath the necessary revision of the official history which we are being sold, there is a *deeper* layer still, namely, that which is *moving* these occult groups to attempt a manipulation of history, via the conversion of a plenitude of techniques known as 'social engineering'. At this deeper level, there exists a still deeper form of pathology, of which the 'puppet masters' (we must assume) are mostly oblivious, and victims of.

Ellul writes, 'The individual who is a servant of technique must be completely unconscious of himself. Without this quality, his reflexes and his inclinations are not properly adapted to technique' (Ellul, p. 138). And: 'True technique will know how to maintain the illusion of liberty, choice, and individuality; but these will have been carefully calculated so that they will be integrated into the mathematical reality merely as appearances!' (Ellul, p. 139). The serial killer attempts to embody the state—*is* an embodiment of the state—by becoming a 'pure', unconscious force, indistinguishable from a machine whose actions are predetermined and driven only by necessity. It is here that the premise of Satan/Ahriman, of controlling invisible entities, becomes useful, perhaps even necessary, as a means of introducing a more rarefied, or metaphysical, level of conspiracy and control.

> [T]echnical progress tends to be brought about according to a geometric progression … Thus, almost without deliberate will, by a simple combination of new data, incessant discoveries take place everywhere; and whole fields are opened up to technique because of the meeting of several currents … Technique reigns alone, a blind force and more clear-sighted than the best human intelligence … A hybrid but not sterile being, and capable of self-generation, technique traces its own limits and fashions its own image.
>
> (Ellul, pp. 91, 94)

This blind force leads inexorably to a technocratic oligarchy that refers to cybernetics, and a host of related techniques, to measure human behaviour, determine what moves human groups, and *apply* this social science by turning it into technique. It thereby hopes to regulate the system that it has mapped and convert it into (the equivalent of) *a living machine*. As Daniel Bell wrote in *The Coming of Post-industrial Society* (1976, i.e. almost *50 years* ago):

> In 1947, Norbert Wiener published his *Cybernetics*, which spelled out the principles of self-regulating mechanisms and self-adjusting systems. If the atom bomb proved the power of pure physics, the combination of the computer and cybernetics has opened the way to a new 'social physics'—a set of techniques, through control and communications theory, to construct a *tableau entière* for the arrangement of decisions and choices. In those years, the basic relationships between science and government were laid out ... The rise of the new elites based on skill derives from the simple fact that knowledge and planning—military planning, economic planning, social planning—have become the basic requisites for all organized action in modern society. The members of this new technocratic elite, with their new techniques of decision-making (systems analysis, linear programming, and program budgeting), have now become essential to the formulation and analysis of decisions on which political judgments have to be made.
>
> (Bell, pp. 347, 362)

Since all this 'computing' both provides the specifics of the problem and formulates the solution, the nature of technocratic rule, though apparently (and actually) oligarchic, is also more or less automatic. Just as decisions within a corporate environment have until recently been wholly based on profit (things have become more complicated with identity politics, not to mention 'the Great Reset'), hence not decisions but *calculations*, there is less and less room, or need, for human agency within the rule of technocracy. The levers that regulate the machine become a higher kind of cog within it.

> The combination of man and technique is a happy one only if man has no responsibility ... Man must have nothing decisive to perform in the course of technical operations; after all, he is the source

of error ... In the same way that military machines condition strategy, organizational and other techniques condition the structure of
the modern state ... The state is no longer caught between political
reality and moral theories and imperatives. It is caught between
political reality and technical means. The problem is to find the
state form most adequate to the application of the techniques the
state has at its disposal.

(Ellul, pp. 132–133, 277)

In *Neoliberalism and Political Theology*, Carl Raschke condenses this rise
of *techne* to the throne of Leviathan in a few deft strokes:

The history of 'high modernism' has been the irreversible replacement of *mētis* [contextualized understanding] with *epistêmê* [rule-
based, rigorously deductive knowledge]. [T]he development of the
modernist epistemology has gone hand in hand with the evolution of *techne* ... Where *mētis* is contextual and particular, *techne* is
universal. Scientific universalism—what Kant referred to as 'pure
reason'—cannot be separated from the quest for global dominion ...
The goal of an all-encompassing *mathesis universalis*, however, was
not so much the glory of the sovereign as the creation of a new form
of human solidarity that would replace, at least in the West, the
organismic with a smooth-running Baconian *orbis terrarum machina*
('world machine'), the *corpus Christianorum* with something like
Hobbes' Leviathan.

(1999, p. 99)

'The intrinsic rationality of the natural world', Raschke adds, 'no longer emanates from divine design, but from the technological genius
of human beings themselves, who bring the *mathesis* to bear on political life itself' (1999, p. 99). Raschke cites the famous opening lines of
Hobbes's classic:

Nature (the art whereby God hath made and governs the world)
is by the art of man, as in many other things, so in this also imitated, that it can make an Artificial Animal ... For by Art is created
the great LEVIATHAN called a COMMON-WEALTH, or STATE ...
which is but an Artificiall Man.

(1999, p. 99)

'The social', Raschke concludes, 'is no longer a predicament but a project' (1999, p. 100).

The difference between the top and the bottom of this societal Leviathan is that the new technical priest-class experience a degree of (illusory) freedom (freedom from responsibility or moral concerns for others, for example, like Rand's superman), while the mechanised mass is more and more oppressed and alienated by the 'choices' being dictated to it under the guise of 'individual freedom'. (Environmentalism, for example, is introducing more and more 'ethical' requirements of the individual, from which the technocratic over-class is exempt.) This understanding diverges from the traditional conspiratorial viewpoint, insofar as the agendas being implemented no longer meet the basic criteria of 'conspiracy', being neither secret (because openly implemented in every sphere of society) nor criminal (because laws are either rewritten or cancelled out by new 'mandates' and government policies, due to 'emergency', etc.). It isn't even a case of clearly identifiable human groups conspiring (Davos, Bilderberg, World Economic Forum, etc.), though these exist. The conspiracy, such as it is, is now systemic. It includes everyone and everything inside the technocratic society, all of whom are under 'the rule of technique'.

I hasten to add that none of this is meant to imply that regular conspiracies don't continue to happen; only that, like everything else, they are subordinate (even when seemingly opposed) to the over-arching technocratic agenda. But to reach this third, deeper layer of systemic manipulation by *truly* hidden forces—to get at the *actual* conspiracy of invisible anti-human forces—requires first uncovering the *second* layer—the one that has been popularised and trivialised (and weaponised) as 'conspiracy theory'.

As Ellul writes,

> everything which is technique is necessarily used as soon as it is available, without distinction of good or evil. This is the principal law of our age ... It expresses the deep feeling of us all: 'Since it was possible, it was necessary'. Really a master phrase for all technical evolution.
>
> (Ellul, p. 99)

Technique has this 'everything is permitted' credo in common both with Satanism and 'woke' culture.

> a principal characteristic of technique ... is its refusal to tolerate moral judgments. It is absolutely independent of them and eliminates them from its domain. Technique never observes the distinction between moral and immoral use. It tends, on the contrary, to create a completely independent technical morality ... Not even the moral conversion of the technicians could make a difference. At best, they would cease to be good technicians.
>
> (Ellul, p. 97)

Moral concerns are irrelevant to technical questions, with one exception: when morality *itself* can be incorporated into a given technique and turned into an instrument of control. (Totem and taboo; examples are many and multifarious, two obvious ones being intersectionality—diversity hires, reparations, etc.—and environmentalism.) Satanism (in the sense I have discussed it here, pertaining to ritual, not in its current trendy incarnation via The Satanic Temple, as a 'secular religion' for LGBTQIA+ SJWs) applies a technique that pertains to moral inversion. It exploits not just our socially conditioned moral sense but, more importantly, the innate biological sense of goodness that is—or rather, once was—the basis for it.

Simply stated, satanic ritual as a technique of evil employs morality—specifically moral horror and repulsion—as a *lever* to prize open the human psyche, collectively and individually, and tinker with its internal parts.[100] But who or what is doing the tinkering, at the end of the day? Serial killers are given a false appearance of autonomy by the narratives they are cast to create. The actual truth reveals that they are almost wholly lacking in autonomy and are, like Deckard in *Blade Runner*, blunt instruments of a corporate agenda, replicants programmed to hunt and kill their own kind. The narrative created around these killers is one of autonomous predatory agents with superhuman capacities that strangely complement, as well as derive from, their moral vacuity. The reality is very different. One might even say that the serial killer—as a media image—approximates how the higher-level sociopaths (the cartel leaders and the technicians of evil, in their various forms) wish to see *themselves*, as a higher species directing (in Ellis' words) 'the potently plastic force of the imagination' to form 'the individual man, not only apart from his fellows, but in opposition' to them, thereby 'creating [their] own paradise'.

A Hell on Earth, with nothing human in it.

* * *

> I loved the darkness, the darkness would excite me, it really was
> sort of my ally.
>
> —Theodore Bundy

Ted Bundy's involvement with Satanism has been convincingly argued by the Australian author Bernard East, who corresponded over many years with two of Bundy's fellow inmates at Florida State Prison, Kenneth 'Mad Dog' McKenna (a serial murderer and contract killer) and Gerard Schaefer (serial killer and author of *Killer Fiction*). According to East, 'explanations of demonism had currency among several members of the serial killer fraternity inside Florida State Prison' (East, pp. 121–122), with Ted Bundy being no exception. East claims that, after murdering several hitchhikers in 1973, Bundy, believing his arrest was inevitable, wanted to 'secure the protection of metaphysical forces'. Via 'contacts in the pornography underworld' he met McKenna and was introduced to 'an organization known as the Church of the Process, established in 1963'. McKenna's own criminal history 'convinced Bundy that he could indeed kill with impunity provided certain guidelines were followed'. McKenna

> offered Bundy a contract to sign which would enable him to
> commit murder and avoid detection as long as he acted as a
> representative of Satan and not simply indulge his own desires.
> A ritual was enacted, with Bundy becoming a practitioner of
> Satanism. The first murder committed by Bundy under satanic
> contract was of Lynda Healy on 1 February 1974 in Seattle,
> Washington. McKenna required a victim involved in 'communi-
> cations' via the air, Healy being the reader of a ski report on local
> radio. The terms of his contract required Bundy to retain the
> clothing of victims, for offering before a Satanic altar ... Bundy
> followed directions provided by McKenna ... in the commission
> of a crime (... the type of victim chosen, the day on which the
> murder would occur, and what should be done with the victim's
> clothing).[101]

Bundy's 1974 murder of Healy, allegedly, *'was the first in which he felt no remorse afterwards, a state of being which made him delighted and one which had been thirteen years in the making'* (East, p. 55, emphasis added). The fact (if true) that Bundy was killing for well over ten years (starting in 1961) before 1974, the year of Healey, his first documented homicide, is not a matter of public record. Also, the sadistic manner in which he killed many of his victims—as if too monstrous for public consumption—has been obscured, partially by Bundy himself, but also by investigating officers (it being something few of the victims' family members would wish to know). East believes Bundy concealed the darker elements of his psychopathy to retain sympathy with his captors, and only let rip when talking to fellow killers: 'The preferred identity of Bundy backstage was of the killer as artiste knowledgeable of the various elements of occult power and hidden knowledge which can be put to service for such ends' (East, p. 115). It's ironic to consider that, as one of the two or three most notorious serial killers of the period, Bundy's 'image' had to be sanitised in order to then be sensationalised, so it could be turned into a lucrative cottage industry.

> Bundy's claim that he 'received no pleasure from harming or causing pain to the person he attacked' [was] an absolute falsehood compared to what he told [prison] friends. Sadism, meaning sexual arousal from physical suffering, humiliation, and control of the victim, is posited as being at the core of serial homicide, and that is certainly correct in [Bundy's] case ... Torture is rendered silent in some of the official discourse, the urban myth being that Bundy was not overly sadistic.
>
> (East, pp. 64–65)

The terrible reality that few members of the public are willing to contemplate is that sexual sadism and satanic technique are bound together so tightly as to be almost inseparable.* In ritualised murders of this

---

*What seems to have been Bundy's most sadistic murder, in 1974, was also the most explicitly a satanic ritual. According to McKenna, 'Bundy wanted Donna Manson to agree to become a spiritual guardian over the cave; applying obscure logic, he is said to have believed that through physical torture the cave would become an area subject to metaphysical protection—her "shade" would remain in the area beyond death to prevent it from being accidentally discovered ... Manson is still listed as a missing person' (East, p. 65).

sort, so the practitioners believe, the victim's soul, or at least their life force, is 'harvested'—via pain and terror—as a means of powering the satanic machinery which the killer (and the forces and factions behind him) wishes to assemble. A feeling of being intensely alive is generated by the act of extinguishing the life force of others, in a kind of energy transference or vampirism. And in fact, drinking his victims' blood is something Bundy claimed to his prison confederates, and openly acknowledged, briefly, while in captivity in February 1978, when he called himself a 'vampire … speaking in a literal sense, not a metaphorical one' (East, p. 127).

The horror and remorse that came after his acts, in roughly those first 13 years, indicates the recurring re-emergence of Bundy's ordinary, everyday consciousness, once the adrenalin 'high' of violence had passed. Over time, the feeling of remorse was reduced until it was no longer an issue. This suggests the gradual annihilation of a core-self, of anything resembling affective empathy, of any conscious connection to the soul, and its replacement by *an invading entity* being fed, fattened, and given full occupational rights over the body, via the satanic techniques being applied. East suggests this process was even observable on the outside:

> Several people who had contact with [Bundy] noticed profound physiological manifestations and changes, including the appearance of a white line … across his face during his 'speculations' about [his] crimes … Also his blue eyes would turn noticeably darker and his voice change to take on a 'stony' quality … Beyond these disturbing physical effects there was an aroma. [One legal investigator] reported seeing Bundy's face changing color and his body emitting a strange odor … 'negative electricity, and along with that came that smell' … resembling 'burning carpet' … Bundy attributed these profound physical manifestations to demonic possession. [H]e felt that as he was getting into killing, a force would come over him that made him turn savage. In other words, there seemed to be elements beyond his control.
>
> (East, pp. 113–114, 116)

A serial killer like Bundy may, in an almost literal sense, become a kind of monster. But if so: a) the true monstrousness of his actions have been strangely but strategically downplayed by the media, and even obscured entirely, even as the crimes are being sensationalised for effect; b) the

process of 'becoming a monster' is intrinsic to the acts being committed; c) this process is not restricted to serial psychopaths but central to
the militaristic mindset; as Che Guevara advocated: 'Hatred as an element of the struggle; a relentless hatred of the enemy, impelling us over
and beyond the natural limitations that man is heir to and transforming
him into an effective, violent, selective and cold killing machine' (2002,
p. 174). This is the same Che Guevara whose image adorned teenagers'
walls in the 1960s and 1970s.

It is not so much that Bundy-the-monster committed these crimes,
then, as that the crimes *made* a monster out of Bundy. What appears to
be an end was rather the means: a process of dark self-transformation
through the ruthless persistence in satanic techniques.

* * *

> In today's technical society, magical and mystical tendencies
> which traditionally were in opposition are all mutually satisfied
> by technique and hence made one. Technique fully satisfies the
> mystic will to possess and dominate. It is unnecessary to evoke
> spiritual powers when machines give much better results …
> Ecstasy is subject to the world of technique and is its servant.
> Technique, on the most significant level, integrates the anarchic
> and antisocial impulses of the human being into society.
> —Jacques Ellul, *The Technological Society*

Ahrimanic forces—in Steiner's own terms—are equivalent to Ellul's
technical mind: that is, a form of consciousness that is now directing
all human affairs, almost or perhaps entirely blindly, in predetermined
ways, to an unknown but perhaps equally predetermined end. This
machine-mind, by its very process and means of progression, creates
problems that are exponentially harder to solve, that are so configured
that only *it* can offer solutions:

> technique, in its development, poses primarily technical problems
> which consequently can be resolved only by technique … These
> problems all exceed the powers of private individuals. Technique,
> once developed to a certain point, poses problems that only the
> state can resolve, both from the point of view of finance and from
> that of power.
> (Ellul, pp. 92, 237)

So what does this 'technical mind' look like? An eyeball can only look at itself by using a mirror. That mirror is our society and culture. For example, the FBI agent or policer in a movie or TV show is usually referred to by supporting characters as 'the best there is'. This is what defines him as the hero. The goodness refers to efficiency rather than integrity. Prowess is explicitly related to *technique*, and technique is the measure of mettle. This is so fundamental to our culture that it goes unquestioned, even unnoticed. In the technical society, a man (and now a woman) *is* what he *does*. And like the good soldier (or serial killer), what he does is what he has been trained to do. He is a means to an end, and the end is one he is not privy to understanding, does not need to know.

'Man is caught like a fly in a bottle. His attempts at culture, freedom, and creative endeavour have become mere entries in technique's filing cabinet' (Ellul, p. 418). The way we all keep a close eye on time (as measured by *machines*), for example, and quantify our activities compulsively, is an obvious example of how the technical mind imprisons the natural body. Electricity is another. Our once-natural rhythms of life have been supplanted by artificial ones. Our lives are now almost wholly regulated by technical factors and considerations. Organic functions obey the mechanical.

> The more rapidly our machines operate, the more precise they must be, and the less we can allow ourselves the luxury of using them arbitrarily. This is as true of the machines we have in our houses as of the machines we meet on the street. Our movements must approach perfection to the degree that the machines approach it and continue to increase in number. Our motions are no longer entitled to express our own personalities. It suffices to take one look at distracted and panicky elderly people in the middle of a Paris street to understand that modern velocities render motion abstract and no longer tolerate imperfect motions just because they are human.
>
> (Ellul, p. 331)

Human beings have always had, and to some degree always relied on, technical abilities; but the progress of mechanisation has moved the focus from innate, instinctive abilities (which to some degree are shared by all, but which naturally develop as distinct *qualities* in different individuals) to specific, *learned* techniques. Learned technique is then used to define humans (even though anyone can learn them), and assign them a place in the collective. A technically defined individual is seen, not so much in relation to others, but in terms of how he or she fits, functionally, into the social organisation. 'He is no longer a man in a group, but an element of the group', no longer 'situated in relation to other men, but in relation to technique' (Ellul, pp. 335, 305). This is known as *specialisation*, and it has led, not only to the requisite skills to organise society, but to a form of human consciousness that is adapted to larger populations (towns and cities), to ever-higher levels of organisation and complexity, and to the values, standards, and methods that such increased technical complexity demands.

> Whenever technique collides with a natural obstacle, it tends to get around it either by replacing the living organism by a machine, or *by modifying the organism so that it no longer presents any specifically organic reaction* … This means that man participates less and less actively in technical creation, which, by the automatic combination of prior elements, becomes a kind of fate. Man is reduced to the level of a catalyst. Better still, he resembles a slug inserted into a slot machine: he starts the operation without participating in it.
>
> (Ellul, p. 135, emphasis added)

When tools become machines, men become tools. Everything is instrumentality, everything becomes means. The end of such a society is as incomprehensible as the machine to the cogs, or time to a clock. And the more incomprehensibly complex these social arrangements become, the more mechanised, the more disoriented and alienated human beings grow within them. What is still mistakenly viewed as 'culture' (especially popular culture) adapts to this—not so much cynically as automatically—by providing *compensatory forms of activity* that reduce the pressure and stress of biological organisms in an antipathetic environment.

In this degenerative process, the arts become more and more the business of an entertainment industry whose main purpose is to distract and placate the workers and keep them from losing their marbles. (Social media has now largely supplanted entertainment media; meanwhile, alcohol and drug use, including prescription drugs, continue to play an indispensable role.) Humans are addicted to stories and images of horror, pain, and suffering, not only in the form of fiction but real-life ('true crime') reporting. This fascination with destruction even extends to our own lives, in which boredom and numbness causes us to thrill to bad news—though few admit it—provided it doesn't get too close to home. Children in the past devoured grisly fairy tales because they provided relief from—by reflecting—the inchoate horror, dysfunction, and despair of their home or community environments. Today, adults locked inside a machine-regulated maze of death seek images of Hell to amuse and distract them. They have their space-cake and eat it: they get to secretly identify with the savage killer and relieve their innate rage and evil, while openly sympathising with the mass-victim, thereby affirming their goodness.

> This content is not the product of chance or of some economic form. It is the result of precise psychological and psychoanalytical techniques. These techniques have as their goal the bringing to the individual of that which is indispensable for his satisfaction in the conditions in which the machine has placed him, of inhibiting in him the sense of revolution, of subjugating him by flattering him.
>
> (Ellul, pp. 95–96)

The arts have become less and less a means for confronting reality than avoiding it. Their trivialisation and conversion into prize-propaganda for boobies required that they be entirely stripped of logical inquiry in favour of sentimentality and 'catharsis' (emotional-manipulation). Their function is to meet the growing needs of human beings locked inside an increasingly unsatisfying social arrangement, a machine world. They are cultural propaganda, not merely for distorting or rewriting history, but for delivering an implicit message. Within the true crime genre of non-fiction, HBO and Netflix documentaries, and (even) privately created podcasts, the message is always affirmative, not merely of lawmen and women—with their advanced techniques and technology—who at least *try* to stop these monsters, but of the private citizens who hunt them via the internet. Most implicitly of all, it is a *way of life* that is being affirmed, both via the monstrous attacks on it and the heroic attempts to protect it. The notion of hero in the technocratic society has sunk below even the level of blunt instrument; now being a *victim* is enough to make you a hero. The complementary pole that balances out the idea of the serial killer-as-monster is: the victim-as-hero. Merely *surviving* evil becomes the proof of goodness.

Like all binaries, the two classes reinforce one another: the more monstrous the predator, the more heroic the victim who survives it. The booby prize serves not just to placate the terrorised, but to further conceal the real agendas being pursued. These monsters are not under but *over* us, being to whatever degree employed (or at least exploited), protected, and promoted by the same technocratic structures that patronise and flatter their victims by branding them as heroes. This secret society predates (and predates!) ordinary society. There is literally a world of difference between giving into the primal urge to murder—using it to define oneself through techniques of evil—and experiencing it vicariously via the passive consumption of violent mass media. It is roughly the difference between the over- and the under-class in a technological society. The doer and the done to.*

Fascination with serial murderers, by allowing ordinary people to vicariously experience the thrill of evil, lays the ground for the subsequent experience of *conscious* complicity with murder, via the legal execution of the killer, in mass scapegoating rituals. The righteous satisfaction of 'retribution' absolves the public of their previous, *unconscious* complicity with the killer, giving them a similar, now more fully conscious release, one that can only occur via a willed possession by collective hatred of evil. ('Hate Week' in Orwell's *1984*.) The two forms of evil balance and mirror one another, a boomerang of satanic technology. There is the serial killer's brutal attack on the collective in an insane bid for total individualisation (to become a superman); then there is the ordinary man or woman's total submersion into the collective, via a shared conviction of the killer's guilt, and the public ritual of scapegoating. As René Girard wrote, violence is mimetic. The scapegoating ritual is the means by which the community (now 'the public'), rather than tear itself apart, binds itself more tightly into a mass, a mass of global villagers with pitchforks, chasing the virtual monster.

Mob rule posing as justice is the predetermined, pre-programmed reaction to psychopathic murder that aspires towards freedom.

---

*Drug-taking as an ecstatic rite (ecstasy pertains to escaping the body) has a similar function to that of vicarious release through exposure to violent mass media. It is a form of 'blood sacrifice' vouchsafed to the masses, a kind of impotent Dionysian revolt. Contrast this with the secret rituals of serial killers, sorcerer kings, and technocrats, in which blood sacrifice and bodily destruction takes on far more literal dimensions, as a means to 'liberate' primal energies.

CHAPTER 21

Killing Time: Internal Abusers,
Autists, & Psychopaths

T̲he M.O. of the impure insider is to identify and denounce impurity outside itself, and then move to eradicate it. The interloper perceives the
host as impure in relation to its own 'purity'. Its central purpose then
becomes to seek and destroy impurity, and so make a home for itself.

In fact, as a virus makes a home for itself, it destroys purity. It does not need
to do anything besides exist to achieve this. Yet it cannot exist except via the
automated 'act' of opposition to the host body which houses it.

If God made Man in His own image, what did Man make? And in whose
image?

* * *

The idea that violence is necessary to break free from the Borgian
hold of the group-mind—the matrix of cultural identity—is evidence of how our culture depends on a form of emotional and
psychological violence to impose its spell upon us.

—The author, 'Autism and the Other
(Perceptual Warfare)', 2013

While working on this book after a long period away from writing, I noticed a resurgence of simmering rage within me. It was observable with every obstacle and setback I encountered, no matter how small; anything that got in the way of my mind's purpose triggered a rage-response. When I would take a break from writing to work in the garden, I used a gas-powered strimmer to destroy the brambles, weeds, and long grass that was turning our recently cleared land back into a wilderness. Here my rage found its full expression. At one point, I remembered how, as a prepubescent child, I had gone through a public garden with a long stick, slicing the heads off daffodils with satisfaction. Evidently, something in me needed to assert its existence through the destruction of its environment, above all by the destruction of *living things*.

As I mentioned at the start of the book, the material that informs the first two chapters of *Big Mother* was originally part of a long-form essay on autism that included an in-depth look at the (somewhat tenuous but culturally promoted) parallels between autists and psychopaths. I gave special attention to the spate of school shootings that began, roughly, at the end of the 1990s with the Columbine school shootings. I researched a number of cases and reported them in detail, with special attention to Adam Lanza and Sandy Hook. Curiously, the spate of serial killings in the US that started in 1969 tailed off at almost exactly the same time that school shootings amped up (1999, though you would never know it from all the TV shows—maybe the Phoenix Program relocated to Scandinavia?).

How serial killers gave over to school shooters in so precise a fashion is beyond the scope of the present work, but suffice it to say that there is plenty of evidence that school shootings are embedded in a similar disinformation matrix as serial murders. Although I have excised all of the material about *We Need to Talk About Kevin*, Sandy Hook, and the many false narratives about school shooters, I find myself, on the home stretch of this latest work, through no conscious decision, once again devoting time, space, and energy to psychopathic killers. Apparently their relevancy to the subject—or their centrality to my own consciousness—cannot be denied. (My interest in serial killers dates back to probably as early as age 15, when I read Colin Wilson's *A Criminal History of Mankind*.)

Looking back over that 2013 material, I found several nascent questions that I am still trying to unravel. For example, I cited a 2005 series of papers by J. Arturo Silva and colleagues that suggested that some mass killers, including Jeffrey Dahmer and 'Unabomber' Theodore Kaczynski, showed evidence of being Aspergerian (AD). I quoted the now-defunct journal *Crime Times*, referring to the Silva article:

> While very few people with AD are violent, studies do suggest that the prevalence of AD may be elevated in violent criminal populations. Dahmer's treatment of his victims, they say, is consistent with the fact that individuals with AD have trouble both in 'theory of mind' (the understanding that other people have thoughts and feelings) and in distinguishing between people and objects ... Silva et al. say their characterization of a subset of serial killers as having high-functioning autism could lead to a greater understanding of the etiology [sic] of both serial homicide and autism.[102]

It takes a perfect storm of elements, social, psychological, and metaphysical, to make a Ted Bundy, an Ed Kemper, or an (alleged) Adam Lanza, a storm that begins before they are even conceived. To give an example: the spate of US serial killings that began in 1970 can be traced back to the generation born and raised in the late 1940s and early 1950s, in the period following the Second World War (also, incidentally, the period when the CIA was created and the MKULTRA programme initiated). Because so many fathers were dead, wounded, or heavily traumatised after the war, many of these children were raised by dominant, if not domineering, mothers (or grandmothers, as well as, no doubt, violently dysfunctional fathers and grandfathers). The previously cited MKUltra operative, Dr. Louis Jolyon West (described without irony by the authors of *The Only Living Witness* as 'an expert on abused children'), opined of Bundy: 'Somewhere in that man's boyhood ... a woman beat him with a stick' (Michaud and Aynesworth, 1999, p. 331). The 3-year-old Bundy, surrounding his aunt with knives while she was sleeping, also signifies latent hostility towards his mother (and/or grandmother), which perhaps could never be expressed *directly*.

This was also the period in which countless pulp novels, comic books, and magazines (e.g. *True Detective*) were on display in the local drug store, sporting extremely graphic depictions on their covers of nubile women, tied and bound, with knives at their throat or being strangled to death. Ted Bundy's claim that these images seeded his early fantasies is certainly backed up by the evidence!* The possibility Bundy never identified the original source of his rage is also evidenced by the fact that his last two phone calls, hours before his execution, were to his mother. Her last words to Bundy were, 'You'll always be my precious son' (Michaud and Aynesworth, 1999, p. 341).

The aetiology of autism indicates a similar combination of early trauma with early imprinting. Originally, theories of autism tended towards the psychogenic, as a physical condition with psychological causes. This viewpoint has been largely pushed out by the increased bias towards the (so-called) 'hard sciences', and autism is now mostly attributed to genetic and neurological factors. When environmental factors *are* allowed, they usually pertain to chemical toxins (including vaccinations) rather than the domestic or ancestral kind.** One early theory—now totally marginalised—is that autism is related to 'refrigerator mothers', women who were cold and distant, for whatever reasons, and the resultant lack of a safe or loving maternal bond. (This factor, ironically, is heavily emphasised in the genesis of the autist-psychopath in *We Need to Talk About Kevin*).

When a child is conceived from, gestated within, and born into adverse conditions—when they are deprived of the necessary energetic support from their natural family system—it is dissociation and psychic fragmentation that provides the relief. Companionship and support comes via the 'imaginary friends' or the sub-personalities that result. If the childhood conditions are sufficiently abusive to create a propensity for violence, such early traumatised, early fractured, and early imprinted children can later be 'recruited' into military service, intelligence programmes, or criminal organisations; alternatively, these individuals are compulsively drawn to such environments, by a desire to commit the kinds of violence that make them useful to the organisations, as if seeking a home.

---

*They directly inspired one serial murderer in the 1950s, Harvey Glatman, who posed as a crime magazine photographer, hired models to pose for him, bound and gagged them, took pictures of them, then raped and killed them and photographed the bodies.
**Alice Miller, a lifelong researcher into the effects of child abuse, maintained that autism is psychogenic, with early abuse as a central causal factor. What prevented this from being discovered, she claimed, was the intense fear of talking about the subject of child abuse, not only on the part of mothers and children, but also of doctors. 'No one, however, was willing to take these facts seriously', she wrote in 1991 (Miller, pp. 48–49).

In her work with many murderers suffering from dissociative identity disorder, Dr. Dorothy Otnow Lewis observed how it was common, if not universal, for early victims of abuse who later became violent offenders to have created *an internalised abuser* within themselves. This internalised abuser (IA, the shadow of AI?) that protected them as children later acted out the abuses on others. The last killer Lewis spoke with was Ted Bundy, and the way Bundy described his own 'entity' to Lewis was consistent with her understanding of DID: 'I think that there's more an integration here', Bundy told her,

> an interrelationship, which [is] when the malignant portion of my personality or consciousness, call it what you will—the entity—is more or less directing the mood and the action. I'm still on another level conscious of this, I'm not totally unconscious of, or unaware of it.
>
> (Nelson, p. 287)

Before he was executed, Bundy was charged with around 30 murders. While his body may have committed many more (East opines between 50 and a 100), based on the many anomalies of the evidence (which a number of researchers have emphasised, though you would never know it by listening to the mainstream media), it seems irrefutable that there are missing pieces that have been deliberately suppressed, whether by Bundy, by officers of the law, or by biographers and documentarians, in order to keep the narrative 'clean and tidy'. Even after a brief period looking at this anomalous evidence, it seems likely to me that: a) some of the murders attributed to Bundy were committed by others (involved with organised crime and Satanism), making Bundy wholly innocent of them and useful as a convenient 'patsy' to create a lone-killer explanation for disparate acts of organised crime (e.g. Debra Kent's murder or Carol DaRonch's attempted kidnapping, since it is virtually impossible for him to have done both);[103] b) some of them were committed with little or no memory of doing so, Bundy being fully 'possessed' (dissociated) at the time, making him at least innocent in his own mind; c) some of the killings were assisted or done as part of a team, making Bundy more like a soldier in a military operation*

---

*When asked where he got the money after his prison break escape to travel across the country and start a new life in Tallahassee, Bundy replied: 'Well, man, there's other people. Other people are in on it' (McGowan, p. 197).

(Chi Omega is a likely example; others closely linked to some of the killings are Colorado police chief Ben Meyers—undersheriff in Aspen, Colorado, who resigned after Ted Bundy escaped from Aspen jail—and serial killers Stanley Bernson and Thomas Creech; all of these men were linked to organised crime);[104] d) some of the killings were performed alone, driven by his personal demons and compulsive, degenerate desires, sourced in early abuses.

Clearly, there is not only a lot more to the alleged killings, but to Bundy himself. By the end, he may well have transformed himself into some mythical monster that simply had to be destroyed; but the process by which he became a host to that entity was a complex and tragic interweaving of good with evil and everything in-between. *Part* of Ted Bundy was evil, certainly, and that was the part that won out in the end. And Bundy, while himself not whole, was wholly (if not solely) accountable for the acts that his body committed. But it would be a mistake to assume that dissociation, psychic fragmentation, and entity possession only occur in psychopaths, or only through obvious acts of aberrational sex or violence. Contracts with invisible entities can provide many different kinds of 'benefits' to victims of abuse, some of which may even be seen as visionary gifts to humankind. The serial killer's rape, torture, and murder of 'innocents' is the flip side of the autistic geniuses' invention of Facebook, Microsoft, Tesla, or Apple Mac. Both are indispensable to the creation of a technocratic surveillance state, and as such are complementary—like the autist and the psychopath are complementary.

* * *

> I am an ontologist and an existentialist and I am willing to risk extinction in order to try authentically to be, since in this moment one has only the choice between extinguishing oneself voluntarily or fighting. I chose to fight and won, and what I won was my own soul.
>
> —Philip K. Dick, *The Exegesis of Philip K. Dick*

Another thing that got my attention back in 2013 was the parallel between autistic and psychopathic types in their relationship to objects. I noted:

> The psychopathic type regards living beings, including human ones, as objects, and treats them accordingly. Autists are known to

regard objects as living beings, and to develop relationships with them—which is usually seen as evidence of their lack of connectedness to people. Maybe the psychopathic perspective is that nothing is alive, the autistic one that everything is? In that sense, they might be said to overlap, because both fail to differentiate between forms of life or consciousness—'All is one'.

While children who grow up to become killers are often said to get started by cutting up animals, autistic children frequently bond with *inanimate* objects, and thus have a special affinity for technology (as discussed in Part I). Are we looking at two sides of a mirror? If the psychopathic type exists in a kind of dream world filled with either obstacles to destroy or objects to possess (or both), is this a defence against the overwhelming loss of identity that the autistic type (the low-functioning kind) experiences? Unable to separate their sense of self from the world around them, it is as if everything exists *except* themselves. (A fairly close match for how enlightenment is sometimes described.)

Marshall McLuhan described all forms of violence as quests for identity. And what better way for the identity-disordered psychopath to create an identity separate from the world than to treat the world (and the human being) as an object, by dismantling its parts? Nor would this only be a desire to reduce humans to automatons, to torture at will (like Descartes with his natural automata), but a need to *become* like a machine, to be impervious to all suffering and outside the limitations of society and of the flesh. All of this is driving the psychopath to become the expression of *pure technique*. In the case of my rage against the brambles, I was even *using* a machine to empower me.

My tentative conclusion in 2013 was that the *apparent* proximity between autists and psychopaths was that both, 'in their respective ways, are rejecting the culturally imposed limitations of identity, forging their own *asocial* path into and through the world'. Certainly, one of the strangest and most intriguing things about this unexpected diversion back into the realm of serial killers and other psychopaths is to discover that my identification, my affinity, is still somewhat with the 'monster', rather than the 'victim'. I view the 'monster' as I always have—as at least *somewhat* aware of the evil he is trapped inside, as at least struggling—however misguidedly—to break free of it (Ted Kaczynski is an obvious example).

The problem is that the struggle is futile and only takes them deeper *into* evil rather than through and out. In attempting to defy the psychosocial (and metaphysical) forces they feel trapped by, these killers are unconsciously submitting to higher, deeper *strata* of those same forces, becoming only dimly conscious agents of them. Gladiator-slaves made to kill for the Empire are still slaves. The idea that they at least get to die as warriors is hardly much to boast about. In the end, they are only killing their own kind, for the entertainment of an Emperor they will never get to sit beside, for whom their only value is their capacity to kill in entertaining and terrifying ways.

It's a curious fact that my whole life's 'work'—thinking, talking, writing, creating artefacts, attempting to make sense of my own existence—has involved the ongoing effort to investigate apparently good things and rebrand them as, if not actually evil, as *not*-good. It has also entailed, in a certain sense, the reverse: to look closely at evil and find ways to turn horror into understanding, compassion, and even redemption.

My strange affinity for serial killers, in fact and fiction, began in my early teens, and coincided *exactly* with an immersion in destructive cinematic fantasies of rape and murder (see *Seen and Not Seen*, *16 Maps of Hell*). With hindsight, I would say this was the period I became a witting host to the sort of murderous entity that drove Bundy and others, albeit at a much milder level. Unlike Bundy, I never acted on those corporate-created fantasies—except in my dreams. One of the factors that ensured I did not act on them was my awareness that I *had* this capacity in me, and a willingness to try and understand what it was doing there, rather than simply suppress or disown it. This process happened partially, maybe even primarily, by looking at cases of other human beings who *were* overcome by their fantasies, fully possessed by some entity, and above all, by looking *with compassion*.

And so I find myself returning to this same time, place, and subject matter, again and again, as often as it takes for some full and final resolution to occur.

* * *

> Look here, it isn't easy to take human life.
>
> —Thomas Berger, *Killing Time*

This last part of *Big Mother* is partly a text about a text (Dick's *Exegesis*) about a living text. As such, it can't be insignificant that, as I was finishing up the notes for the final chapters, reading the last pages of the *Exegesis* (a mere nine years after starting it), the other book I was reading, for simple pleasure, was Thomas Berger's *Killing Time*. *Killing Time* is about an inspired lunatic called Detweiler who kills several people (including two women), as a means of 'killing time'. The phrase has a triple meaning for Berger: the time for killing, a meaningless or motiveless activity (which the killer claims his act was), and, most difficult of all to sum up, *the eradication of Time*. It's here that the intersection with Dick's *Exegesis* becomes unmistakable. Berger's book explores the killer's mystical philosophy of 'Realisation', and includes long passages of dialogue about time, reality, God, and the nature of human beings and other objects.

The book, published in 1967, is strikingly prescient of the sort of motiveless motives for murder given by Charles Manson and his 'family'. For Manson, 'human life has no individual value. If you kill a human being, you're just killing part of yourself; it has no meaning'.[105] For family member Tex Watson, murder was like 'breaking off a minute piece of some cosmic cookie … Death is to be embraced because it exposes the soul to the oneness of the universe'.[106] André Breton's 'pure surrealist act' was shooting random passers-by on a street; Mickey Knox's rationale in *Natural Born Killers* was 'a moment of purity is worth a lifetime of lies'.

The spiritually deranged Detweiler (or inspired, it's hard to say how Berger views him) holds a similar belief. Since everything is God, one cannot kill God, only liberate humans by killing the time allotted to them. He is trying to stop time by 'Realising' his victims (shifting them from time to a timeless state). 'I could not have killed those three people without God's faith in me', he says. 'To kill Time is to know God' (1967, p. 244). Most eerily of all, Detweiler finally achieves Realisation when, during his trial, he has an experience of being in two timestreams simultaneously—an exact match for Dick's own vision, post 2-3-74!

I came upon this *before* I had begun to write about serial killers, though I was aware of being on the trail of *something*, like a cop hunting a killer or a predator its prey. I was unaware of what it was, except in the most general way. My hope, as always, was that, by arranging the pieces of the puzzle—scribbled responses in a notebook to the various books I was reading, as I pursued the avenues of inquiry that opened up—they would fit together as a piece of literature, and that this would allow for the uncovering of the truth. I knew that it was far less likely to happen the opposite way—that I would hit on the truth and then know how to finish the book! Life—or time—is rarely that straightforward.

The question of technique (introduced only after I started to read Jacques Ellul's book) is pertinent here: every writer has a technique, or a bag of them. Writing itself is a technique, one that almost all of us have been obliged to learn. By their very nature—that of syntax and the rules of grammar—words resist spontaneous arrangements. William Burroughs tried to break out of this trap with his cut-ups method, but it never really worked (it was a technique!). The content of these last few chapters has been made up of largely spontaneous, free-flowing responses to equally spontaneous choices to read certain books. The Berger book was most especially spontaneous, since I had no idea it would be relevant to what I was working on, *having not yet begun writing about serial killers, and having no conscious intention to do so.*

Spontaneity comes from response. If we listen to what someone is saying to us without thinking about our answer, in that space of listening, a natural response comes. It will not be constituted by the contents of our mind, but by those elements that the other soul has introduced to us, moments ago, via our dialogue. This has the effect of *neutralising* the technical mind—which is put on hold by the act of listening, or reading—and allowing the body, the natural mind, to take over.

This process was never more apparent to me than when I found myself hitting on a number of key passages for this last part of the book while listening to audiobooks of transcripts from old Rudolf Steiner lectures, in bed at night. I was not listening to them for information, or even pleasure, merely as a sleep aid. The audios had been selected weeks before, while I was reading the Gospel (they were from Steiner's lecture on Matthew). I am not a fan of the advocates of 'synchronicity'; there seems a kind of narcissism at work in thinking that existence is sending messages to us (it sounds more like the devil's MO to draw our attention to the world); but there was no doubt, when I heard these particular passages, that they were relevant to this analysis and could help to pull it together. This was the most pertinent passage:

> all evil in the world, everything that in its physical image must be called dark and sinful, was not originally so. [T]he wolf, for example—which in a certain way represented something savage and evil, an outcome of the working of the Ahriman-principle—was regarded [in Zarathustrianism] as having degenerated; when left

to itself, the Ahriman-principle could become active in it. Thus the wolf had descended from a being in which the presence of the good cannot be denied … Evil comes into being because something that was good in the form in which it existed in an earlier epoch retains this form in a later age; in failing to transform itself, it becomes retrogressive, for it preserves the form suitable for an earlier time … Evil is not absolute evil but, rather, good manifesting out of its appropriate time, something that once, in an earlier period, was good but is no longer so. *Evil in the present, therefore, manifests in the form of events through which conditions suitable for the past are carried into the present.* When there is as yet no conflict between the earlier and the later, *Time is still undifferentiated, not divided into single 'moments'.*[107]

The vision that Dick shared with Berger's Detweiler was a vision of existing in two timestreams simultaneously, transcending both time and space, turning time *into* space by making it 'undifferentiated, not divided into single "moments"'. Berger called this experience 'killing time', linking it to the deranged belief of a serial killer that killing people was a way to liberate consciousness (theirs and his own) from time and enter eternity. As a last point of strange correlation, Berger himself tapped into the near future, by conceiving his *Übermenschian* murderer: there *were* no (well-known) serial killers when he wrote the book, and certainly not ones with mystical philosophies for rationales.

* * *

> Today the sharp knife of specialization has passed like a razor into the living flesh. It has cut the umbilical cord which linked men with each other and with nature.
> —Jacques Ellul, *The Technological Society*

Serial killers are a strange combination of a delusional spiritual impulse to evolve (they are 'progressives'!) with a 'reactionary' return to the primal ways of the predator (wolf), to ways that were once essential to human survival, and to war and conquest. Some of these practices don't look so good today. Ed Kemper severed the heads of co-eds and then took them back to his bed and slept with them (a practice he apparently had in common with Bundy). When he contemplated what he was doing, he was conflicted about it:

> As I'm sitting there with a severed head in my hand talking to it,
> or looking at it, and I'm about to go crazy, literally, I'm about to
> go completely flywheel loose and just fall apart. I say, 'Wow, this
> is insane'. And then I told myself, 'No it isn't, you're saying that
> and that makes it not insane'. I said, 'I'm sane and I'm looking at a
> severed—Wait a minute, wait a minute'. I'd seen old paintings and
> drawings of Viking heroes and talking to severed heads and taking
> them to parties, old enemies in leather bags. Part of our heritage.[108]

This heritage goes back to Cain. While it is difficult to make an argument that murder was *ever* 'good', that's very much the point. Everything has its time, place, and justification. In their confused attempt to bridge the past with the future, serial killers bring something that was once essential to human survival—wildness, ferality—out of the past and into the present. What remains is a severed head: a frozen image of the past, transported into a present that can only regard it with horror, as an image of death, as 'ultimate evil'. In a final irony, to transcend time—as Steiner describes it—is to attain a perspective in which there *is* no evil, because acts are no longer only viewed in the context of the time frame they occur within. They become 'realised'—moving objects in a transtemporal landscape that has sufficient space for beasts, men, and headless angels.

Adolf Hitler saw no reason why man should not be as cruel as nature. For the Phoenix Program in Vietnam, and the death squads in Central America, CIA assassins were trained in acts of terror that resembled grisly forms of butchery usually associated with ancient warlords like Vlad the Impaler or Genghis Khan. At the same time, they were harbingers to the serial murders in the US—the common thread being a satanic technique that 'transcends' historical time by predating it. The justification of these barbaric methods overseas was what it has always been: to defeat evil (whether it's communism or terrorism), it's necessary to adopt the methods of the enemy, when not to do so would be a strategic disadvantage. As Ellul wrote, the adoption of the techniques of evil is never based on moral criteria but only on efficiency. The principle of 'ends justifying means' is a more prosaic version—or perhaps an inversion—of the Zarathustrian idea which Steiner spoke of, that the evils of today ensure the good of tomorrow. Meanwhile, the warrior-killer deployed to protect his community in wartime, becomes in peacetime the bad man that must be dealt with (cf. *Rambo: First Blood*).

'The world needs bad men', says Rust Cohle in *True Detective*. 'We keep the other bad men from the door'.

The technological society has supplanted transcendental religious myths of an eternal afterlife with the myth of progress and evolution. Time for the technical mind is a means without an end: an endless line that we are destined to keep moving down, getting closer and closer to some final destiny but never quite arriving. Within this frame of reference, ultimate good lies always in the future, and the past becomes the locus of our sins, where all the bodies are buried.[109]

The confusion of our culture juxtaposes its horror at the social reality of the serial killer (a 'monster' that embodies our predatory past) with his glorification as a form of entertainment in which he is seen as a kind of *Übermensch* (Hannibal Lecter, Dexter). It glosses over the gaping abyss of contradiction by dismissing it as the difference between reality and fantasy—even while fantasies of this kind can sometimes get a person convicted.[110] Similarly, the idealisation of supposed cultural pioneers heralding the future turns them into heroes, but only until their sins are found out, at which time they are consigned to the dungeon. But today's hero is *always* tomorrow's monster, because protecting the community from evil requires men who not only understand evil, but who know how to *handle* it. Anthropologically, shamans were often said to live on the outside of the village for this reason: they were necessary to the tribe but not especially welcome in it. What becomes of these men (or women) when they no longer have evils to fight against? Not every wolf can be tamed; in which case, it either goes back to the wilderness or it gets hunted and killed as a dangerous predator.

As without, so within. This moving line of evil can also be seen in the form of the serial killer afflicted with dissociative identity disorder. The originary example of *a protecting agency that must assume the characteristics of its enemy* is that of the abuse victim who internalises the abuser. The psyche under attack defends and protects itself by dissociating from the abuse, splitting off the wounded part and placing it under the protection of an aggressive-alter. The victim then experiences the power and control of the abuser by identifying *with* them. This protective mechanism is good and necessary at the time the abuse is occurring, because without it, the whole psyche might collapse. But as the child grows older, it becomes both a frozen image of the past and an aggressive offence-strategy that attacks even when not itself under attack. Eventually, if allowed to continue unhealed, unintegrated, and un-rehabilitated, the controlling entity will destroy the host and seek another to possess. So the sins of the past are passed on, generationally.

In milder forms, all human beings who grow up in adverse conditions (and there *are* no other kind in a technological society) make similar pacts with protective forces and become trapped by them in later life, often until they die. This is our 'state', out of which the 'State' arises: a once good, now evil, that still knows how to disguise itself as 'good' in order to *do* evil. Central to that disguise is the creation of overt forms of evil separate from itself (using images of past abuses), evil which it can contrast itself to and do combat with, so that its role of false protector can continue.*

We can apply this principle to *all* forms of technique: in the beginning, whether it's fire, the wheel, or the microchip, they are there to rescue us—if not from death, from hardship and discomfort—and thrust us into the future. Like the apple of knowledge, it seemed like a good idea at the time. Yet there's no technique so beneficent that it won't end up being the death of us. Not counting Jack the Ripper, the prototype for the serial killer was Ed Gein, who began his career by digging up his mother's corpse, removing her head, and attempting to 'shrink' it for a trophy. He dug up several more dead female bodies before graduating to live ones and murdering several older women, dismembering them, and/or removing their skin. Besides using the pieces to make lampshades and items of clothing, he stitched parts together to create a 'woman suit' to hide inside.

As one article drolly states: 'Gein's beloved mother had been dead almost 12 years, and by all accounts he had missed her terribly'.[111]

---

*Witness the problem-reaction-solution of covid-lockdowns–mRNA driving the medical dictatorship in the early 2020s.

CHAPTER 22

King Batty (who has more children in his basement: Sam Harris or Ted Bundy?)

*I*dentity experiences itself most tangibly in contrast or opposition to the world and others. The quest for identity involves violence because we are mostly firmly convinced we exist when our consciousness collides with existence, via an event of overwhelming intensity.

Living inside the artificial mind is like being in solitary confinement to unreality, a constant sense of disconnection or derealisation. It is blah-world syndrome. Like Dick's androids yearning to be real—or Roy Batty driving a nail through his palm to keep from going numb—the sufferer seeks pain just to feel anything at all.

Experiences of joy, bliss, peace, or happiness entail a loss of awareness of our separation, a dissolving into existence, like a foetus inside a womb. Absolute opposition to existence is then the fullest assertion of identity—like a simulation of a painful birth. While happy experiences tend to pass us by, terrible tragedies mark us for life; they mark us both with and in time.

The ultimate horror is not of something incomprehensibly awful happening to us, but of having caused it to happen to another. It is like being in a nightmare that we can never awaken from, like awakening into a nightmare. From here, the only escape is back to unconsciousness.

The artificial mind is driven to seek pain—of the self and of others—to find out what life is made of. Overwhelmed by reality, it seeks to disappear into that *life, to become one* with *it. Sexual murder satisfies both these urges—to kill the mother* and *to merge back into her body.*

* * *

> Imagination does not breed insanity. Exactly what does breed insanity is reason. Poets do not go mad; but chessplayers do. Mathematicians go mad, and cashiers; but creative artists very seldom … The men who really believe in themselves are all in lunatic asylums.
>
> —G. K. Chesterton

In the week before submitting *Big Mother*, Sam Harris went viral after making some ontologically indefensible comments. (A popular author and speaker, Harris was dubbed one of the 'Four Horsemen of New Atheism', along with Richard Dawkins, Christopher Hitchens, and Daniel Dennett.) Discussing mainstream media attempts to suppress some highly compromising material found on Hunter Biden's laptop (President Biden's son), Harris insisted that, whatever it was, it could only distract from the *primary mission* of keeping Donald Trump out of office. 'At that point', Harris said, 'Hunter Biden *literally could have had the corpses of children in his basement—I would not have cared'.*

While admitting that a 'left-wing conspiracy' to deny the presidency to Trump was blocking attempts to look at Biden's laptop (Twitter had just shut down the *New York Post*'s account for trying), Harris insisted that it was warranted:

> It doesn't matter what part's conspiracy, what part is out in the open, if there was an asteroid hurtling toward earth and we got in a room with all of our friends and have a conversation about what we could do to deflect its course … Is that a conspiracy? … Politically speaking, I consider Trump an existential threat to our democracy.[112]

Harris was once known for a proud adherence to logic and rationality, for upholding the dogged pursuit of truth at whatever cost to personal belief or ideology. Yet here he argues that Trump is as dangerous to the planet as an asteroid, and that this 'truth' justifies the suppression of facts—including facts about the most heinous high-level human crimes imaginable—by any and all means necessary. Curiously, as if to pre-empt any such charges, Harris introduced himself in the same interview with an equally extravagant claim:

> I think there's one algorithm I'm running more than most which is, you know, what I would call 'Intellectual Honesty'. The burden is not to be who you were yesterday. The burden isn't to join some tribe, who, you know, you'll get some social reinforcement from for, you know, conforming to … I mean even having an identity itself is too much. You know, not only can you not conform to a tribe, you can't really even conform to who you were yesterday, if your master value is to be honest and rigorous and available to new data and new arguments and new insights.

Doth the Horseman protest too much? Harris' statement is diametrically at odds with one he makes later, in the heat of the moment: 'Now the question is, what can you do *with your own biases* and get the outcome you think is actually better, not just for yourself personally but for the world?' Since Harris believes Trump represents 'a once in a lifetime moral emergency', even while knowing with one part of his brain that this is a personal bias, his algorithms are directing him to the most craven and brazen forms of intellectual dishonesty to cover this fact up—from himself, if no one else. Harris' algorithmic intellect is like FBI behavioural sciences profiling—an occasionally effective technique that more reliably serves as an instrument of deception, misrepresentation, and reality-distortion, sloppily disguised as a truth-seeking missile.

Why am I spending so much time on this at the 11th hour? First, because it showed up and caught my attention, and thereby got pulled into the spontaneous unravelling of the BM thesis. Second, to the point, because Harris' controlled meltdown may provide an indication of how technical minds eventually and inevitably wind up insane, as they become ever-more restricted by the 'algorithms' they have created to run themselves by. The fool who persists in his folly will become wise, said Blake; and the rationalist who insists on his rationality, shows Harris, will eventually become a complete fool.

The technical mind is born from problem-solving; yet the solutions it creates always give rise to new problems, each one greater than the last. This is how the technical mind thrives, like a flesh-eating virus, on the host it purports to be saving. (Harris wishes to undermine democratic process to save democracy from a candidate he dislikes.) To conceal this reality—that the technical cure will always turn out to be exponentially worse than the disease—technical propaganda (ideology) must continuously spin false narratives to justify its existence and rationalise evermore extreme measures. Central to the narratives and measures created is a gross exaggeration of the problem that the technical mind perceives itself as 'morally'—i.e. technically!—obliged to solve. *A delusionally inflated idea of its own goodness is a natural correlate to this exaggeration of evil.*

Harris' algorithmic mind is asserting its superior goodness in exact proportion (and direct opposition) to the 'evil' it has identified (Trump). Paradoxically, by this justification, it becomes increasingly extreme in its means of addressing the problem, and even boldly admits its complete lack of a moral centre (who cares about murdered children?) as irrelevant to the mission. Like a psychopathic predator or a deadly virus, it disguises craven self-preservation as an altruistic service to the whole.

The value system Harris is defending and promoting is that of tastefulness and the war against vulgarity (i.e. covert monstrosity as opposed to overt, which Trump represents). *Vulgarity* refers to the common people, and Trump appeals to that same class, which is his real 'sin'. To the smooth-functioning, orderly algorithms of Harris' technical mind, vulgarity is immeasurably worse than depravity. It is 'an existential threat'. A threat to what exactly? Not democracy, clearly—since Harris has already thrown that to the wolves—but to Harris' own sense of 'decency' and to a social reality worth living in (and for). Harris' mental algorithms are—like Bundy's predations—*exclusively built for the protection of his identity.**

* * *

---

*The reference to 'dead children' is like Jimmy Savile's 'jokes' about abusing minors. Harris dismisses the reality of the sex trafficking of children by acknowledging it as (potentially) real, but irrelevant. (It's only the President's son, not the President.) Harris is battling something more deplorable—more of an existential threat—than raping and murdering children. To Harris, Trump is worse than Ted Bundy, he is the embodiment of the primary 'evil' that the technical mind recognises: vulgar or uncultured presentation. Harris' fear and loathing of vulgarity relates to a hatred of visible monstrosity. This is why Charles Manson is the official face of the serial killer—even though he wasn't one—because he was vulgar, uncultured, clownish, and obviously 'mad'. Jeffrey Epstein, on the other hand—who moved in similar pseudo-scientific circles to Harris—belonged to the techno-progressive class and presented in the right way. Very little, if any, moral consternation was expressed, among the technocratic class, when the truth about Epstein came out, even though many of them had rubbed shoulders with him for decades (as had Trump, admittedly).

> It becomes possession. They are part of you … You then possess them and they shall forever be a part of you. And the grounds where you kill them or leave them become sacred to you, and you will always be drawn back to them.
>
> —Theodore Bundy, on his victims

In my unexpected revisit to the troubled terrain of the serial killer, as must by now be obvious, I found myself taking particular interest in Ted Bundy. This was a curious thing in itself, because my brother, before he died, told me he had read *ten* Bundy biographies. (The context for this strange admission was that he knew more than I did about Bundy, hence my suggestion that Bundy got help escaping from prison was beneath his contempt.) Apparently, this fascination runs in my family and is somehow ancestral. Like my brother, I find myself experiencing a peculiar sympathy for Bundy that I can't easily explain. Speaking for myself, my interest in/affinity for Bundy can't be uncoupled from how closely his sexual pathology resembles my own traumatically induced, media-fuelled fantasy life as an adolescent, stirring to life a paraphilia that is still latent in my psyche, however inactive, and that to this day renders the experience of my sexuality far from problem-free.

A number of things Bundy talked about in his last interview, with Dr. Dorothy Otnow Lewis, stood out for me. His descriptions of the entity that possessed him have already been explored. His all-too-brief admission of horror at his acts of violence also struck me, and it tugged on my awareness for several days after reading it:

> There are times I've, the rage and the madness was just so strong, I was just so … I'd be screeching, screeching, cursing, you know. That's when I was, deep down inside I was watching this, I said, You're absolutely mad. This is just madness. Oh, yes … Initially, of course, I was just absolutely … again I was nauseated and horrified, just frightened, more than I can say. I couldn't sleep for days, the first two times this happened. I just couldn't sleep. I was just, let's just say, appalled by what had happened. Now as the years passed and the incidents happened, I reached the point where I just suffocated. I would always feel that sense of … a sense of … despair and horror kind of combined, but it wouldn't really last for more than a few hours.
>
> (Nelson, pp. 288–289)

Bundy may have misrepresented, in this admission, just how thoroughly he killed his conscience; but there is still some undeniable poignancy, for me, in his words. Imagining his horror, and the awareness Bundy must have suffered in witnessing his own monstrousness, I felt a strong sense of compassion for him. I also had a sudden insight into *why* Bundy committed these monstrous acts. Not in the philosophical sense, but in terms of *what for*, i.e. what the acts did for him at an *internal* level.* I realised that the 'gain', so to speak, might be inseparable from the horror—and that the horror was a means to another, deeper goal. To be clear, Bundy talking to Lewis of his moral horror should not be seen as an expression of remorse *at that time*. As already discussed, Bundy was almost certainly beyond remorse by that point. But it did provide me with a clue as to the sort of soul-killing satanic techniques Bundy was applying, and the ultimate cost of them—not only for the victims but for himself.

The inevitable horror and remorse undergone in the early 'training' period of the satanic 'technician'—remorse which it took Bundy 13 years to get free from—is the price paid for the equally intense *frisson* of sadistic pleasure he experiences, via acts of abduction, rape, torture, murder, and *the complete objectification of the other*. The pleasure Bundy took was in exact proportion to the pain he caused his victims. This makes it perhaps the starkest and most viscerally appalling example of *how an oppositional identity is formed and fortified*.

* * *

> Ordinary people find the need for violence as they lose their
> identities. It is only the threat to people's identity that makes
> them violent.
>
> —Marshall McLuhan

In a passage from my 2013 essay on autism, I made an early attempt to untangle the knots of mimetic violence, scapegoating, and the complementarity of good and evil:

---

*Note: 'Bundy becomes angry when Keppel doesn't want to hear about *why* he killed the girls. "I told him I wasn't interested in why", said Keppel, "that 'why' never caught anybody. And he took a little offense at that"' (Michaud and Aynesworth, 1999, p. 337).

The alienated youth-turned-killer is unwittingly volunteering to be the sacrificial Other, the scapegoat, thereby strengthening the solidarity of the group. They are acting out the deepest, most disowned (because unsafe) desire of the group, which is to reject the safety of belonging and forgo the need for group identity to individuate from it (if necessary by violence). [Compare this to Harris' pitiful claim to be free of tribal identifications.] Perhaps this is why the heroic impulse towards autonomy is always 'shadowed' by the psychopathic urge to destroy (and self-destruct)—why the cop always has his evil doppelganger and the Batman is forever haunted by the mocking laughter of the Joker … Simon Baron-Cohen's idea is that autists and psychopaths are like mirror opposites of one another.

A 'monster' like Ted Bundy—when taken at face value, as the mainstream narratives would have us do—exists to deflect our awareness from the ordinary, everyday psychopaths—such as Harris—that move in circles high and low, around and above us. Sam Harris may even be demonstrating, as his precisely regulated tech-brain starts to go on the fritz and do a 'HAL', just what happens as the natural self—the organic sentience and biological limitations of the body—begins to crumble and fragment, under the pressures of transhuman ideologies and the accompanying technologies (no surprise that Harris staunchly advocated the mRNA 'vaccine' technology). What happens as human beings become ever more overwhelmed and colonised by these techno-progressive invasions, as the proximity of Big Mother's artificial body-womb grows ever more suffocating? The zombie apocalypse is what happens—in gory eschatological tango with a loss of identity that, verily, *is not* enlightenment.

As ordinary humans like Harris (neurotypicals) become increasingly at sea in a world of technology and hyper-objectification; as they are having experiences less and less experientially *real* to them; they are also becoming more and more dissociated from their bodies. They are caught, like infants with still-unformed identities, between the terror of separation from the mother's body and the terror of annihilating re-immersion into it. Instinctively, they seek ways to re-assert that unstable sense of identity through forms of violence—by finding traction, resistance, surfaces to *push against*. This eventually comes down to attacking designated objects around them, objects that are perceived as existential threats, enemies, asteroids from the beyond.

Within the creeping chaotic 'blahness' of the *nöösphere*, acts of opposition, even of violence and depravity, become the only remaining means to re-establish a choate sense of identity and reconnect to organic existence, however psychotically.* If Harris truly believes he is fighting back the zombie apocalypse of deplorables and saving the Earth from a giant asteroid, suffice to say, he did not get this belief via any kind of logical or philosophical reasoning. Like a runaway horseman, with his total belief in his own algorithms and the corresponding duty to obey them, Harris is *leading* the zombie apocalypse. *Bundy and his ilk, likewise, belong to hidden 'tribes' of apocalyptic identity-regeneration whose only modus operandi is violence.*

Insofar as the organised psychopath understands all this through direct experience, he is 'superior' to the ordinary man or woman, whom he designates as victim (rather than an active threat) and uses as a means of separating himself from that mass. Bundy's momentary flashes of awareness regarding what he had done, Kemper's time spent with his severed heads, provided the most intense *shock of reality* imaginable, the fullest experience of existing (inseparable from the horror and remorse, as much as the vicious pleasure), by *recalling their acts*. The severed heads drew them *back* to the 'ground' of the original murders, in which they were *merged* with the object of their rage and dark pleasure, back in mother's arms—together but also apart (just as the women's heads were separated from their bodies).

Their identities—as perpetrators of abominations—were cemented and secured, within themselves as much as in 'history'—while paradoxically being *subsumed* into that of their victims/mothers. There is no gain involved in this false individuation, this artificial union ritual, save the gain of madness, infamy, and death. Yet there *is* a form of self-sacrifice that, while it cannot be admired, much less emulated, in no way can be dismissed or despised as merely aberrational. For in that sacrifice is the most profound and terrible wisdom available to human beings, regarding the true cost of Lucifer's fall. It is the price of a life, conscripted into the Hell-service of a false identity.

The man who cannot look at a Bundy or a Kemper (or a Trump, if you are Sam Harris!), and know—really *know*—that 'there but for the

---

*Identity politics and so-called 'sexual liberation' involves violence in ways that are not so obvious, perhaps, though transgender does make self-mutilation intrinsic to the quest for identity.

grace of God go I'—that under even slightly different conditions we are capable of making the equivalent choices and winding up in a similar place—has failed to understand this scapegoat's tragedy. By extension, they have missed the true implications—the cost and the challenges, and the always-possible consequences—of being human. That is to say, the consequences of choosing not to be.

* * *

> Once a man has begun to use violence he will never stop using it, for it is so much easier and more practical than any other method. It simplifies relations with the other completely by denying that the other exists. … The fact is that once violence is loosed, those who use it cannot get away from it … Violence imprisons its practitioners in a circle that cannot be broken by human means.
>
> —Jacques Ellul, *Violence*

The invisible junction between the monster and the victim is where the ordinary, 'decent' person, strictly aligned with the victim-hero identity-pole, takes vicarious pleasure (through works of entertainment) in the violence and horror of the monstrous behaviours of serial killers, and the little 'shocks of reality' they provide. At the same time, his or her sense of identity is fortified, in contrast and opposition to the monster, by virtue of an *imaginarily clear* dividing line between them. (It is also dependent on never acknowledging the secret affinity). Bundy-the-boogeyman paints the 'monster' large and so prevents us from noticing the smaller, subtler symptoms of monstrosity, as metastasising on the fevered brow of a Sam Harris, for example (or in our mirror or selfies). We fail to realise that a legion walks amongst us, and that it frequently passes for the best of minds, and the best of men.

The localised violence of organised criminals and predatory psycho-paths, then, widely disseminated via news stories, true crime media, and fictional forms of entertainment, provides a necessary sense of identity to the masses—just as Trump does for Harris—and a cor-responding feeling of collective security: a safe space. By so doing, it prevents this sort of 'random', aberrational violence from breaking out, mimetically, into society at large. This is a factor that may be one of the less-considered functions of these sorts of covert, State-sanctioned acts of domestic terrorism (to be distinguished, emphatically, from the mostly fictionalised 'domestic terrorism' of 'deplorables'). They help to keep a lid on the seething rage of the collective.

What if, by their very aberrational nature, the appalling crimes of a Ted Bundy or an Ed Kemper serve to *reduce* the level of violence within greater society, by concentrating it into isolated areas? This is a rather shocking hypothesis, admittedly, but can it be dismissed? It's been well-documented (by René Girard and others) how the presence of the 'monster'—the shared awareness of it and the collective agreement about its guilt—prevents a community from literally tearing itself apart. There may even be palpable evidence of this in the way in which the very obvious monster of the serial killer has transmogrified over time, first into the school shooter (our own children), and then, in more recent times, to include just about anyone who owns a firearm, who finally snaps under pressure and shoots up the local church, mosque, or supermarket.

This sort of thing is now happening in the US at a rate of around two mass shootings per day.* The violence is getting closer and closer to home, the monster less and less possible to distinguish from the victim—or the hero. One way in which this internalised violence is co-opted, or contained, by the technocratic propaganda machine is, wherever possible, to frame the acts of violence inside narratives of '4chan', 'white supremacists', 'anti-Semites', 'homophobes', and 'right-wing extremists'. It's a dark irony that, after decades of suppressing the truth of domestic terrorism inside the Empire walls—such as the Phoenix Program behind the creation of many 'serial killers'—the 'domestic terrorist' has now been fashioned out of the ordinary 'deplorable' man and woman—Harris' 'existential threat'—thereby making the internal threat an 'other' that can be scapegoated: an other amongst us. (This scapegoated demographic now includes conspiracy theorists, at your service!)

If what was once good has become evil, it may eventually be perceived, truly, within the context of the totality of Time, as good once again—or at least necessary. What choice do we have? It's only by

---

*The Gun Violence Archive listed almost 700 mass shootings in the US in 2021. The war in Ukraine has experienced a per capita murder rate for the first half of 2022 (12.9 per every 100,000) well *below* that of several American cities. (The top three were New Orleans, with 36.8, Baltimore, 29.1, and Birmingham, 28).

understanding souls like Ted Bundy—truly, madly, deeply *understanding* them—that we can avoid collectively *becoming* Ted Bundy. Because what drives Bundy, also drives Harris, drives Trump, drives Horsley, drives the collective body of humanity and its many parts, into the Hell of its own making. Ignorance is no substitute for innocence. It is rather the guarantor of complicity.

When a person has cancer, we don't say their organ has it or that certain cells have it, but that they do. We don't blame the cells, the organs, or the person, however, and we certainly don't blame the symptoms (though we may hate them). We blame the cancer. In the body of humanity, the tumour is the satanic system, the cancerous cells are the individuals that have organised to create that system; the 'serial killer' is just one of the symptoms that lets us know something is metastasising under the surface. But the cancer itself remains unidentified, save by the effects.

If all of us are connected by, or in, that cancerous body, even if we are unaware of one another, then we are all accountable for what that body does and for what happens *to* it, regardless of our degree of awareness or our conscious complicity. We have all been conscripted into the same service, and it is to an evil that knows how to use *all* the parts—that converges on the human body itself, as the image of the divine that most offends it. The evil, like the cancer, remains undefined outside of what it does: a mystery. Evil, like cancer, like Satan, is a necessary place-keeper for that mystery. But we must eventually *go* to that place that is being kept for us, to know the nature of the beast. For there is nothing more dangerous than the cure that is prematurely formulated.

CHAPTER 23

Original sin-tax: God's original dilemma

*T*he mathematician posits infinity as a necessary hypothesis for the rest *of his equations to work; yet doing so in no way means the mathemati-cal system can now explain (much less contain) the infinite. The infi-nite is by definition incomprehensible and inexplicable, and the same applies to God.*

Word-concepts are necessary because of our felt sense that there is a reality beyond words and concepts. We need words to arrive at the awareness that words are pointers towards something far beyond, that is at the same time within them (immanent and transcendent).

Words span the abyss between Lucifer and God, making Christ the Logos, the ratio between the two.

In the beginning was the word. In the end, what?

* * *

Someone *must* come along and play the role of Plato to my Socrates.

—Philip K. Dick, *The Exegesis of Philip K. Dick*

As must be obvious, the final sections of *Big Mother* have been partially informed, if not actually inspired, by the author finally getting around to reading the second half of Dick's *Exegesis* and, shortly after that, reading Jacques Ellul's *The Technological Society*. I now have the task of weaving all of these new strands together so I can close the book (and then you can).

While I was ploughing diligently through the *Exegesis*, I found myself wondering about the fascination that all these writers have for Dick (myself included). Was it due only to our investment in the *belief* that Dick was really on the trail of God/VALIS, and the inability to separate that vain hope from a feeling of compassion for Dick's desperate search for meaning? What writer doesn't secretly believe that he really *can* save his soul by reading and writing? Language makes gladiator-slaves of us all?

If Dick hadn't written his many works of fiction, if he hadn't gained the status he did or received the blessing of pop culture, and 'the arts', it's clear that no one would have ever taken the time to plough through 2 million words of his journals to make any *Exegesis* fit for publication. Now that this *has* been accomplished, what is the net gain? Further deification of Dick and the *reification* of his delusional fantasies? Is all of this effort only to strengthen the hallucination that we can eat soup with chopsticks—that using language can become a valid way *out* of the death-maze of our Ahrimanically incepted mind-selves?

As ever, at the 11th hour, I find myself attempting to somehow redeem this devilish conundrum by exposing the hidden machinery behind it. A Dickian task that involves *disproving* my theory by *proving* it: if I can show that PKD was only creating more diabolic mind-mazes to hide inside (and for future Dick-heads to get lost in) under the *pretence* of finding the way out, maybe I can turn that Chinese mind-trap into a *genuine* exit? Is there a way to complete Dick's unfinished project by establishing that it should never have been started in the first place?! Or am I, at the end of the day, just trying to write myself into a better place? Is there a difference? Where is Dickian pie-in-the-sky, if not in my own eye?[113]

The flip side of the goal of exposing the conspiracy of the counterfeit (Satan), which aims to supplant goodness with evil *disguised* as goodness, is to isolate 'Ubik': the omnipresence of the Holy Spirit; to find it at work even in the most 'degenerate' of souls. To save one soul (mine) requires saving every soul. The last shall be the first. The quest for

God (reality, the natural) thus becomes a seemingly unending attempt to identify Satan, in the hope that, once everything that is not God (is unnatural, devilish, artificial) is identified, the contrast provided by the revealed darkness will make the light fully known, leaving no other option but to submit our souls in service *to* it. This methodology—roughly 'Neti, neti', not-this, not that—is consistent with one of Philip K. Dick's (innumerable) descriptions of God-as-Valis in the *Exegesis*: 'A total system that perpetually chooses through a binary process of rejection that is cumulative' (2011, p. 709).

But is it by rejection or is it by integration? The soul's impulse to identify what *appears* good as not so good at all, and turn *away* from it, has, like all things, a shadow side or counterfeit. It also serves as a covert means to put myself—the dogged exposer of the inferior product (in this case Dick's 'intellectual error')—in a perennially superior position. This is a satanic impulse, akin to Lucifer's pride and envy. It is the urge to accuse, condemn, and debase everything that is good, and bring it down to our own fallen level. As the necessary corollary to the Pauline saying 'Unto the pure all things are pure' (Titus 1:15), Nietzsche wrote, 'To swine, all things are swinish'. Seeing Satan under every rock makes me, the seer, most easily and necessarily ID-ed as the prime locus of the satanic: the eye that beholds only ugliness. Get me behind thee, Dick! The first *shall* be the last. This question is pertinent to the BM thesis, and not merely the author's trademark expression of self-doubt. It comes down to the question of technique—are we using it, or is it using us?

On the *other* hand (since there are always more hands to an octopus), identifying the devil in myself is what the process of 'spiritual autoly-sis'[114] is all about; there's no sense in mapping Hell if it doesn't lead to the exit. So—all so good, so far?[115]

And then lo!—the day after writing the previous section (the one that begins 'As must be obvious'), I read, for the first time ever, of Dick's 'theophany' of 17 November 1980:

> Thus my exegesis has been futile, has been delusion, *and*: has been a hell-chore, as I was beginning to realize, but God delivered me from it, from my own exegesis; and he pointed out the one truth in it: the infinity expressed in it was—but this was overlooked by Satan who does not possess absolute knowledge—a road to God, and did lead there; but *only* when I recognized the exegesis as futile

and a hell-chore and delusion. Hence God permitted this deluding by Satan, knowing when it would end … I have sinned in this exegesis; it is one vast edifice of hubris, of Satan in me questioning and accusing.

(2011, pp. 643, 648)

Hallelujah! Then, a few pages later, Dick goes a step further: 'All my speculations have been about the world, so world has me fast! It has been a trap! … My exegesis, then, is both a delusion in which I am trapped and, in addition, a delusion *I am creating for others*' (2011, pp. 654, 658).

It was an eerie, Dickian experience to hear my words echoed back to me by the subject *of* them. Then, in a further redemptive movement: in the same segment, Pamela Jackson—the only woman to work on the *Exegesis*—hits the crucifixion nail on its head, when she comments (in a footnote):

Even in his most megalomaniac moments Dick never suggests that the Exegesis *itself* will ever be read. But the fact that, improbably, we are reading these lines gives the question he poses here and elsewhere—what is the value of all this *thinking*?—a certain urgency for us as well. If the Exegesis is his delusion and 'hell-chore', it is now ours too. Dick is never more honest, nor more passionate, than when he's questioning, then defending, the solitary path of his inquiry that his life has become … *But what is it for us?* This question was often in my mind as I read the eight thousand manuscript pages that shared my Berkeley apartment these past years.

(2011, p. 658n)

Dick's view (if I dare paraphrase it, and I shall) was that we exist in a language-based reality in which time is illusory and events are being absorbed continuously into the body of a Christ-like meta-organism that reorganises them according to *meaningful associations*, until all seemingly unconnected, random, otherwise incoherent events are transformed, redeemed, and rendered part of the eternal tapestry of Christ's Body. From Dick's own point of view, my writing what I wrote above *may just as well have retroactively caused Dick's theophany of 42 years earlier* (17 November 1980), and I then went on to read about it the following day! In contrast, Dick's own account is infinitely more

dreary and mundane: his vision of God happened under the influence of marijuana!* Which reading of events would Dick have chosen?
Which would *you*?**

* * *

> No human activity is possible except as it is mediated and censored by the technical medium. This is the great law of the technical society. Thought or will can only be realized by borrowing from technique its modes of expression. Not even the simplest initiative can have an original, independent existence. Suppose one were to write a revolutionary book. If it is to be published, it must enter into the framework of the technical organization of book publishing. In a predominantly capitalistic technical culture, the book can be published only if it can return a profit. Thus, it must appeal to some public and hence must refrain from attacking the real taboos of the public for which it is destined. [P]resent-day methods of communication exclude all intellectual activity except what is so conventional that it has no decisive value.
>
> —Jacques Ellul, *The Technological Society*

For Philip K. Dick, God/reality was *dialogue*, a discourse between two or more people holding different points of view in order to establish the truth through reasoned argument. In many ways, *all* of my books since 2010 have been dialogues, usually with non-present, sometimes deceased, other parties of generally opposing viewpoints: my brother with *Paper Tiger*; Jonathan Lethem, Pauline Kael, and my brother again for *Seen and Not Seen*; Whitley Strieber for *Prisoner of Infinity*; Aleister Crowley in *Vice of Kings*; Roman Polanski, and by extension all of Hollywood, for *16 Maps of Hell*; Stanley Kubrick with *The Kubrickon*. Writing about Dick's *Exegesis* (with its two editors and many

---

* 'I gave up on the exegesis and kicked back and massively turned on' (2011, p. 647).
**A more historically engraved example of this phenomenon would be how William Burroughs anticipated an inevitable fusion between Dick's plasmate (living information) and his own 'word virus', when he wrote the otherwise vanishing text, *Blade Runner (a Movie)*, in 1979, thereby providing the title for the Hollywood version of Dick's *Do Androids Dream* (DAD!). It would be hard to imagine an uncannier avocation of Dick's 'world-as-information-linkage'.

commentators) has been a dialogue with a dialogue (a trialogue?). It is like an ongoing argument between the word 'now' and the word 'then' (no reference to Jimmy Savile intended). Or perhaps, a continuously evolving interface between nouns and adjective-verbs, by which all are categorically and essentially transformed?

One of the more interesting ideas in the *Exegesis* (apparently from Wagner's *Parsifal*), and one Dick returns to throughout the 900 pages, is: 'Here time becomes space' (an idea Steiner also spoke about, rather more coherently than Dick). At one point, Dick gives a brief example of how he perceived this interdimensional wedding/transmutation, describing how words may have a greater perceivable depth due to their longevity *as* words. His first example is the title of the Linda Ronstadt album, *ASHER*,

> lying very deep, since it is an ancient Hebrew word. So a message can be put together using it as a linking device. For example, when I looked at a page in *Tears* I saw the word FELIX at a different depth from the words surrounding it, and this was before I knew it was a Latin word as well as a name. I did not estimate the depth by age; I estimated the age by depth, by the various different depths.
>
> (2011, p. 676)

Ancient words are more established in time. This means (one imagines) that, in a text seen from a 'time = space' perspective, the older the word, the deeper the spacetime tunnel behind it. I may have discovered a similar principle while writing *Seen and Not Seen*. In that book, I began a dialogue with my past self, transporting passages from my first published work, *The Blood Poets*, into the current text, analysing them and responding to them with a present-time commentary. The result was to bring past insights into the present, and to discover within them meanings, clues, innuendos, that I had been unconscious of at the time of writing them. This had the effect of deepening my present understanding of myself, and of the subject matter, *via my responses*.

Applying Dick's model, the older passages in my book have more temporal *depth* (in a non-metaphorical sense) and provide context, dimensionality, to the more recent text that surrounds them (which hopefully is deeper in the metaphorical sense, i.e. more *conscious*). The example Dick uses is the relationship between the Old and New Testament, and how not only does the New Testament comment on the Old, but the Old Testament anticipates and feeds into the New, in a linking of 'objects' (words) in time, through special arrangement. The internet (the womb for the technological body of evil that is Big Mother) is the artificial counterfeit of this metaphysic: hyperlinking past to present objects to create a 'maze of death' in which memory becomes artifice. The aim of any good dialogue is for the different perspectives, with their varying degrees of depth, to complement and contrast each other, and so provide a richer canvas for the consciousness of the reader (in the present moment) to interact with, immerse in, and bounce off of.[116] The living, present-time dialogue of any collection of words is that between the writer(s) in the past, and the reader in the present.

Thus, the act of writing/reading becomes itself a linking of 'objects'— living bodies—by which time becomes space, and every dialogue, no matter how fraught the discourse or how wide the gulf, becomes a potential reconciliation of opposites.

* * *

> Technique erects a screen between the author and his readers. Miniature fireworks issue from the magic bottle, but not revolt. A few printed pages out of the deluge of printed matter will never make the butterfly a revolutionary.
>
> —Jacques Ellul, *The Technological Society*

At one point in Berger's *Killing Time*, the policeman interviewing the killer formulates 'a definition of a maniac: he who accepts nothing on faith, a kind of *scientist of the soul*' (1967, p. 161, emphasis added). The context for this statement is Detweiler's account to the policeman of attempting to *sever his own penis* (in order to remove the distractions of his sex drive), and stopping when he finds it simply too painful (something the cop opines anyone sane would know in advance). 'Being mad, he had to test it for himself'.* Though this might be applied to Dick *some*

---

*Berger may have been thinking of William Burroughs when he wrote this. Burroughs cut off the end of his little finger and sent it to a boyfriend. Various motivations have been attributed to the act: romantic despair, to avoid the draft, emulating Van Gogh, even copying a Crow Indian initiation ceremony. Ginsberg claimed that Burroughs cut off his finger to prove he did not feel pain, which is the explanation that best fits here, as well as with my own memory, which is that Burroughs claimed he wanted to know what it would feel like.

of the time, when he was in his *Exegesis* mode, it is a closer match for the transhumanist or Ahrimanic impulse—the technical mind. With its total lack of faith, and the corresponding compulsive need to test, measure, categorise, and control everything, the technical mind functions *to the absolute exclusion of spontaneity or natural human expression.* The expunging of these qualities of spontaneity is perhaps the end, as well as the means, of the satanic agenda. 'Every human initiative must use technical means to express itself. These technical means *ipso facto* "censor" initiative' (Ellul, p. 420).

This is like a left-handed writer (I am one) smudging the ink with the same hand that's writing—until his words are no more than a black smear—in a kind of auto-redaction. The question, then, is not so much: can we identify the Ahrimanic internal command mechanism within us; but rather: with *what* are we attempting to identify it? Is the act of identifying 'Satan' compatible with, and therefore exploitable by, the same underlying evil which we are trying to get free of? Or is it a genuine injection of the truly natural, soulful, *human* spirit, by which we may switch over from a falsely-engendered allegiance to satanic technique, to a free-falling and unconditional surrender to—what is outside all rules and regulations, formless and unknowable, and truly outside the reach of the Black Iron Prison?

'Everything in human life that does not lend itself to mathematical treatment must be excluded—because it is not a possible end for technique—and left to the sphere of dreams' (Ellul, p. 431). The goal of the technology of evil is to capture the human soul *by making human beings subject to mathematical treatment.* Language (written and spoken word) is the means to this end. It is the bridge between human consciousness and the mathematical formula of machines. While consciousness is unquantifiable, words—as shown in gematria and even the simplest spy codes—can be translated into numbers and thereby turned into quanta. This makes language—and by extension human beings possessed by language—the *sine qua non* of the ingress of the technical or Ahrimanic mind *into* the organic realms.

Turning human beings into text, code that can be used to generate pseudo-reality (i.e. a simulation), is the apotheosis, the making manifest, of the cybernetic method and the technocratic goal. It is technique taken to the highest and deepest levels of human existence (the so-called 'internet of bodies'). Compare this to children being traumatised through extreme acts of violence and sexual abuse, incepted with specific word combinations (commands) as a means to 'programme' them—cause dissociative identity disorder—and create artificial personalities through the appliance of specific techniques, and it would appear that this ultra-modern technocracy depends on the most *ancient* of principles to maintain itself. To call this principle Satanism, sorcery, or even the more neutral 'magic', is to attempt to use words to understand a system that has used words against us, since language began, to ensure we never, ever escape its influence. The conspiracy that can be named is not the true conspiracy.

* * *

> And what about the novelist? Has he lost *his* original face? I think everything we do in the West is so readily absorbed by the culture that it is very difficult for works of art to become dangerous. The culture works in such a way that it has a reflex that enables it to absorb danger as soon as it appears.
> —*Don DeLillo: The Word, The Image, and The Gun*
> (BBC documentary)

For text to truly be alive as a carrier of spiritual wisdom means not only writing from the body but, symmetrically, to embody the words in, as, and through *acts*. This is why, when it comes to words, practicality is of immeasurably greater value than profundity on the spiritual journey. This is a maxim that I think Dick's *Exegesis* proves time and time again.

In my own writing, I have strived for two primary outcomes. 1) To render my own experience more coherent and meaningful, and if possible to pass that enhanced meaning, or wisdom, on to others (similar to what Steiner believed was possible, though not quite so ambitious).[117] 2) To hold myself—and by extension others—to the ever-higher account which an ever-deepening understanding of existence demands.

Dave Oshana's view on spoken and written language—ironically expressed through this very same medium—is that it is the devil's tool (a liar and the father of it): a Babel-esque noise, embedded in the human nervous system via, or in conjunction with, an original wounding caused by the Serpent's venom back in the Garden. What techniques did the Serpent teach Eve and Eve teach Adam? Whatever it was, it led to the fig leaf as the first bit of 'artifice' in God's creation.

When he talks about words being meaningless, Oshana is like the Cretan saying all Cretans are liars. He beseeches anyone who will listen, time and time again, not to listen to his words, because words only feed and fatten the false identity programme that has already—matrix-like—captured and co-opted our consciousness and generated a dissociative, disembodied simulation world around us. Whenever we use language, Oshana says, we are fighting fire with fire: not only tithing to Satan (original sin-tax, geddit?), but potentially tightening the *nöös* of the language-based, Ahriman-Lucifer, technical mind around our necks.

This is the never-ending conundrum of culture, the Gordian knot that no book has ever been able to slice through (not even the Good Book). Even the most benign of cultural influences may be doing us more harm than good, precisely *because* of the system it is serving to bolster, validate, and reify—in its attempts to subvert it—by injecting novelty and meaning *into* it. Throw away this book, and all of culture along with it.

> [T]hese phenomena, which express the deepest instinctive human passions, have … become totally innocuous. They question nothing, menace nobody. Behemoth can rest easy; neither Henry Miller's eroticism nor André Breton's surrealism will prevent him from consuming mankind. Such movements are pure formalisms, pure verbalisms. No one has ever carried out the famous 'pure surrealist act'. And as for the self-styled revolution in ethics of Miller and the 'black novels' of Boris Vian and others, all they amount to for the normal man is an invitation to a brothel (something which has never passed for revolutionary or as an affirmation of freedom). It is harmless to attack a crumbling middle-class morality. True, persecutions, seizures, and lawsuits have been directed against the 'Black' authors. But I would like to point to the tidy profits that such minor scandals have brought them. I am somehow unable to believe in the revolutionary value of an act which makes the cash register jingle so merrily.
>
> (Ellul, pp. 416–417)*

---

*The best I can say in my (or Dave's) defense is: I still haven't heard the jingle. This book is for the tiny, tiny few.

If Oshana's message is 'don't listen to this message', my own literary output seems more and more to be, *kill* the messenger, throw away the message, get the Hell out of Sodom, and don't look back. By such a contradictory message, this author aspires not merely to trump all previous authors, but to abolish the act of authorship entirely. The only value of these words is if they serve to disrupt and neutralise (even for a moment) the internal value system of language that continues to put stock in words. Can we *grok* these apples?

Put somewhat differently, this is from a 2018 piece I wrote about Oshana:

> Oshana said recently that there is hope but there is also no hope. This is a clear-cut example of how he uses words to reconcile opposites: he is literally stating a truth and its polar opposite in the same sentence. Yet the result isn't gobbledygook but a higher kind of coherence. The only real hope is the hope that can withstand full immersion in a state of no hope, and a hope that exists beyond hope is like a light that can exist even in seemingly absolute darkness, a flame that cannot be extinguished even when all air is gone. A light that's subtler than the human eye can see and yet is somehow detectable opens the senses to a layer of our being that we have previously ignored. It invites us to see—with something other than the mind's eye—that there is no darkness, only varying shades (or densities) of light that allow form to exist. In a similar way, words *can* express the inexpressible, but only when they are carried by—in service to—that which they are formed to express. Bizarrely, they become an expression of something via its apparent negation, a hope conjured by the evocation of no hope.[118]

The above passage amply demonstrates—for me—the power of the word to link disparate 'objects' in time via a shared consciousness in space. This is the first time I have incorporated dialogues with Dave Oshana into one of my books (I am usually at odds with my subjects!), and each time I have read back this passage, I found myself profoundly moved, as if touched by a living presence within the words (what Dave calls the Enlightenment Transmission?). Such a strong response can't be attributed to words alone; it suggests that words act as a channel, a link, between souls.

The genesis of this book has been influenced by everything happening around me at the time of writing. The choice to read certain books is only the most unmistakable and demonstrable of these influences. Spontaneous action *is* possible, even when applying a technique such as writing. Both how I write and what I write are determined by *why* I write—what moves me or inspires me to do it. To be consistent with the moral of this story, I cannot write to reach 'humanity' (the monster *or* the victim). I can only write to reach *you*, the self-selected few. As Rudolf Steiner said in 1910,

> Your own hearts and souls ... will take more from these words as time passes ... By allowing them to echo in your hearts, you will acquire more than if you simply commit them to memory. What I have said here was intended to be a stimulus. If you look for its results and effects in your hearts, you may discover something completely different from what I have said.[119]

Essentially, I am only writing this for one soul, and one soul only, hoping and trusting it reaches it. Only you can know if it did.

POSTSCRIPT: DEAR DICK

> If what we possess in the form of a book (info) is actually a
> world, then what we experience as world is perhaps only info—
> a book. Everything is backward.
>> —Philip K. Dick, *The Exegesis of Philip K. Dick*

Somewhere in that excretory morass of the *Exegesis*, Dick writes: 'All
that is colossal is fraud' (2011, p. xxi). And the *Exegesis* is nothing if not
colossal. The Cretan exposes himself again.

In the final stages, after I had reasonably considered it complete, *Big
Mother* expanded by 25 per cent due to a spontaneous impulse to 'finish reading the *Exegesis*', and then by another 25 per cent after reading
The Technological Society! Words *are* viruses—whether diabolic or divine;
they either replicate through acts of love or acts of war.

Somewhere near the start of this book, I wrote that the subject of
everything I write lately, implicitly but with growing explication, is:
why am I unable *not* to write? Only now, with these final (?) black notes
does it occur to me that this may be the best description of the subject
matter of Dick's *Exegesis*. This is (also) the only sense in which writing

could be called Dick's 'spiritual discipline': PKD was trying to get *free* of his own compulsion to narrate himself into existing. He quite literally wrote himself to death.*

The question remains unanswered: what *is* the cure for writing? Dick (like myself, like any 'serious' writer) wrote above all else in order to think more clearly. But the ultimate goal of thinking more clearly is—always has been, always must be—not to think at all. Which is to be as God is –

> for God there is no distinction between what he knows and what he does. Ratiocination—logic itself, thinking itself—does not occur because it is not required. God does not figure out; he does not reason because he does not *need* to reason.
>
> (2011, p. 841)

Amen.

When natural mind finally ousts the cuckoo of the Ahrimanic double, there will be nothing left to think, and therefore, one supposes, verily, nothing left to write (only fields to plough). That is, unless there are others still trapped inside the BIP nightmare of his-story who are not beyond saving. In which case, there may be no choice for us, Bodhisattvas of the pen, but to enter *back* into the dream-maze and give the slumberers one last kick. Of course, that may be another trick of Hell, to keep us forever-spinning inside and never exiting from its endlessly revolving doorway.

Either way, in this game of God it is, assuredly all for one, or it is all for nought.

Bless you, Phil, and may our Father who art in Heaven prize us forever out of the Ahrimanic arms of Big Mother (BIP), and back where we belong.

---

*As I first wrote that line in my notebook, I became aware of the distinct smell in the bedroom of something cooking. I called my wife to ask if she had left something on the stove. She claimed not to smell anything, and asked: 'Are you having a stroke?' 'That's what Dick died of', I replied. 'Are you tuning into him?' she said. What else is reading a writer's words good for, if not tuning into their soul's aroma?

AFTERWORD: SCIENTISM

Much (though not all) of the following is taken from an unfinished 'redaction' of an old work by the artist-formerly-known-as Aeolus Kephas, *Homo Serpiens* (2009), first written in 2019.

> The very meaninglessness of life forces a man to create his own meaning.
>
> —Stanley Kubrick

The whole notion that human beings are a form of divine technology has special appeal for males who grew up on 'Star Trek', Arthur C. Clarke, Isaac Asimov, Robert Heinlein, and other science-fiction fantasies (especially *2001: A Space Odyssey*, the uber-text for transhumanism). Its companion memes are those of the gods as space aliens, of God Himself as cosmic energy or simply the Universe ('the force'), and the quantum mechanical, what-the-bleep, spiritual scientism of the New Age.

The assumption is 'as above, so below': what men create in imitation of God will provide a suitable—and applicable—model by which to understand and experience 'God' (now squashed down into synonymity with 'the Universe'). This leaves out the question of where 'Satan' is in this translation of paradigms from spiritual to material;

it conveniently banishes the possibility that there is something in human beings—a self-deceptive, self-sabotaging, God-defying, *anti-life* element—that causes us to create diabolic imitations, not as the means to return to our true nature, but in order to perpetuate our separation from it and, if it were possible, to prolong that separation indefinitely.

New Age spirituality and scientism remove Satan from the equation, leaving only a de-spiritualised version of God as 'energy'. (Making Satan entropy or inertia, perhaps? Or simply inert matter.) At the other end of the pole, Jung's 'Problem of the Fourth' proposed establishing Satan as the fourth principle, thereby expanding the Holy Trinity to incorporate the Unholy One. The problem with this 'fourth' is that it is based on two assumptions. First, that God or Spiritual Reality is an unfinished proposition that is changing over time (evolving), presumably in tandem with human culture and consciousness. This assumption contradicts the (I would say necessary) orthodox religious assertion of God's eternal, absolute, unchanging nature (how can you increase what is infinite?). The second assumption that Jung's proposal makes is that Christian doctrine is itself incomplete or unfinished, due to the inadequacy of the revelation that gave rise to it, and that Jung is transmitting a fuller and more profound revelation, via his proposed reformation. (Jung was a Gnostic.)

Ironically, the domain of objective reality seems to have become the exclusive province of orthodox religion, while science seems to have less and less use for it. It stands to reason that, once God was declared dead, objective reality wouldn't be far behind. As a result, objectively subjective reality—the domain of psychic phenomena—has supplanted objective reality and is being taken as the closest we can ever get to it, since the psychic is 'higher' and deeper than the material. In tandem with this error, the psychic domain is being conjured up to (re-)animate gross material reality. Since the human imagination, like Nature, cannot tolerate a vacuum, when God is denied access to reality, enter the Dragon.

This may be why ardent materialists are the most superstitious and fantasy-prone of individuals, and why the most proactive and 'progressive' types are closet nihilists. If nothing is true, everything is permitted: where no absolute objective meaning is allowed, there is the prerogative to create our own meanings and 'establish' them, before that void swallows us up forever. More paradoxically still, the denial of God makes it an absolute necessity that we create God *in our own image*;

the loss of access to or belief in Heaven drives us to storm its gates, if only to prove there is nothing there.

* * *

> The sciences, each straining in its own direction, have hitherto harmed us little; but some day the piecing together of dissociated knowledge will open up such terrifying vistas of reality, and of our frightful position therein, that we shall either go mad from the revelation or flee from the deadly light into the peace and safety of a new dark age.
>
> —H. P. Lovecraft, 'The Call of Cthulhu'

Occultism was born out of a negative identification with—a push against—both science *and* religion. Transhumanism (the belief that humans are destined to merge with machines and transcend death) is occultism for atheists, and modern computer science has even been called 'applied demonology' (by Marcelo Rinesi, from The Institute for Ethics and Emerging Technologies). The Enlightenment raised rationality to the highest plateau of human endeavour; its attempt to banish the shadow of *unreason*, the human unconscious, only provoked that shadow to intensify its darkness—like a cancer that is untreated. This gave rise to a growing appetite for gothic horror, for art that expressed— and invoked—*the terror of the irrational*. The more humans believed in the power of reason, the more terrifying the irrational became to us, because it undermined the thing we were basing our lives upon.

Lovecraft's 'Call of Cthulhu' is an exact psychological equivalent to the idea of science facilitating the apocalypse; the paradox that paralyses us is that the very same scientific method that we employ to reduce existence to measurable quantities eventually leads us to an encounter with the infinite. The only 'rational' response is to double down and impose limits on the limitless—to fix the fluid—which of course, only makes it madder still. Ahriman and Lucifer, dark and light, in an endless war for supremacy over the human soul.

It is my view, then and now, that autism as a condition is a side-effect, an early, misunderstood signifier, of human beings' collective attempt to free ourselves from this schism. What Steiner called Ahrimanic entities, Christians call the devil, and a secular viewpoint might describe as social indoctrination and the prison of language. *This is metaphorised in the sci-fi stories about technology taking us over and/or replacing us, turning us into* it, *in order to turn itself into* us. (As everyone who ever ended up in a sci-fi dystopia enslaved to machines will tell you—if they dare— *Presume Intelligence.*)

The result of going passively and unconsciously along with this is that, as the pinball finally drops and we realise what we've been complicit with, we wind up, collectively and individually, with a backlog of 'horror' to deal with. Rudolf Steiner also anticipated 'gothic horror' as a prerequisite to enlightenment, in *The Fall of the Spirits of Darkness*, as follows:

> 'When human beings are filled with spiritual wisdom, these are great horrors of darkness for the Ahrimanic powers and a consuming fire. It feels good to the Ahrimanic angels to dwell in heads filled with Ahrimanic science; but heads filled with spiritual wisdom are like a consuming fire and the horrors of darkness to them'. If we consider this in all seriousness we can … build a place for the consuming fire of sacrifice for the salvation of the world, the place where the terror of darkness radiates out over the harmful Ahrimanic element. Let those ideas and feelings enter into you! You will then be awake and see the things that go on in the world.

God is a religious term, and within the understanding of orthodox religion, if God can be known at all, it is not by our own efforts but by God's grace. Science, on the other hand, and especially *scientism*, presumes there is a material basis (however subtle) to everything, including 'God'. Enamoured of this premise, it presumes that, when it encounters evidence of intelligence in Nature, it has found God—not in a religious but a scientific sense, i.e. God has been reduced to a scientifically measurable quantity.

* * *

> What has never been seen before is the erection of an entire civilization on something purely negative, on what indeed could be called the absence of principle; and it is this that gives the modern world its abnormal character and makes of it a sort of monstrosity … Individualism [is] the mainspring for the development of the lowest possibilities of mankind, namely those

possibilities that do not require the intervention of any supra-human element and which, on the contrary, can only expand freely if every supra-human element be absent, since they stand at the antipodes of all genuine spirituality and intellectuality.

— René Guénon, *Crisis of the Modern World*

To say we cannot know everything about a God who is infinite is to understate things. We can't know everything about our spouses, our children, or our pets, all finite beings. If God is infinite and absolute, as finite beings, what little we can know about God is infinitesimal compared to what we *can't* know. This means it would be more correct to say we can't know *anything* about God, except, perhaps (and since to use the word at all requires some definitions), that He is infinite, absolute, transcendent and immanent, and that He is all-wise and all-good.

There is a Christian riddle about God: if He is omnipotent, can He create a rock so heavy that He can't lift it? Can God go against His own Nature? Can God act in ways that are evil or foolish? Can God bring about His own destruction? Clearly, there are things that are either impossible to God or so absurd that they may as well be. God could create a rock too heavy for Him to lift, but then He could reduce it in size or increase His own strength. And so on, *ad nauseum*.

For this reason, science must always become scientism when it aspires to supplant religion. It must invert and invalidate its own premises and principles in order to pretend to have explained all of existence (or even that all existence can be explained), because existence—both scientifically and religiously speaking—is infinite and eternal (or otherwise non-existence is). Scientism is like a mathematics that makes ∞ into a really big number and then pretends that the new value is close enough to infinity to make no difference to subsequent calculations. All of which are then wrong.

Metaphysical principles in contrast, *when correct*, are like a bridge over an abyss that can never reach the other side but that can extend *just far enough* for the traveller to get pulled over—by forces beyond his ken. This force is not itself a metaphysical principle, but it nonetheless *responds* to those principles by somehow—inexplicably—completing them and fulfilling them. In the same instant, it cancels them out entirely, by revealing them to be illusory aids to divine revelation. Under grace, there is no law.

While it is true that the psychic realms are in a certain sense more real than the purely physical (because the psychic realm infuses, even contains, the physical, where the physical cannot access the psychic), on the other hand, it is also *less* real because *more* subjective, and hence extremely difficult to distinguish from our projections. Add to this the fact that an experience being more *real* doesn't mean it is more beneficial to us. A head trauma is also more 'real' than a haircut, insofar as its effects are more profound, intense, and long-lasting. That hardly makes it better.

The common error is one the author Charles Upton describes very well: because both the psychic and the spiritual realms exist outside of our physical awareness, from a purely sense-based perspective, there may appear to be no difference: anything that emerges from outside or above the material plane we take for spiritual, meaning good, wise, and true. How much licence does this give to psychic entities, whether previously human ('ghosts') or otherwise, to influence us? Already endowed with certain powers, combined with the experience of being perceived as good and wise, how quickly might such psychic agents be corrupted by such an experience of power?

What we see on the human and grossly material plane, in society—in terms of how power is given to those who will most ruthlessly abuse it, and how this creates a vicious circle of increased abuses of power—could well be playing out, over vastly greater periods of time, in the 'astral' or psychic dimensions. This is not a reassuring thought for the optimistic New Ager to entertain.

There has always been an element of elite social exploitation in the establishing of religious doctrines, beliefs, and practices in the world. Without the support of ruling elites, no religion—just as no scientific discovery—could become established. But there seems to have been a steady progression over the centuries, or a degeneration, further and further away from flawed systems of belief sourced in divine revelation, and closer and closer to whole-cloth simulations that are cynically devised for social exploitation and control. In the 21st century, it is all but impossible to separate potentially benign, or at least well-meaning, attempts to 'update' myths and religious models to make them more 'user-friendly' to modern man (e.g. Carl Jung or Joseph Campbell), from consciously destructive efforts by secret organisations to debase, and if possible destroy, the ancient wisdom.

Whether occult fraternities or intelligence agencies, these modern groups apply at least rudimentary metaphysical knowledge as a means to increase and extend their power and influence in the world. Once again, metaphysical knowledge misapplied soon becomes distorted, and distorted metaphysical knowledge can only be misapplied. This creates a negative feedback loop that has accelerated exponentially to the point that it is currently observable at the most mundane of social levels (e.g. transgender). Elites abuse metaphysical knowledge (and occult or psychic powers) to control the masses; in the process, they pass down even more debased versions of that knowledge to the masses, handing out matches in a nursery, with the certainty that people will sabotage their own spiritual development and become increasingly susceptible to, and reliant on, external forms of guidance and control—all the while believing they are becoming 'liberated' (cf. psychedelics).

Transhumanism—which both anticipated and is set up to follow on the heels of transgenderism—is the final stage of this degeneration of metaphysical principals into their total inversion. It is the synthesis of New Age, quasi-spiritual and secular-religious beliefs with scientism and postmodernist political correctness. It is the apotheosis of the self-willed 'ascent', by which God becomes subject to Man, and the fully socialised human gets to remake hir self in hir own unique self-image. When the relative replaces the Absolute, human error becomes infinite.

Rudolf Steiner said that whenever the soul strives to express esoteric truths, words are feeble means of expression, because they are only good for talking of things that have been known of and talked about for centuries, things which have not changed significantly over the years. When it comes to esoteric truth, however, words can only ever approximate it, and must be delegated to kinds of fables.

Postmodernism—and now 'woke' culture, identity politics, etc.—is happy to erase this distinction between exoteric realities (such as biological sex) and esoteric ones. Trans-ideology, as 'the programming language of the transhumanist experiment',[120] conflates the two and tries to argue that words cannot describe *anything* accurately. This leads to a paradoxical situation in which words, seen as essentially meaningless and therefore subject to endless redefinitions in service to the prevailing ideologies (i.e. what is 'fair'), end up being the sole designator of meaning. The insistence that there is no objective reality that words point towards, because everything requires a subject to be experienced, ironically disconnects subjectivity from ultimate reality, replacing it with subjective fantasy. (What Nietzsche meant by 'God is dead and Man has killed Him'.) To deny the objective reality of God/eternity is to uncouple time from space, and end up like a severed head in a jar, gazing narcissistically at a frozen image of the past, forever.

A (pseudo-)metaphysical set of principles that aspires to build a bridge all the way across the abyss is like a Tower that aims to reach God (or a rocket ship, or a metaverse). The attempt to attain a full understanding of God (or even of a human being, made in God's image) must at some point lead to *a falsification of its own findings* in order not to give up the goal in despair. Once new findings are falsified, it is only a matter of time before the original set of principles (which has already been misunderstood enough to create the erroneous goal) is recalibrated to match the false conclusions.

What remains is a *counter*-tradition and a *counter*-initiation, a satanic counterfeit and inversion of truth. We are left staring at a 'God' made in Man's image, a God who creates Man in order to become conscious of Himself, an *unconscious* God who acts irrationally (as Jung has it in *Answer to Job*), or a God that is a kind of impersonal universal energy to be wielded and directed by humans for their own ends. We are left with Crowley's ruling principle, 'There is no god but man', ergo: 'Do what thou wilt is the whole of the Law'. These are all inversions of the divine truth that make Satan equivalent to (i.e. the only) God. The truth is that it is not God who needs Man to become conscious, but Satan:

> *Satan is the law of matter come alive through the divine spirit.* Satan lies dead in matter, *as its law*, until with its own life the divine spirit makes him come alive. Whenever man's consciousness identifies itself with the law of matter so that his thinking, words and deeds, instead of serving the divine law, serve the law of matter, *man is bringing Satan to life*, man is becoming satanic himself. Without man Satan cannot exist; for without the *self* of man, Satan is only an unconscious force, a necessary natural law of matter.
>
> (Haich, p. 234)

Any false set of principles always leads to a distorted form of being and action that, over time, becomes the inverse of everything natural and good. False beliefs have to be constantly 'validated' by more and more distorted and extreme behaviours, and storming Heaven always leads to (and stems from) the violation of one's own soul and body (God-given truth and essence), and consequently to the violation of others, i.e. to embodying satanic principles and techniques.

On the other hand, since distorted behaviours and abuses are not only common within religious communities—orthodox or otherwise—but typical of them, it would be too simplistic to make a dichotomy of, say, monotheism and pantheism, or religion and occultism, and attempt to equate it with true and false values. The problem is *the loss of spiritual awareness*, the closing down of the spiritual senses, and the subsequent, inevitable distortion of metaphysical knowledge formulated by those lacking either spiritual awareness or senses.

This loss of a true metaphysics, or spiritual science, means, on the one hand, that any religions that continue to hold sway over human consciousness become further and further divorced from the esoteric principles that once gave rise to them. On the other hand, in a diabolic form of complementarity, there arises an increasingly scientistic, 'post-modernist', sorcery-based worldview in which the *subjective* perspective is reified over any form of shared, *objective* reality. It is a world where every 'truth' comes with its own possessive pronoun.

* * *

> Technique has become the bond between men. By its agency they communicate, whatever their languages, beliefs, or race. It has become, for life or death, the universal language which compensates for all the deficiencies and separations it has itself produced.
>
> —Jacques Ellul, *The Technological Society*

Technique, from fire-building to coding to CRISPR, evolves in tandem with the growth of human populations and their increased interlinking and interdependence. The larger the population (and the greater the connections between them, however artificial), the more the need arises for techniques of cohabitation, trade, healthcare, prosperity, and the like. It is then down to technology to optimise these techniques and meet those needs. Over time, the will of the mass-mind—and its methodology of technical, non-spontaneous, predetermined behaviours—becomes supreme, and the 'Mother-State' that serves it becomes god-like.

> Science brings to the light of day everything man had believed sacred. Technique takes possession of it and enslaves it … Nothing belongs any longer to the realm of the gods or the supernatural. The individual who lives in the technical milieu knows very well that there is nothing spiritual anywhere. But man cannot live without the sacred. He therefore transfers his sense of the sacred to the very thing which has destroyed its former object: to technique itself.
>
> (Ellul, pp. 142–143)

This is scientism: what people least understand, they are quickest to believe; and then to worship (and suffer). From the first huddling together of nomads around a fire, and the invention of the wheel to allow for transportation between settlements, all the way to the global Smart Village, technology has both arisen from and accelerated the *binding together of increased numbers of human beings*, both physically and psychically. To partake of 'global consciousness' and subscribe to an identification with 'humanity' is to place one's dependency on, faith in, and allegiance to the machine, in both literal and metaphorical, mundane and metaphysical, senses of that word.

The solution is accordingly unthinkable: to dis-identify from humanity and to cancel one's allegiance, not merely to the machine, but to the whole *idea* of 8 billion human beings forming a collective of which one is a part, as a victim-hero pitted against a monster. It is this belief in, and identification with, an unconfirmed (because unconfirmable) collective of heroic victims which has made the technocratic society we are being victimised by indispensable to us. It is also what renders the idea of abandoning it to its own devices, as opposed to endlessly tweaking it and trying to secure a safe space within it (for 'marginals', and for oneself), unthinkable—inhumane if not actually inhuman. As unthinkable as understanding the mind and motives of a serial killer.

To unsubscribe from the technocratic lie of humanity (the monster *and* the victim) leaves a new/old formula, that of only believing in or caring about those life forms, and those aspects of existence, with which we have a *direct, living, and unmediated connection*, and to Hell with the rest. Ironically, this point of view is one that is levelled at the supposed ruling elite, as is the (increasingly open) goal of reducing the planet's population, which is perhaps an unnecessary literalisation of the above formula—though also, possibly, a necessary consequence of embodying it. (If so, it is also not our business.)

Artificially-induced *cognitive* empathy for billions of faceless humans we will never meet feeds into a mechanised simulation of virtue, meant only to signal our participation in and allegiance to the dominant ideology and power structures. As a result, it overwrites any real-time, lived, *affective* empathy for the human beings we encounter directly, in our day-to-day lives—or would do, if we weren't too busy scrolling for 'likes'.*

The *idea* of being (and feeling) connected to a collective humanity, and of that feeling signifying true compassion, is a ruse and a snare, meant to lure us into identifying with the mass-mind (the technocratic state), while disconnecting us both from human community and our own humanity. The technologically-enhanced immersion into a mass-identity (McLuhan's global village) is what allows for—makes unavoidable—the sweeping tide of mimetic violence, or 'zombie apocalypse'. By the same token, lived, non-mediated relations with our immediate community, with Nature and with other bodies, human and otherwise, is the only possible way—besides hermit-like isolation—*not* to be swept up in that killing tide.

I suspect that those who take the mRNA implant into their bodies—though ostensibly out of a fear for their survival, combined with a misplaced sense of responsibility to the human herd—do so most of all as the result of being successfully indoctrinated into the belief in the machine-mass-mind of 'humanity'. The belief that fusing human biology with technology is the necessary and unavoidable next step in human evolution inexorably leads to the presumption that survival depends on submitting to the Internet of Bodies. It is a *transhumanist faith* that is being enacted, even if most of the actors have never heard of the Singularity, and would not consciously subscribe to it if they had. Actions speak louder than words.

The steepening insanity curve of political correctness—as it asserts such progressive beliefs as a man = a woman (the new definition of a woman being anyone who identifies as a woman) and 2 + 2 = 5—is at the point of crashing in on itself. When the very criteria of argumentation are instantly vaporised by the arguments being made, the result is a self-negating system of beliefs that hinges upon the denial of physical,

---

*This distinction between cognitive empathy and affective empathy was one that I underlined in the 2013 essay series, 'Autism & the Other: Perceptual Warfare', as the difference between the psychopath and the autist.

as well as spiritual, reality (i.e. of everything but the solipsistic self). When a world built on and by cybernetics, computers, and every kind of engineering techniques that human beings can invent and apply, becomes a world in which 2 + 2 is no longer *allowed* to equal 4, not just bridges but the entire infrastructure must fall. Such is the 'karmic' push-back of the unconscious against a runaway reductionism and a 'reign of quantity'. The hegemony of technical thought and action (so-called progress) is forcing human beings to crash headfirst into the limitations of their reduce-everything-to-nothing scientistic viewpoint, through the fatal impact of the death-clown world it has given rise to.

In this sense, those human beings who believe themselves to be the most intelligent and progressive of the species, who are behaving in the most demonstrably unintelligent and regressive of ways (whether serial killers or 'SJWs'), may turn out to be, ironically, at the cutting edge of the evolutionary curve, after all. They may be the canaries in a collapsing coal mine, whose function is to alert those of us at the *back* of the line—whose doubt and trepidation prevented us from ever quite getting behind the myth of progress—that it is time to back *away* from the spectacle, and begin retracing our steps—all the way back to the Garden, if need be.

BIBLIOGRAPHY

Arnold, Kyle (2016). *The Divine Madness of Philip K. Dick*. Oxford University Press.

Bell-Villada, Gene H. (2014). *On Nabokov, Ayn Rand and the Libertarian Mind: What the Russian-American Odd Pair Can Tell Us about Some Values, Myths and Manias Widely Held Most Dear*. Cambridge Scholars Publishing.

Berger, Thomas (1967). *Killing Time*.

Berger, Thomas (1982). *Reinhart's Women*. Methuen.

Blakeman, John R. (2010). *The Merger of Fact and Fiction: Philip K. Dick's Portrayal of Autism in* Martian Time-Slip. Blakeman.

Browne, David (2009). *Goodbye 20th Century: A Biography of Sonic Youth*. Da Capo Press.

Carrere, Emmanuel (2017). *I Am Alive and You Are Dead*. Henry Holt and Company.

Castaneda, Carlos (1992). *Tales of Power*. New York: Simon and Schuster.

Chomsky, Noam (1992). *What Uncle Sam Really Wants*. Odonian Press.

Dick, Anne R. (2010). *The Search for Philip K. Dick*. Tachyon.

Dick, Philip K. (1964). *Martian Time-Slip*. Ballantine.

Dick, Philip K. (1999). *The Shifting Realities of Philip K. Dick: Selected Literary and Philosophical Writings* (ed. Laurence Sutin). Vintage.

Dick, Philip K. (2011). *The Exegesis of Philip K. Dick* (eds. Pamela Jackson and Jonathan Lethem). Gollancz.

East, Bernard (2021). *A Dramaturgical Approach to Understanding the Serial Homicides of Ted Bundy: Impressions of Murder.* Rowan & Littlefield.

Ellul, Jacques (1964). *The Technological Society.* Vintage.

Guevara, Che (2002). *Guerrilla Warfare.* Rowman & Littlefield Publishers.

Haich, Elizabeth (2000). *Initiation.* Aurora Press.

Horsley, Jasun (2015). *Seen and Not Seen: Confessions of a Movie Autist.* Zero Books.

Horsley, Jasun (2017). *Prisoner of Infinity: Ufos, Social Engineering, & the Psychology of Fragmentation.* Aeon Books.

Horsley, Jasun (2018). *The Vice of Kings: How Fabianism, Occultism, and the Sexual Revolution Engineered a Culture of Abuse.* Aeon Books.

Horsley, Jasun (2020). *16 Maps of Hell: The Unraveling of Hollywood Superculture.* Auticulture.

Howard, Scott (2020). *The Transgender-Industrial Complex.* Antelope Hill Publishing

Huxley, Julian (1941). *Man Stands Alone.* Harper.

Kephas, Aelous (2004). *The Lucid View.* Adventures Unltd.

Laing, R. D. (1969). *The Other Self.* Random House.

McGowan, Dave (2004). *Programmed to Kill: The Politics of Serial Murder.* iUniverse.

Michaud, Stephen G. and Aynesworth, Hugh (1999). *The Only Living Witness.* Authorlink Press.

Michaud, Stephen G. and Aynesworth, Hugh (2019). *Ted Bundy: Conversations with a Killer.* Mirror Books.

Miller, A. (1991). *Breaking Down the Wall of Silence: The Liberating Experience of Facing Painful Truth.* Dutton.

Nelson, Polly (1994). *Defending the Devil: My Story as Ted Bundy's Last Lawyer.* William Morris.

Pearce, Joseph Chilton (1977). *Magical Child: Rediscovering Nature's Plan for Our Children.* Dutton.

Pulé, Paul M. and Hultman, Martin (2021, editors). *Men, Masculinities, and Earth: Contending with the (m)Anthropocene.* Palgrave Macmillan.

Raschke, Carl (1999). *Neoliberalism and Political Theology.* Edinburgh University Press.

Rotman, Brian (2008). *Becoming Beside Ourselves: The Alphabet, Ghosts, and Distributed Human Being.* Duke University Press.

Sammon, Paul M (1996). *Future Noir: The Making of* Blade Runner. Orion.

Steiner, Rudolf (1986). *Background to the Gospel of St. Mark.* Rudolf Steiner Books.

Steiner, Rudolf (1993). *The Fall of the Spirits of Darkness.* Rudolf Steiner Press.

Steiner, Rudolf (2004). *Secret Brotherhoods and the Mystery of the Human Double.* Rudolf Steiner Press.

Steiner, Rudolf (2014). *How the Spiritual World Projects Into Physical Existence: The Influence of the Dead.* Rudolf Steiner Press.

Strieber, W. (1987). *Communion: A True Story.* Beech Tree Books.

Teilhard de Chardin, Pierre (1969). *Human Energy* (trans. J. M. Cohen). Collins.

ENDNOTES

Introduction and Part I

1. The fact that autism—and the individuals being diagnosed as autistic—presents such a challenge may have a lot to do with why it's being seen in such negative and disparaging terms, as a 'plague' that must be understood only in order to be cured or prevented. The term neurodiversity, on the other hand, was coined by a neurodiverse self-advocate, as a contrast to neurotypical behavior. The naming of a condition—'autism', say—as something 'other' made it necessary to introduce the counter-idea of the neurotypical (also coined by a neurodeviant). When neurotypical science, psychology, and medicine attempts to diagnose and define autism, it is, somewhat ironically (because unconsciously), attempting to understand what it means to be human.

2. Somewhat related, there is 1992 film by Nick Zedd called *War Is Menstrual Envy*.

3. 'The Intense World Syndrome—an Alternative Hypothesis for Autism', by Henry Markram, Tania Rinaldi, and Kamila Markram, 2007: www.ncbi.nlm.nih.gov/pmc/articles/PMC2518049/

4. If the Monolith of *2001* has metastasised into the smartphone, this was only after TV became the civilised adult's fireside protector. People put on Netflix to go to bed so as not to have to peer into that darkness. Both

fire (light, reason) and stories (movies, TV) provide comfort and shelter from the darkness. They shield us from the unknown. Even before fire was, perhaps the original form of external technology, clothing. The primary uses of technology are, firstly, to deepen, enrich, and transform our relationship with the environment; secondly, to separate ourselves from it by transforming ourselves; in both cases, the fundamental transformation that occurs is in, or at least acts upon, the human body. The fig leaf in Genesis denotes Adam and Eve's fall from Paradise, their loss of 'oneness' with God. Knowledge of good and evil—the fundamentals of every narrative—is practical knowledge, in other words, technology. It means independence but also estrangement: separation from Nature gives humans the option of controlling and dominating it.

5.   'Perfecting a robot that bridges the gap will call for advances in almost every facet of modern robotics: artificial intelligence, machine vision, mechanical and electrical design, signal processing'. 'The New Face of Autism Therapy', www.popsci.com/science/article/2010-05/humanoid-robots-are-new-therapists

6.   Ibid.

7.   The book was called *Tape Delay: Confessions from the Eighties Underground*. Oddly, I first heard about the author Paul Bowles—who also became a major influence—from an interview (published elsewhere) with Swans. One medium (music) was leading me deeper into another (literature), like the right brain sending messages to the left?

8.   *Sister*, Sonic Youth's 1987 album, was the first of theirs I ever heard, and it indirectly led me to the book. The album was in part inspired by the life and works of Dick, and it was named as a reference to Dick's fraternal twin, who died shortly after birth, and who haunted Dick his entire life. 'Sister' was also the original title for the song 'Schizophrenia'.

9.   'Time Perception in Autism Spectrum Disorder', by Adrienne Warber: http://autism.lovetoknow.com/Time_Perception_in_Autism_Spectrum_Disorder

     See also 'Slipping Through Time In Autism', 2011: http://blogs.discovermagazine.com/neuroskeptic/2011/04/25/slipping-through-time-in-autism/#.Uh01aDDuAaA

10. 'Philip K. Dick: Interview with Charles Platt, from 1979', *Dangerous Minds*, 17 November 2011: https://dangerousminds.net/comments/philip_k_dick_interview_with_charles_platt_from_1979

11. In the 1979 Charles Platt interview, Dick describes taking a psychological test with a friend who was training to be a psychological profiler for the army. The results showed him to be paranoid, cyclothymic (mildly bipolar), neurotic, schizophrenic, and a pathological liar!

12. 'Philip K. Dick: Interview with Charles Platt, from 1979', *Dangerous Minds*, 17 November 2011: https://dangerousminds.net/comments/philip_k_dick_interview_with_charles_platt_from_1979 (Emphasis added)

13. Ibid.

14. *The Shifting Realities of Philip K. Dick*, Vintage Books, 1995, pp. 172–173, emphasis added.

15. Quoted in *Autism and the Edges of the Known World*, Olga Bogdashina, p. 109.

16. Cf. Jimmy Savile

17. A number of researchers have tried to connect perseveration with a lack of memory inhibition (the person repeats the answer because they have not been able to forget a past question and move on to the current subject); however, this connection could not be found, or was negligible. This links perseveration to the anomalous perception of time already connected to autism.

18. Precogs are produced by identifying the talent within a 'subject' and developing it in a government-operated training school—for example, one precog was initially diagnosed as 'a hydrocephalic idiot' but the precog talent was found under layers of damaged brain tissue. The precogs are kept in rigid position by metal bands, clamps and wiring, which keep them attached to special high-backed chairs. Their physical needs are taken care of automatically and it is said that they have no spiritual needs. Their physical appearance is somewhat different from that of ordinary humans, with enlarged heads and wasted bodies. Precogs are deformed and retarded, 'the talent absorbs everything'; 'the esp-lobe shrivels the balance of the frontal area'. They do not understand their predictions.

19. At time of completing the first draft of this piece, I had made it through Parts I and II to the midway point. However, just as when I read the Holy Bible, it would be more accurate to say that my eyes passed over every word. I certainly didn't take all of it in consciously.

20. An inside-reference to the author's own current trajectory.

21. Possibly at least. '*kindred* (n.) c.1200, *kinraden*, compound of kin (q.v.) + -rede, from Old English ræden "condition, rule", related to rædan "to advise, rule"': www.etymonline.com/index.php?term=kindred

22. *The Grasshopper Lies Heavy* is a book within a book about our present world that exists in a parallel world (that of *The Man in the High Castle*) in which the Axis (Japan–German alliance) won the Second World War and the world is a fascist super state. So within Dick's fiction, reality exists *as a book*. The book is banned by the ruling powers.

Part II

23. 'The Mystery of Larry Wachowski', by Peter Wilkinson, *Rolling Stone*, 12 January 2006: https://archive.is/PYeMs#selection-669.1-681.196 (Emphasis added).

24. 'Money's interventions in debates about pedophilia, arguing that there is a clinical distinction to be drawn between "affectional pedophilia" and "sadistic pedophilia", and appearing ambivalently supportive of elements of the propedophilia movement, led controversy to dog his reputation', 'Pervert or sexual libertarian?: Meet John Money, "the father of f***ology"', by Lisa Downing, Iain Morland, and Nikki Sullivan, *Salon*, 4 January 2015: www.salon.com/2015/01/04/pervert_or_sexual_libertarian_meet_john_money_the_father_of_fology/

25. 'Lana and Lilly Wachowski: Sensing Transgender', by Cáel Keegan: https://caelkeegan.com/lana-and-lilly-wachowski-sensing-transgender/

26. Reference to Shakespeare's *Macbeth*, in which the titular character is told by the witches that he need not fear 'any man born of woman'.

27. 'Autism and Gender Dysphoria', *Transgender Trend*, 24 October 2020: www.transgendertrend.com/autism-gender-dysphoria/

28. 'Gender-Affirmative Therapist: Baby Who Hates Barrettes = Trans Boy; Questioning Sterilization of 11-Year Olds Same as Denying Cancer Treatment', *4thWaveNow*, 29 September 2016: https://4thwavenow.com/2016/09/29/gender-affirmative-therapist-baby-who-hates-barrettes-trans-boy-questioning-sterilization-of-11-year-olds-same-as-denying-cancer-treatment/

29. Claims that the process is reversible are just more gobbledygook. One of the charges against the Tavistock Gender Identity Clinic—which was closed in 2022 due to parental and victim-patient pushback—was that it never followed up on its victim-patient cases to check how they were responding to gender-reassignment treatment. This is hardly surprising, since doing so would make it impossible to continue to claim irreversibility, in the face of the many 'desistors' attempting to reverse their transition, and the damage that has been done to them.

30. 'TMI: Genderqueer 11-Year-Olds Can't Handle Too Much Info About Sterilizing Treatments—But Do Get On With Those Treatments', *4thWaveNow*, 13 April 2021: https://4thwavenow.com/2021/04/13/tmi-genderqueer-11-year-olds-cant-handle-too-much-info-about-sterilizing-treatments-but-do-get-on-with-those-treatments/

31. Ibid.

32. Ibid.

33. 'Forget What Gender Activists Tell You. Here's What Medical Transition Looks Like', by Scott Newgent, *Quilette*, 6 October 2020: https://quillette.com/2020/10/06/forget-what-gender-activists-tell-you-heres-what-medical-transition-looks-like/

34. 'How To Tell If Your Baby is Trans', by Rod Dreher, *American Conservative*, 12 April 2018: www.theamericanconservative.com/dreher/how-to-tell-if-your-baby-is-trans/

35. 'Father arrested for discussing child's gender transition in defiance of court order', by Jesse O'Neill, *New York Post*, 18 March 2021: https://nypost.com/2021/03/18/man-arrested-for-discussing-childs-gender-in-court-order-violation/

36. '"Insistent, Consistent, Persistent": Autism Spectrum Disorder Seen as no Barrier to Child Transition—Or Sterilization', *4thWaveNow*, 29 October 2015: https://4thwavenow.com/2015/10/29/insistent-consistent-persistent-autism-spectrum-disorder-seen-as-no-barrier-to-child-transition-or-sterilization/

37. 'The Sterilization of Trans Kids: Pesky Side Effect, Or Modern-Day Eugenics?' by worriedmom, *4thWaveNow*, 26 January 2018: https://4thwavenow.com/2018/01/26/the-sterilization-of-trans-kids-pesky-side-effect-or-modern-day-eugenics/

38. See 'MKUltra, Transgenderism, and the Feminization of Men', by Rachel Wilson, 9 January 2022: https://rwilson.substack.com/p/mk-ultra-transgenderism-and-feminization

39. 'Media Contagion and Suicide Among the Young', by Madelyn Gould, Patrick Jamieson, and Daniel Romer: www.columbia.edu/itc/hs/medical/bioethics/nyspi/material/MediaContagionAndSuicide.pdf The report offers a series of recommendations to reduce the danger of social contagion resulting from fictional depictions or factual reports of suicide. It encourages against 'inadvertently romanticizing suicide or idealizing those who take their own lives by portraying suicide as a heroic or romantic act'. It warns that 'the danger is even greater if there is a detailed description of the method … Presenting suicide as the inexplicable act of an otherwise healthy or high-achieving person may encourage identification with the victim'. It recommends that 'whenever possible stories [should] include the important role of mental disorders such as depression and substance abuse as precursors to the act'.

40. LGBTQ individuals are said to have a higher than normal susceptibility to psychological disorders such as depression, addiction, substance abuse, and self-harming behaviours. The predominant belief is that this is due to the effects of social prejudice. If culture is partially or even primarily responsible for such psychological wounding, as

evidenced by most gender dysphoric individuals, this is *not* because of too many bigots or intolerance for social anomalies. The psychological damage evident in so many of these classes of individual occurs *long before any kind of sexual orientation or gender dysphoria has become sufficiently apparent to provoke social condemnation* (discounting claims that gender dysphoria is identifiable in infants!). It's logical to suppose that the damage or the dis-orientation is due to psychic and physical toxins in the child's environment stemming from caregivers and close family members, quite possibly starting in the womb. These would also include general environmental toxins, the mother's diet, and other maternal, paternal and family behaviours. Simply stated (if increasingly inadmissible): certain sexual orientations and gender identifications might themselves be symptoms that co-exist with other forms of social maladaptation, i.e. *they share a common aetiology relating to early trauma, psychological fragmentation, and/or cultural contamination.*

41. 'Children Thrive When Parents and Schools Work Together': www.sogieducation.org/parents/

42. 'SOGI Backgrounder', *Culture Guard*, 4 May 2017: www.cultureguard.com/2017/05/04/sogi-backgrounder/

43. See www.dragqueenstoryhour.org/

44. 'Children Could Be Taught About Transgender Issues Using Penguin Story Books', by Nicholas Reilly, *Metro*, 21 September 2015: https://metro.co.uk/2015/09/21/children-could-be-taught-about-transgender-issues-using-penguin-story-books-5401433/

45. See www.sexysexed.org/ and https://twitter.com/realchrisrufo/status/1501225322401787904

46. 'Kentucky Summer Camp Teaches Children to Masturbate and Have Sex On Drugs', by Jeremiah Poff, *Restoring America*, 8 March 2022: www.washingtonexaminer.com/restoring-america/community-family/kentucky-summer-camp-teaches-children-to-masturbate-and-have-sex-on-drugs

47. 'Owner of "Sexy Summer Camp" for Teenagers Says She Has Been Forced Into Hiding After Backlash Over Her Encouragement of Masturbation for Toddlers and "Self-Managed Abortions"', *Daily Mail*, 19 March 2022: www.dailymail.co.uk/news/article-10629957/Owner-Sexy-Summer-Camp-forced-hiding-backlash-masturbation-toddlers.html

48. 'Melissa Harris-Perry Says Your Kids "Belong to Whole Communities"', by Ari Armstrong, *Objective Standard*, 8 April 2013: https://theobjectivestandard.com/2013/04/melissa-harris-perry-says-your-kids-belong-to-whole-communities

49. 'It's the White House Siccing the FBI on Parents who Question CRT Nonsense', *New York Post*, 22 October 2021: https://nypost.com/2021/10/22/its-the-white-house-siccing-the-fbi-on-parents-who-question-crt-nonsense/
50. 'Covid Teams Can Vaccinate Pupils Against Parents' Wishes, Schools Told', by Richard Adams, *The Guardian*, 15 September 2021: www.theguardian.com/education/2021/sep/15/covid-teams-can-vaccinate-pupils-against-parents-wishes-schools-told
51. 'Is Munchausen Syndrome By Proxy Really a Syndrome?' by Geoffrey C. Fisher and Ian Mitchell: https://adc.bmj.com/content/archdis-child/72/6/530.full.pdf
52. 'Maternal Enmeshment: The Chosen Child', by Dee Hann-Morrison: http://journals.sagepub.com/doi/pdf/10.1177/2158244012470115
53. Ibid.
54. Ibid.
55. 'Munchausen Syndrome by Proxy: A Complex Type of Emotional Abuse Responsible for Some False Allegations of Child Abuse in Divorce', by Deirdre Conway Rand: www.ipt-forensics.com/journal/volume5/j5_3_1.htm
56. https://twitter.com/EliErlick/status/1560330329977651201
57. Admittedly, gender reversal surgery is far from being a common practice—but this should hardly come as any surprise (reversing gender-altering surgery and hormonal changes is a *lot* harder than removing tattoos). A London-based specialist in genital reconstruction, Prof Djordjevic, 'has performed just 14 surgeries to date' (in 2017). The procedure is extremely complex and can cost over $20,000 (£15,965), and Djordjevic's 'services aren't easily-accessed. He only treats patients who have undergone a one-year psychiatric evaluation, and he stresses the importance of post-surgery aftercare. So far, he 'has exclusively treated transgender females who have asked to recreate their male genitalia'. 'Gender Reversal Surgery is More In-Demand Than Ever Before', by Olivia Petter, *The Independent*, 3 October 2017: www.independent.co.uk/life-style/gender-reversal-surgery-demand-rise-assignment-men-women-trans-a7980416.html
58. 'WEF Founder: Must Prepare for an Angrier World', CNBC International TV (*YouTube*), 14 July 2020: www.youtube.com/watch?v=LJTnkzl3K64
59. 'Martine Rothblatt is responsible for launching several satellite communications companies, including the first nationwide vehicle location system (Geostar, 1983), the first private international spacecom project (PanAmSat, 1984), the first global satellite radio network (WorldSpace, 1990), and the first non-geostationary satellite-to-car broadcasting

system (Sirius, 1990). As an attorney-entrepreneur s/he was also responsible for leading the efforts to obtain worldwide approval, via new international treaties, of satellite orbit/spectrum allocations for space-based navigation services (1987) and for direct-to-person satellite radio transmissions (1992)'.

60. 'Robot Rights Violate Human Rights, Experts Warn EU', by Alice Cuddy, *Euro News*, 13 April 2018: www.euronews.com/2018/04/13/ robot-rights-violate-human-rights-experts-warn-eu The Sherpa project was set up for this purpose and received funding from the European Union's Horizon 2020 research and innovation program.

61. 'Postgenderism: Beyond the Gender Binary', *Sentient Developments*, 20 March 2008: www.sentientdevelopments.com/2008/03/postgenderism-beyond-gender-binary.html

62. 'Don't Call Pregnant Patients "Mothers": Doctors Are Banned From Using The Word Over Fears It Will Upset Those Who Are Transgender', by Stephen Adams and Sanchez Manning, *Mail on Sunday*, 28 January 2017: www.dailymail.co.uk/news/article-4167632/Don-t-call-pregnant-patients-mothers.html

63. 'Brave New World: The Cost of Stability', by Ricky Gehlhaus, Jr, also quoting Neil Postman, *Amusing Ourselves to Death*. https://somaweb. org/w/sub/BNW_CostOfStability.html

64. Ibid.

65. '*Brave New World*—ironically, set in a world in which books are banned—made it into the top ten in third place. Huxley's novel is no stranger to complaints: in 1980 it was removed from classrooms for making promiscuous sex "look like fun", and it has been the subject of frequent challenges in the US over the years'. www.theguardian.com/ books/2011/apr/12/brave-new-world-challenged-books In 2010 it was successfully banned from the curriculum at Nathan Hale High School. Seattle, when a Native girl complained about the treatment of Native people in the book. http://archive.seattleweekly.com/home/ 930387-129/booksauthors More incidents of the book's banning in schools can be found here: https://thecensorshipfiles.wordpress.com/ volume-1/issue-2/brave-new-world/

66. '*The Future of Mankind*, by Pierre Teilhard de Chardin, Chapter 21: From the Pre-Human to the Ultra-Human: The Phases of a Living Planet', *Religion Online*: www.religion-online.org/book-chapter/ chapter-21-from-the-pre-human-to-the-ultra-human-the-phases-of-a-living-planet/

67. 'Pierre Teilhard de Chardin's Transhumanism and the Cult of the Fourth Industrial Revolution', by Matthew Ehret, *Strategic Culture Foundation*, 26 October 2021: www.strategic-culture.org/news/2021/10/26/

pierre-teilhard-de-chardins-transhumanism-and-the-cult-of-the-fourth-industrial-revolution/

68. Another obvious example is the way human beings have been becoming more and more robotic in their behaviours, working bureaucratic jobs, operating telephone switchboards, while having to refer to computers to make their decisions. Now we have recorded telephone switchboards passing for human beings, making it harder and harder to know when we're talking to a digital recording (AI program) or a human being. Likewise, artificial intelligence image synthesising software is taking existing images of people and creating fake video footage (mostly fake sex videos for revenge porn, or putting a celebrity's face on pornography). There is also Photoshop for voice with which you can take a recording and make anybody appear to say anything. Fake news gets real, because no one can tell the difference; and meanwhile, a Reality TV show host becomes a real-time POTUS.

69. 'Gender Dysphoria in Children', by the American College of Pediatricians, June 2017: https://pubmed.ncbi.nlm.nih.gov/29108153/ The ACP is a very small (about 500) splinter group of 'apostates' from the American Academy of Pediatrics (AAP), the foremost national professional organisation regarding pediatrics in the country, which consists of 66,000 members. The ACP holds Judeo-Christian, traditional values but is open to paediatric medical professionals of all religions provided that they hold true to the group's core beliefs that life begins at conception and that the traditional family unit, headed by a both-sex couple, poses fewer risk factors in the adoption and raising of children. The AAP, on the other hand, holds that same-sex parenting has no inherent differences for child development than traditional both-sex parenting. The ACP has been listed as a hate group by the Southern Poverty Law Center for, in their words, 'propagating damaging falsehoods about LGBT people'. Despite this, ACP takes a clear and medically supported viewpoint on gender dysphoria (previously known as gender identity disorder), as follows: 'Gender dysphoria (GD) of childhood describes a psychological condition in which children experience a marked incongruence between their experienced gender and the gender associated with their biological sex. When this occurs in the pre-pubertal child, GD resolves in the vast majority of patients by late adolescence. Currently there is a vigorous, albeit suppressed, debate among physicians, therapists, and academics regarding what is fast becoming the new treatment standard for GD in children. This new paradigm is rooted in the assumption that GD is innate, and involves pubertal suppression with gonadotropin releasing hormone (GnRH) agonists followed by the use of cross-sex hormones—a combination that results in the

sterility of minors. A review of the current literature suggests that this protocol is founded upon an unscientific gender ideology, lacks an evidence base, and violates the long-standing ethical principle of "First do no harm"'.

70. Ibid. In the 1960s, Johns Hopkins University was the first American medical centre to venture into 'sex-reassignment surgery'. It 'launched a study in the 1970s comparing the outcomes of transgendered people who had the surgery with the outcomes of those who did not. Most of the surgically treated patients described themselves as "satisfied" by the results, but their subsequent psycho-social adjustments were no better than those who didn't have the surgery'. Hopkins 'stopped doing sex-reassignment surgery, since producing a "satisfied" but still troubled patient seemed an inadequate reason for surgically amputating normal organs'. 'Transgender Surgery Isn't the Solution', by Paul McHugh, *Wall Street Journal*, 13 May 2016: www.wsj.com/articles/paul-mchugh-transgender-surgery-isnt-the-solution-1402615120 Despite this, gender reassignment surgery has been available on the British National Health Service for more than 20 years. This means that the UK government will pay for your 'reassignment', provided it establishes that you are experiencing 'gender dysphoria', whereby a person recognises a discrepancy between their biological sex and their gender identity. Since then a new condition has arisen, 'Rapid Onset Gender Dysphoria': 'a new kind of trans-identifying youth, primarily natal females, who during or after puberty, begin to feel intense unhappiness about their sexed bodies and what it means to feel/be/present as a woman. Let me emphasize: What is "rapid onset" in this population is the dysphoria, not the gender atypicality. What distinguishes these young people from the early-onset populations studied previously is that they may have been happily gender nonconforming throughout childhood (though some were more gender typical), but they were not unhappy (which is all "dysphoric" really means), nor did they claim or wish to be the opposite sex. The unhappiness set in suddenly, in nearly every case only after heavy peer influence, either on- or offline'. 'WPATH & The Advocate Aim to Suppress New Research On Adolescent Gender Dysphoria', by J. Brie, *4thWaveNow*, 25 February 2018: https://4thwavenow.com/2018/02/25/wpath-the-advocate-aim-to-suppress-new-research-on-adolescent-gender-dysphoria/

71. Ibid.

72. 'Eli Erlick, 27, is under fire after posting his plan to ship cross-sex hormones to young people through the internet without any medical oversight or prescription. "If you need hormones, I work with a network of distributors to give you access. Everything is free, no

questions asked", Erlick wrote on 23 May in an Instagram post. "We have hundreds of doses of Testosterone, Estradiol and Spironolactone available right now. All are prescribed by doctors and unused". Erlick deleted the post shortly after it was shared by high-follower Twitter account @libsoftiktik and political commentator Matt Walsh, but archived copies of the declaration remain. Erlick also stated the move was in direct defiance to an increase in proposed legislation that would prevent minors from accessing medical "gender affirming" hormones. The legislation has largely come in response to increasing evidence calling into question their risk for long-term negative side effects … Erlick gained popularity due to being the youngest openly trans person in California. He became the first person under 18 years old in his home state to be approved by his insurance company for sex reassignment surgery (SRS). Two years after his surgery, Erlick wrote on his Tumblr blog, "I feel as though getting surgery was not my own choice, but rather coercion … I still bought into the stigma that I wouldn't have 'truly' been a trans woman had I not sought out the 'correct' medicine". At the age of 16, Erlick established TSER (Trans Student Educational Resources) in 2011 alongside another trans identified teenager, Alex Sennello. Erlick's activism gave him access to trans-identified teenage girls, and several have since come forward with allegations that Erlick raped them. [One] alleged victim … called Erlick her "rapist" and "abuser", something that he did not deny. Erlick apologized and said he would seek therapy'. 'Trans Activist Accused of Sexual Assault Offering Hormones to Youth', by Shay Woulahan, *Redux*, 6 August 2022: https://reduxx.info/trans-activist-accused-of-sexual-assault-offering-hormones-to-youth/

73. 'Blessings of the Abyss: On the Internet of Non Binary Bodies', by Schwabstack Schwab, 30 July 2022: https://schwabstack.substack.com/p/the-internet-of-non-binary-bodies

74. 'James Poulos: "Human, Forever"': Being Human in the Digital Catastrophe. A Dialogue', by A. Niederhauser, *Piped*: https://piped.kavin.rocks/watch?v=W5G_j5vl-Zg

75. Schwab offers the example of 'DNABLOCK, a 3D creation platform for virtual avatars, virtual worlds and their digital content', whose creator has argued that neither Facebook nor game designer studios can effectively run the metaverse. What is required is a community of independent creators, equivalent in scale to the metaverse itself. Top-down social engineering now depends on bottom-up cooperation in 'mapping the interiority of decay. This will allow managers and cyberneticians to predict erratic behaviors, wrangle retards, and otherwise constrain these wildly mutating "gifts of the abyss"'.

76. 'No One Should Be Forced To Declare Their Pronouns', by Joanna Williams, *Spiked*, 29 June 2022: www.spiked-online.com/2022/08/16/trump-is-still-scrambling-the-minds-of-the-elites/ 'Only one in ten people (10%) think that everyone should generally display or state their pronouns, with the largest number of Britons tending to think that only those who wish to should display their pronouns (48%). Another 17% think people should generally not bring up their pronouns unless asked'. 'Should People Have To Display Their Pronouns?' by Connor Ibbetson, *YouGov*, 25 January 2022: https://yougov.co.uk/topics/lifestyle/articles-reports/2022/01/25/should-people-display-their-pronouns

77. 'More than a Media Moment: The Influence of Televised Storylines on Viewers' Attitudes toward Transgender People and Policies', by Traci K. Gillig, Erica L. Rosenthal, Sheila T. Murphy, and Kate Langrall Folb, *Sex Roles*, 78(7–8), 2017: 1–13.

78. 'Kellie-Jay Keen: Why I'm Fighting the Transgender Cult', *The Brendan O'Neill Show*, 28 July 2022: www.youtube.com/watch?v=TdFOacqCv3c&t=980s

Part III

79. 'Maternal Enmeshment: The Chosen Child', by Dee Hann-Morrison: http://journals.sagepub.com/doi/pdf/10.1177/2158244012470115

80. In *The Lucid View*, I equated Lucifer with Venus, via the symbolism of the Morning Star, as well as with Kundalini, also known as 'the serpent goddess'. In other words, I saw Lucifer as a female archetype. One obvious correlation is the one between Lucifer and matter/mater/mother. In the Garden of Eden story, Lucifer, the Serpent, enters into the female body of Eve, as a means to get access to Adam, and thus to God. It is as if Lucifer is trying to be God—replace the Father—and become a demiurge, a creator in his own right (or his own image). Yet he has to enter into a woman's body to do it. The urge of the male to transform himself into a female—or vice versa—is transgenderism. It is the urge: a) to recreate the original movement from Spirit to Matter; b) to assert freedom from the restrictions of materiality, in the most absolute way possible, by reversing sex.

81. Obviously Dick was aware he was playing around with religious preconceptions and to some degree he was no doubt attempting to bake his own noodle thereby. There are subtler examples of possible satanic deceptions, however, that don't indicate so much awareness. In a passage towards the end of the *Exegesis*, Dick describes his salvific higher-dimensional beings in such a way that seems more compatible with Steiner's Ahrimanic imposters—than the unfallen Angelic hierarchy: 'I then saw how they see us; I saw from their viewpoint, and to them,

we are the gods and they are the apes! Yet we view it the other way around … And this is why our soul … "descends" into incarnation into this, our world, Purgatorio. Our world is superior because here there is atmosphere, hence music. This is the motive for the voluntary fall, and it is quintessential wisdom … They venerate us and yearn for us; we venerate them and yearn for them. It is as if when we die we go to our just reward we go there [sic]; and when they die and go to their just reward they come here, as willingly and voluntarily and easily as we go there' (2011, p. 862). Shortly after his disturbing ode to inhuman-to-human congress, Dick declares, 'This is the first time in my life … that I have ever been *truly* enlightened—beyond even Buddha or Christ or Mani, beyond all wisdom of East and West—beyond even another realm (heaven), Christ and God' (2011, pp. 863–864). Dick, shall we say, was not in his *natural* mind at the time of these particular visions. How much of Dick's distorted, entity-ridden pseudo-vision of human evolution stemmed from cultural contamination would be impossible to say, but clues are there in the *Exegesis*: 'Evolution-wise we must be like the apes in *2001*; we are on the lip-edge of evolving to where we'll see Valis/the plasmate. It's like *Close Encounters* at the end. A life form, sacred and beautiful, right here. An information life form' (2011, p. 673). Kubrick and Spielberg, sitting on the right and left sides of Dick, dictating his Hollywood Babylon vision.

82. If there is now a Body of Dick that is its own counterfeit, making all who have been in-formed by 'VALIS' part of that cultural eggregore, then it includes some seriously deluded advocates and practitioners, philosophies and proclivities, all the way from Stanford Research Institute (SRI) to Silicon Valley via Hollywood, and beyond. Wherever Philip K. Dick's soul is now (perhaps still bound up with that of his twin sister?), it may only be as saved as the most duped, deceived, and ensnared of his reader-followers. This question is of primary relevance here. For all his epiphanies and original insights, Dick at the premature end of his life was neither healthy nor whole. That he was delusional is not entirely assuaged by his constant awareness of that fact, or at least, his repeated acknowledgment of the possibility, which often reads more like a disclaimer before wilful re-immersion in delusion. Certainly, Dick never became a cult leader or petty tyrant along the lines of a Carlos Castaneda or Timothy Leary, and he remains, for me, a relatively benign example of a cultural outlier and 'heaven stormer' who achieved mass influence within the culture (hence influenced me from an early age).

83. 'The Connection Between The Legalization of Marijuana in Uruguay, Monsanto and George Soros', *ENCOD*, 30 July 2014: https://encod. org/en/news/2014-6/the-connection-between-the-legalization-of-marijuana-in-uruguay-monsanto-and-george-soros/

84. See 'Marijuana Induced Gynecomastia: Clinical and Laboratory Experience', by J. W. Harmon and M. A. Aliapoulios: https://jhu.pure.elsevier.com/en/publications/marijuana-induced-gynecomastia-clinical-and-laboratory-experience-4

85. See *The Influences of Lucifer and Ahriman*, by Rudolf Steiner, Rudolf Steiner Books, 1995.

86. 'The drugs did work', by Philip Purser-Hallard, *Guardian*, 12 August 2006: www.theguardian.com/film/2006/aug/12/sciencefictionfantasyandhorror.philipkdick

87. Medicines and Healthcare products Regulatory Agency (MHRA) released a report, 'Coronavirus Vaccines Summary of Yellow Card reporting', on 4 August 2022, disclosing that: 1) 4,342 children have now reported injury, harm, or death following a COVID-19 injection, including 82 cases of myocarditis, and pericarditis. Children in the UK are being injected with Pfizer (majority), AstraZeneca, and Moderna injections. 2) Details of the deaths of children following a Covid injection and the number of injuries being suffered by children are not being disclosed by the MHRA. 3) It is estimated by the MHRA that only somewhere between 1 and 10 per cent of all cases of harm, injury or death are ever reported to the Yellow Card Scheme—as such the true number of cases could be 10 to 100 times higher than this number. The long-term impact of these experimental injections is currently unknown. See '4,342 Children Have Reported Injury, Harm or Death Following a COVID-19 Injection—UK MHRA', by Lioness of Judah Ministry, *Exposing the Darkness*, 26 August 2022: https://lionessofjudah.substack.com/p/4342-children-have-reported-injury

88. 'In his teachings, Oshana brings the focus always back to the senses. He counsels continuous observation of what is going on at a perceptual level, both in the outer environment and in our physical, mental and emotional responses. He encourages a ceaseless questioning of every thought, every belief and assumption, always referring us back to what the senses are telling us is actually there. He prescribes total commitment to transformation, hyper-vigilance, and continuous questioning of our thoughts. He does not preach any doctrine or philosophy. He is opposed to conceptual or abstract thinking, belief, and any kind of dogma. From what I have observed on three Oshana retreats, his methods are primarily improvisatory, spontaneous, unplanned and unpremeditated. Oshana claims this is because he follows the Transmission at all times and it is the Transmission that decides what will happen, not him. This means that he has no more of a clue what he is doing than the rest of us, until it happens. His role is as a coach and a guide, more than a teacher. The actual journey of discovery must

be undertaken by the student, and it must be undertaken alone'. 'The Disillusionist', by Jasun Horsley, *Auticulture*, 2012: https://boxes.nyc3. digitaloceanspaces.com/wp-content/uploads/oshana.pdf

89. Kripal writes: *'for Dick, writing and reading are the privileged modes of the mystical life.* Writing and reading are his spiritual practices. His is a mysticism of language, of Logos, of text-as-transmission, of the S-F novel as coded Gnostic scripture. The words on the page, on his late pages at least, are not just words. They are linguistic transforms of his own experience of Valis. They are mercurial, shimmering revelations. They are alive. And—weirdest of all—they can be "transplanted" into other human beings, that is, into you and me via the mystical event of reading' (2011, p. 800n). Kripal performed a similarly suspect coat-tailing-cum-mythologising of the alien abductee Whitley Strieber, to (I would say) an even more disingenuous and reality-distorting degree. The coat-tailing goes hand in hand with the deification, of course, since he who creates gods gets a special place on their coat-tails. This is what I mean, later, by securing a place in the world being antithetical to the salvation of the soul. I like to think that Dick would have been appalled by all such efforts to turn him into a religious avatar, even if he makes similar claims himself, periodically, in the *Exegesis*.

90. 'Modern Slavery: The True Cost of Cobalt Mining', by Hermes, *Human Trafficking Search*, 2017: https://humantraffickingsearch.org/resource/modern-slavery-the-true-cost-of-cobalt-mining/

91. 'Canada Advocates Warn of Worsening Trends in Euthanasia', by John Burger, *Aleteia*, 14 August 2022: https://aleteia.org/2022/08/14/canada-advocates-warn-of-worsening-trends-in-euthanasia/

92. 'Jack Sarfatti—His Ideas About the Tic Tac Came from "A Phone Call from an Alien"', *Hollywood Entertainment News*, 17 March 2021: https://hollywoodentertainmentnews.com/2021/03/17/jack-sarfatti-his-ideas-about-the-tic-tac-came-from-a-phone-call-from-an-alien-unidentified-aerial-phenomena-sci/

93. 'Jack Sarfatti's History', by Joel De Reijden, 8 July 2020: https://isgp-studies.com/bio-of-jack-sarfatti Also see 'NEW AGE PERVERTS: The Epstein-Sarfatti-Oswald-NAMBLA Connection', Subliminal Jihad #58 -(feat. Jimmy Falungong): https://soundcloud.com/subliminaljihad/58-new-age-perverts-the-epstein-sarfatti-oswald-nambla-connectionfeat-jimmy-falungong

94. 'Mathematical Notes Jack Sarfatti Physics Tic Tac V6', by Jack Sarfatti, 17 March 2019: www.academia.edu/38526339/Mathematical_Notes_Jack_Sarfatti_Physics_Tic_Tac_V6_March_17_2019_

95. 'Jack Sarfatti—His Ideas About the Tic Tac Came from "A Phone Call from an Alien"', *Hollywood Entertainment News*, 17 March 2021:

https://hollywoodentertainmentnews.com/2021/03/17/jack-sar-fatti-his-ideas-about-the-tic-tac-came-from-a-phone-call-from-an-alien-unidentified-aerial-phenomena-sci/

96. West was also a prominent member of the False Memory Syndrome Foundation and connected to numerous other covert CIA operations throughout his career. See *16 Maps of Hell*.

97. Apply the following to the commonly held view of the serial killer: 'It is to the extreme individualization involved by the developments of erotic symbolism that the fetichist [sic] owes his morbid and perilous isolation … He is nearly always alone. He is predisposed to isolation from the outset … When at length the symbolist realizes his own aspirations—which seem to him for the most part an altogether new phenomenon in the world—and at the same time realizes the wide degree in which they deviate from those of the rest of mankind, his natural secretiveness is still further reinforced. He stands alone. His most sacred ideals are for all those around him a childish absurdity, or a disgusting obscenity, possibly a matter calling for the intervention of the policeman' (Havelock Ellis, Studies in the Psychology of Sex, vol 5). Or an FBI profiler.

98. No wonder that, on the rare occasion the subject matter is handled by serious technicians, such as Roman Polanski with *Rosemary's Baby* or William Friedkin with *The Exorcist*, it becomes a 'classic' (both these films are based on pulpy novels, however, and even *Rosemary's Baby* limits the social reality of Satanism to 'kooky neighbors').

99. 'What can government do about conspiracy theories? … (1) Government might ban conspiracy theorizing. (2) Government might impose some kind of tax, financial or otherwise, on those who disseminate such theories. (3) Government might itself engage in counterspeech, marshaling arguments to discredit conspiracy theories. (4) Government might formally hire credible private parties to engage in counterspeech. (5) Government might engage in informal communication with such parties, encouraging them to help. Each instrument has a distinctive set of potential effects, or costs and benefits, and each will have a place under imaginable conditions. However, our main policy idea is that government should engage in *cognitive infiltration of the groups that produce conspiracy theories*, which involves a mix of (3), (4) and (5)', (emphasis added). 'Conspiracy Theories', by Cass R. Sunstein and Adrian Vermeule, 2008: https://papers.ssrn.com/sol3/papers.cfm?abstract_id=1084585

100. Rudolf Steiner describes the incarnational body of Christ (the second coming) as being energetically woven into existence through each and every Christ-like thought, word, act, and impulse of human beings, in communal relationship to one another and to existence

(I am paraphrasing). The inverse of this invisible inter-weaving process is—something I have explored for the past 30 years at least—the organised ritual abuse of children (and adults) by 'satanic cults'. The scare quotes are there to disarm deniers, because these agencies *are* satanic, and they are cult-like. They are also embedded within (and the invisible foundation of) mainstream society (see the Netflix documentary *The Keepers* for a 'light' introduction; Carl A. Raschke's *Painted Black*, among other books, for a broad overview; Ross E. Cheit's *The Witch-Hunt Narrative* for a robust debunking of the 'satanic panic' whitewash spin of 'mass hysteria' and 'false memories'). So-called Satanic Ritual Abuse has a specific purpose, above and beyond the many parasocial and parapolitical layers which I have tried to unravel in my last few books. This deeper layer pertains to the disruption—and if it were possible, the destruction—of the 'weave' of the communal body of Christ, and its replacement with a body of Antichrist. This is the esoteric goal of accumulated, intentionally evil acts, committed by human beings on one another, acts that are traumatic at the soul level because they sever the connection between the body and soul, and hence are also mimetic and contagious (extreme abuse creates extreme abusers).

101. 'Social Control and the Violation of Human Rights: The Relationship Between Sociological Variables and Serial Murder', by Bernard East, *Criminology Australia*, 6(3), February 1995: https://media.auticulture.com/wp-content/uploads/More-on-mckenna-and-Bundy-crime-Aust6_3.pdf

102. 'Asperger's Disorder: A Possible Explanation For Behavior of Sub-group of Serial Killers?' *Crime Times*: https://web.archive.org/web/20160801000000*/http://www.crimetimes.org/05c/w05cp13.htm

103. See *Cavedef*, 'Ted Bundy': http://cavdef.org/w/index.php?title=Ted_Bundy#Others_involved Also 'The Enigma of Ted Bundy: Did He Kill 18 Women? Or Has He Been Framed?' by Cheryl McCall, *People*, 7 January 1980: https://people.com/archive/the-enigma-of-ted-bundy-did-he-kill-18-women-or-has-he-been-framed-vol-13-no-1/

104. For Ben Meyers, see *Cavedef*, 'Ted Bundy': http://cavdef.org/w/index.php?title=Ted_Bundy#Others_involved; for Stanley Bernson see 'Satanic Activity In Oregon', alt.conspiracy, Google Groups: https://groups.google.com/g/alt.conspiracy/c/TFKc6-nM9N4; for Thomas Creech, see *Cavedef*, 'Thomas Creech': http://cavdef.org/w/index.php?title=Thomas_Creech

105. 'Charles Manson: The Incredible Story of the Most Dangerous Man Alive', By David Felton and David Dalton, *Rolling Stone*, 25 June 1970: www.rollingstone.com/culture/culture-news/charles-manson-the-incredible-story-of-the-most-dangerous-man-alive-85235/

106. 'Progress in Conversion: From Charles Manson's Brainwashing to Cultivating Discernment', by Paul Axton, *Forging Ploughshares*, 7 November 2019: https://forgingploughshares.org/tag/charles-manson/
107. (Emphasis added), see 'The Gospel of St. Matthew', Lecture II, 2 September 1910, Berne: https://rsarchive.org/Lectures/GA123/English/RSPC1946/19100902p01.html
108. Kemper in 1981, in *The Killing of America*.
109. Everything in the past that doesn't conform to the ideology of the present is proof of humanity's progress and of our ancestors' ignorance, at best their lack of sophistication (technique), at worst their lack of moral compass. No concession is given for context, that ideology is always evolving, or degenerating, that morals change and what seems obviously wrong today might have worked well enough back then. No forgiveness is offered for our ancestors, only cancellation; the sins we inherit are summarily disowned (though others must pay reparations). All statues of patriarchs must be torn down, all racial minorities represented, however falsely, in every manufactured image of the past. ('Logical deductions', as Ellul wrote, 'falsify reality', p. 110.) Progress not only depends on realising the visions of the future but on erasing and rewriting history. The present becomes totalitarian, monolithic. 'Technical modalities cannot tolerate subjectivity' (Ellul, p. 429n).
110. cf. Gilbert Valle and *The Case of the Cannibal Cop*.
111. 'Who Was the Mother of the Most Depraved Serial Killer of All Time?' by Candace Sutton, *NZ Herald*, 25 October 2020: www.nzherald.co.nz/world/who-was-the-mother-of-the-most-depraved-serial-killer-of-all-time/T75XZ2O7K7AGAP5LBGPKDKHVV4/ The Big Mother state is Ed Gein's degenerate mission taken to a global level: an artificial womb through which 'Ahrimanic' entities can incarnate physically. The 'internet of things'—so our technocratic caretakers intend—is establishing an inorganic matrix; 'the internet of bodies' is intended to generate the foetus within it. Human bodies are essential to the assembling, but first they must be converted into hosts for nanotechnology, receiver-transmitters for 'AI' (which some researchers suggest could be a hidden function of the mRNA). It is akin to the amalgamation of cells and organs that forms a foetus inside a womb, only that the child being gestated is looking more and more every day like it will grow up to be Ed Gein, rather than the *Übermensch*.
112. 'Sam Harris: Trump, Religion, Wokeness', *Triggernometry*, 17 August 2022: www.youtube.com/watch?v=DDqtFS_Pvcs
113. Where is the truly dark side of human society in Dick's vision? He may have been paranoid about the FBI and even Satan, occasionally; and he certainly had few illusions about the potential of technology

for evil. But those deeper aspects of the society he was living in—such as the ritualised trafficking, rape, torture and murder of men, women, and children—are, with the occasional, partial exception of his pre-cogs and other exploited autists, entirely absent. They are even less seriously considered—and sometimes even reviled and ridiculed—among the tech-gnostic Dick-lovers of SRI, MIT, and IONS (Institute of Noetic Sciences). These—along with collective humanity (which at least has the excuse of ignorance)—are the weavers of deceit whose devotional, delusional mis-appliance of whatever is good about PKD's revelations have turned him into a false prophet and 'antichrist'. My desire to expose these satanic bellwethers, then, to save Dick from his own Luciferian legacy, and to extricate myself from the spell of cultural counterfeits, may be all one and the same impulse.

114. Cf. Jed McKenna, *Spiritual Enlightenment: The Damnedest Thing*.

115. To resume the counterfeit-busting after that necessary disclaimer, this could be related to—even the other side of—the conspiracy-phobia that is so common among a certain breed of psychedelic-advocates, including some (but not all) Dick-heads and *Exegesis*-commentators: the insistence on seeing everything through a positive, 'numinous' lens, as aspects of a unitive force and principle that places everything political within a 'paranormal' dimension and thereby turns Satan into God's shadow, an ephemeral, abstract, and (outmodedly) academic 'absence of good'. This secularised Satan is devoid of all power to act in or on our world, or to move through or as human beings. (One commentator in the *Exegesis* (Erik Davis) disparages the idea of 'a conspiratorial Satan'—as if Satan had any other way to operate in the world! They also equate it—via Christian fundamentalism—with 'homophobia'!) Admittedly, evil as unconsciousness seems like a solid enough idea, were it not that such reductionism depends on the presumption of consciousness by those who are themselves unconscious. First and foremost (I would argue), they are unconscious of the power and presence of evil in their own lives and actions—of their complicity. Invariably, the conspiracy-deniers, both high and low, are, consciously or not, in cahoots with the very forces they are denying, as made manifest by how 'naïvely' (to give benefit of doubt) they defend, and even advocate, the many instruments, objects, organisations, and institutions in Satan's Ministry. End rant.

116. As it happens, this present work is made up of an unusually wide temporal range of material by the author, spanning a period of some nine years. (It also draws extensively on Dick's work from the 1960s through to 1982, and Rudolf Steiner from the early 1900s; but this is not unusual for a nonfiction work).

117. Despite Steiner's insistence that words were 'feeble means of expression' unfit to describe spiritual realities, his view on language as a spiritual tool was surprisingly optimistic. He once said that all the discoveries of a clairvoyant would be 'extinguished after death' besides whatever 'has been translated into language which, in any given period, is the language of a healthy sense of truth'. The work of clairvoyants, he believed, is to convey spiritual truths—via language, however 'feeble'—in such a way that others can be nourished by them. Most surprisingly of all, Steiner attributed the conveyance of such insights via language with the power to transmit wisdom by osmosis: 'This, then, is the position of the spiritual investigator among his fellow-men. If they are willing to listen to him and assimilate his findings, they make the same progress as he does' (1986, pp. 18–19). Is this a whole new last-minute wrinkle in time for the Dick-heads to slide through?

118. 'Testifying to Love: How Dave Oshana & the Enlightenment Transmission Allowed for an Experience of My Soul', by Jasun Horsley, *Auticulture*, 15 September 2018: https://auticulture.wordpress.com/2018/09/15/testifying-to-love-how-dave-oshana-the-enlightenment-transmission-allowed-for-an-experience-of-my-soul/

119. 'The Gospel of St. Matthew', Lecture I2, 12 September 1910, Berne: www.rudolfsteineraudio.com/accordingtomatthew/matthew12%201.mp3

120. 'Blessings of the Abyss: On the Internet of Non Binary Bodies', by Schwabstack Schwab, 30 July 2022: https://schwabstack.substack.com/p/the-internet-of-non-binary-bodies

INDEX

Milton Keynes UK
Ingram Content Group UK Ltd.
UKHW021421231023
431178UK00035B/450